THE BALLET CALLED SWAN LAKE

GALINA ULANOVA AS ODETTE

THE BALLET CALLED SWAN LAKE

By

CYRIL W. BEAUMONT

Dance Books • Alton

First published in 1952

This edition published in 2012 by
Dance Books Ltd
Charwell House
Wilsom Road
Alton
Hampshire
GU34 2PP

ISBN 978-1-85273-153-3

A CIP catalogue record for this book is
available from the British Library

To

NATALIE RENÉ

(ROSLAVLEVA)

In Gratitude and Friendship

PREFACE

THE favourable reception accorded my previous book, *The Ballet called Giselle*, a study of the evolution of a single ballet from conception to realisation, has prompted me to attempt an account on similar lines of another famous ballet, *Swan Lake*.

The history of that work being largely connected with Russia offers particular obstacles in the collection and assembling of material, quite apart from the normal difficulties of the Russian language. Indeed, it would have been almost impossible for me to describe the early productions of *Swan Lake* without the help of a Russian friend, Miss Natalie René (Moscow), an assiduous student of Ballet, who not only most generously aided me in the acquisition of Russian documentation but also frequently suggested fruitful sources of study. This book owes a great deal to her unremitting interest and her constant encouragement over several years.

I am also much indebted to Dr. France, a Russian friend resident in this country, who with the greatest goodwill translated for me many Russian texts.

I wish to record my sincere appreciation of the courteous assistance afforded by the Bakruskin State Theatrical Museum, Moscow, who had copied for me the text of the Begichev-Geltser scenario, and the cast of the Moscow *première* of the Reisinger production.

I also desire to express my grateful thanks to The British Council and their representative, Miss Tripp, for help in obtaining illustration material from Russia; to Monsieur Pierre Michaut who afforded me information respecting early performances of *Swan Lake* in France; to Monsieur Gérard Mulys, the *maître de ballet* and dancer, who generously placed at my disposal his extensive documentation of ballet performances at the Théâtre du Casino, Monte Carlo; to Monsieur Aurel Milloss, who helped me regarding performances of *Swan Lake* in Italy; to Mr. Svend Kragh-Jacobsen for information respecting performances of *Swan Lake* in Denmark; to Mr. Allan Fridericia for similar information respecting Sweden; to the Yugoslav Embassy for notes on performances in Belgrade; to Messieurs Jan Reimöser and Sacha Machov who obtained for me copies of programmes relating to the performance of *Swan Lake* in Prague; to Miss Margaret Rolfe who found for me certain German texts relating to the Swan Legend; and to Miss Betty Henry, formerly of the

British Embassy, Moscow. I am also indebted to Messrs. Putnam for the loan of the photograph of Spessivtzeva and Lifar, from the latter's book: *Ballet, Traditional to Modern*.

In the recording of the choreography of the four scenes I have had the expert assistance of Miss Margaret Skeaping, Miss Molly Lake, Miss Peggy van Praagh, Miss Gerd Larsen and Mr. Harold Turner. On page 75 I have set out the particular contribution made by each. I should like to have discussed any differences that may exist between the performances of the full length ballet seen here, which were reproduced by the late Nicholas Sergeyev from the stenochoreographic notations made by him during his service as *régisseur* to the Maryinsky Theatre, St. Petersburg, and the performances to be seen in Soviet Russia to-day, but, since duties here have prevented my going there, that has not been possible.

In defining the directions made by the dancers I have made use of the Cecchetti system, which regards the stage as a square having eight imaginary fixed points. These are the four corners of the stage numbered 1,2,3,4 beginning with the front left-hand corner from the spectator's viewpoint and moving anti-clockwise, and the centres of each of the four sides of the stage, numbered respectively 5,6,7,8. A plan for the use of the spectator will be found following page 176.

I have not devoted a chapter to Marius Petipa as his career is fully detailed in my *Complete Book of Ballets*, to which the reader is referred.

There exists a certain difficulty in the terminology of the four scenes because, whereas the original production by Reisinger was divided into four acts, Petipa rearranged the ballet in three acts, the first containing two scenes, corresponding to Acts I and II of the original production. For the sake of consistency, I have adhered to this plan, in all references to productions based on the Petipa–Ivanov choreography, although some present-day productions fall into four acts and some into three.

In conclusion, I have to thank my friend, Mr. Lionel Bradley, for his inestimable service in reading through the proofs.

CYRIL BEAUMONT

CONTENTS

PART ONE: HISTORICAL AND BIOGRAPHICAL

PART TWO: TECHNICAL AND CRITICAL

ILLUSTRATIONS

CHAPTER I

THE ORIGIN AND CONCEPTION OF "SWAN LAKE" (REISINGER VERSION)

FEW lovers of ballet will dispute that *Giselle* and *Le Lac des Cygnes* are the two greatest romantic ballets in the long history of that composite art, and each is endowed with so many virtues that it will ever remain a nice question as to which is the more popular and which can be regarded as the superior of the other.

The ballet called *Lebedinoe Ozero* or *The Swan Lake* was first performed at the Bolshoy Theatre, Moscow, on February 20th/March 4th, 1877. According to the programme those responsible for the various contributions were as follows: Book: V. P. Begichev and V. F. Geltser. Music: Peter Ilyich Tchaikovsky. Scenery: H. Shangin (Act I), K. F. Valts (Acts II and IV), H. Groppius (Act III). Peasants' Costumes: H. Simone. Costumes: Vormenko. Machinery and electrical effects: K. F. Valts. Shoes: Pirone. Flowers: Deladvez. Wigs and coiffures.: Silvan.

How did the ballet originate? In regard to *Swan Lake*, we are less fortunate than in the case of *Giselle*, for, unlike Gautier, neither of the Russian scenarists has recorded the source of his inspiration, or hinted at the extent of his contribution.

It would seem that the seeds of inspiration may first be traced to a certain day in April, 1866, when Tchaikovsky, then twenty-six years of age and recently appointed teacher of composition at the newly-formed Moscow Conservatoire of Music, made friends with an artiste of the Imperial Theatres, K. N. de Lazari; who enabled him to make the acquaintance of V. P. Begichev, Intendant of the Moscow Imperial Theatres, a handsome Court official who was married to a lady once renowned for her singing; a widow with two attractive and youthful sons, Constantine and Vladimir Shilovsky, who even at that early age were greatly interested in music and literature. The last-named, then fourteen years old, became Tchaikovsky's favourite pupil and frequently accompanied him on his travels.

In June, 1868, Tchaikovsky, having completed his first opera, *The Voyevoda*, went with K. N. de Lazari, V. Shilovsky, and V. P. Begichev on a tour of Western Europe, returning to Moscow early in September. They travelled down the Rhine and visited both Berlin and Paris. There is a well-established Moscow theatre legend to the effect that the theme of *Swan Lake* was conceived jointly by Tchaikovsky and Begichev during this holiday, and it must be admitted that the sight of the many romantic castles which line the banks of the Rhine might well have inspired such a plot.

Although Tchaikovsky's name does not figure among the authors responsible for the scenario of *Swan Lake*, it is difficult to resist the feeling that he had some part in it.

On November 18th, 1860, Tchaikovsky's sister, Alexandra Ilyinishna, married Lyov Vasilyevich Davidov, and went to live with her husband on the Davidov estate at Kamenka, in the province of Kiev. Tchaikovsky was much attached to his sister, and the children with which she was blessed were a particular source of joy to him. The composer was never so happy as when taking part in their games. Indeed, his nephew Ivan Lvovich records that during one summer holiday at Kamenka early in June, 1871, Tchaikovsky composed specially for their delight a little ballet called *Ozero Lebedeye*, that is, *The Lake of the Swans*. Ivan Lvovich also declares that he remembers quite well how taken he was with the charming melody of the swan's song, later the theme associated with Odette, which is so vital a part of the score of the ballet we know to-day.

On the other hand, Yuri Bakrushin, the Soviet historian of ballet, is inclined to accept this reminiscence with reserve, contending first, that it depends solely on Davidov's statement, which is not confirmed by any other person, and second, that since Davidov's Memoirs were written when he was very old, it is quite likely that his memory may be at fault, or that he confused certain facts. But while it seems difficult to see how, so many years later, such a statement could be confirmed, when the chief witnesses, apart from the composer, were children at the time it was made, it is true that memory, at an advanced age, does sometimes play strange tricks with actual fact.

Vladimir Petrovich Begichev was born on May 6th, 1828, at Tula. A member of an old-established noble family, he was educated at Moscow University. On graduation he served first in the State Chamber, then in the Council of Guardians, after which he became Intendant of the Moscow Imperial Theatres. He was elected head of the Moscow Assembly of Nobles.

On becoming Intendant, Begichev introduced a number of reforms and innovations, not only in the company, but in the matter of stage presentation, to which he devoted himself with great zeal. He required all artistes to be prepared to undertake both important and minor roles. He also drafted many useful regulations for the administration of the theatre.

In his photograph, Begichev suggests a typical *bon viveur* of the period. Handsome, with refined and intelligent features, broad brow, wavy hair, silky moustache with waxed points, shaven chin, with a fluffy fringe of hair outlining the jaw, he looks every inch a tactful and efficient Court official.

He had a lively disposition and was fond of good company, particularly artistes of every branch of the theatre. He kept open house in Moscow and has been preserved to posterity by Boleslav Markevich, in his novel, *Chetvert Veka Nazad* (*A Quarter of a Century Ago*), in which Begichev is portrayed as Oshanin.

Begichev wrote many books, mainly comedies and vaudevilles for the stage, which were often performed. He frequently appeared on the stage in person and with success. He died at St. Petersburg on November 17th, 1891, of angina pectoris, and was interred in the Volkov Cemetery.

Vasily Fedorovich Geltser was born in 1840. His father, of German descent, came to Russia early in the 19th century and settled in Moscow, where he opened a bakery and eventually married the daughter of a Moscow merchant. In time the German settler so absorbed the manners and customs of his adopted country that he became quite Russian in his outlook. He had three sons and a daughter, all of whom became associated with the theatre. Vassily and Fedor were both dancers, the former in the Moscow ballet company, the latter in the St. Petersburg company; Anatoly was a stage designer and responsible, among other things, for the moving panorama used at the close of the Vision scene in the Moscow production of *The Sleeping Beauty;* while Vera was an actress at the Maly Theatre.

Vasily entered the Moscow School of Ballet in 1848 and completed his training in 1856. He was placed in the *corps de ballet* of the ballet company attached to the Bolshoy Theatre at a salary of 120 roubles a year. He soon won promotion and became a prominent member of the company. In 1860 he was appointed soloist. He was also noted for his abilities as a mime. Six years later, when Saint-Léon revived his ballet *Koniok Gorbunok* (*The Hump-backed Horse*) for Moscow, Geltser was given the leading role of Ivan the Fool and partnered the ballerina Adela Grantzova, the first Tsar Maiden in Moscow.

His interpretation of Ivan the Fool is one of the great performances in the tradition of the Moscow Ballet and established a model for his successors. Geltser himself performed the part for more than 350 times and when he became too old to dance it, he took the part of the Khan until 1906, the year of his retirement, so anxious was he to maintain his long association with that ballet. Another of his famous interpretations was that of the deaf-mute Malay in Simon's opera *The Song of Triumphant Love*. In this role he had to hypnotise Fabius's wife, Valerie, into falling in love with his master, Muscius. Geltser, solely through his facial expression, projected his personality with such force that not only the audience, but even his fellow artists, were deeply impressed.

Geltser was a well-read, cultured man, with a gift for languages. It is probable that Begichev invited his collaboration in the writing of the *scenario* for *Swan Lake*, because of his varied experience of ballet, for not only was he a leading dancer and mime, but he had also occupied the post of *régisseur général* to the Moscow ballet company, to whom he also taught the art of mime. His artistry was reflected in his daughter Ekaterina Geltser, the Moscow *prima ballerina*. Vassily Geltser died at Moscow on December 30th, 1908 (O.S.).

In Chapter II, I give in English translation the original scenario, printed by I. I. Smirnov at Kudrino, Moscow, in 1877. For this I am indebted to the extreme courtesy of the Bakrushin Theatrical Museum, Moscow, founded by the father of the Soviet historian of ballet. The latter expresses the opinion that the whole tone of the libretto is inconsistent with what would be expected of the authors.

The office of Intendant of the Imperial Theatres was an important appointment which not only depended on the favour of Court officials, but had also to receive the personal approval of the Tsar, one of the most autocratic of monarchs. In substance, the theme of *Swan Lake* is a charming conception, akin to the beloved tales of Hans Andersen, but not only does it lack the charm of the Danish author's style, but there are times when it is almost crude in its artless dialogue. Again, some of the speeches and certain of the incidents are invested with an ironic note which hardly accords with the accepted demeanour of an important State official at this period.

Contrariwise, the main episodes of the plot are obviously inspired by some person or persons of culture who had either studied in detail the myth of the swan-maiden or was possessed of a considerable knowledge of the literatures of the world, from which he or they selected and pieced together incidents appropriate to the theme.

A study of the original scenario as printed on February 12th, 1877, suggests that the text, printed privately in the Kudrino

VLADIMIR PETROVICH BEGICHEV

VASSILY FEDOROVICH GELTSER

quarter of Moscow and available even before *Swan Lake* was performed, was not that written by Begichev and Geltser, but the work of a hack engaged by an astute publisher for the purely commercial purpose of writing up the story of a ballet—whose rehearsals he had been permitted to attend—which had received an unusual degree of advance publicity and for which publication a considerable sale might reasonably be anticipated.

It is difficult to establish the date when the scenario for *Swan Lake* was first written, but it would appear that Tchaikovsky was invited to compose the score for the ballet during June, 1875. The composer, in a letter to N. A. Rimsky-Korsakov, dated September 10/22 of that year, thus refers to the commission: "The directorate of the Opera have commissioned me to write the music for the ballet *Le Lac des Cygnes*. I accepted the work, partly because I need the money and partly because I have long cherished a desire to try my hand at this type of music."

The choreography of *Swan Lake* was entrusted to Wenzel Reisinger, an Austrian *maître de ballet* of mediocre talent, who was clearly baffled by the unconventional music. Rejecting the symphonic conception and carefully built-up harmonious whole, Reisinger tried to adapt Tchaikovsky's score to the long-established convention of a series of *divertissements* in a fairy-tale setting, varied with spectacular processions. A sufficient comment on Reisinger's sense of style-atmosphere is the fact that he wished Tchaikovsky to compose a Russian Dance for Odette. As a result of Reisinger's editing, the original score was cut by practically one-third and several of Tchaikovsky's numbers replaced by dances taken from other ballets, for the most part of little value as music.

According to Mukhin[1], Reisinger was a very mediocre choreographer. The dancers composed their own *variations*, and all the dances were produced collectively.

The ballet was produced for the benefit of a *danseuse* called Pelagia Mikhailovna Karpakova, who, apart from the distinction of being the first Odette-Odile, does not figure among the names of dancers whose fame has been preserved to posterity.

Indeed, that Karpakova should have created the principal role at all in a new ballet is something of a mystery, because this privilege should by every right have been accorded to the leading ballerina, A. O. Sobeschanskaya, who did not appear in the ballet until its fourth performance, when it was given for her benefit. Such unusual departure from theatrical custom can only be explained by the exercise of an unusually powerful

[1] *Régisseur* to the Moscow Ballet in the eighteen-seventies. His MS. *History of the Moscow Ballet* is preserved in the Bakrushin State Museum.

influence, since it is clear that, of the two dancers, Sobeschanskaya was definitely the superior. An anonymous writer in the *Annual of the Imperial Theatres* observes: "although Madame Karpakova has assumed the position of ballerina she has not justified the hopes reposed in her. The talent of this artiste and even the tempo of her dances are so uniform that a spectator who had seen her in one ballet could easily visualise her performance in another."

So far as I am aware the only account of Karpakova to be found exists in a rare book by Carlo Blasis, entitled *Dances in General, Ballet Celebrities and National Dances*, published in Russian at Moscow, 1864. Carlo Blasis went to Moscow in the early 'sixties when he not only gave lessons in technique which made a considerable impression and constituted a valuable legacy, but also produced three important ballets, *Orfa*, *Méteore*, and *Faustus*. In addition, he wrote the book mentioned in which he summed up the abilities of contemporary Moscow solo dancers, among these essays being a portrait of Karpakova. A Russian author, Denis Leshkov, reminds us, however, that all the studies consist of uniformly eulogistic tributes which make their value suspect, moreover, the dancers described were all pupils of Blasis, who was noted for his gallantry. And now here is the opinion of Carlo Blasis.

"Mlle Karpakova is a charming and capable pupil. She has made considerable progress and developed those natural gifts which will soon place her among the leading *danseuses*, if she will but continue her manner of dancing, so suited to her physique, her line, and her abilities. She has revealed to lovers of the art and genuine connoisseurs that her talent is adapted to various styles of dancing; the graceful, the passionate, the tempestuous, and both the dance *en l'air* and the dance *à terre*. Her successes in various difficult dances and in her *pas de deux*, Terpsichore and Apollo in *Pygmalion*, serve as a guarantee of a wonderful future in the difficult and brilliant career of choreographic art.

"Mlle Karpakova's charming features and slim waist produce a most harmonious and effective impression. The expression of her face is very sweet."

The famous contemporary critic, Skalkovsky, compares the two dancers thus: "Karpakova is beautiful, on the other hand her dancing is heavy and her miming inexpressive. Had she not the benefit of certain influence she would not have advanced beyond the rank of *coryphée*. Sobeschanskaya dances coldly and heavily, but she is a serious dancer, even if she sometimes overacts through an excess of enthusiasm and from a desire to appear captivating. Another critic, S. M., writing in the *Moskov-*

skie Vedomosti (*Moscow Information*), declares that Sobeschanskaya conquered the public "not by the manner in which she achieved difficult leaps or by the speed of her turns, but by the way in which she built up a role, in which the dances reflected the mime."

No doubt the displacement of Sobeschanskaya in favour of Karpakova exerted a detrimental influence upon the *première* of *Swan Lake*, for, according to Mukhin, "Sobeschanskaya was in every respect incomparably better than Karpakova in the role of Odette."

The cast of the ballet was as follows:

Odette, a Good Fairy . . .	Mlle Karpakova I[1]
A wealthy Princess . . .	Mlle Nikolayeva
Prince Siegfried, her son . .	M. Gillert II
Wolfgang, his tutor . . .	M. Vanner
Benno von Sommerstein, the Prince's friend . . .	M. Nikitin
Von Rothbart, an evil geni . .	M. Sokolov
Odile, his daughter, who exactly resembles Odette . . .	* * * *
Master of Ceremonies . .	M. Kusnetsov
Baron von Stein . . .	M. Reinshausen
Baroness von Stein, his wife .	Mlle Polyakova
Freiherr von Schwarzfels . .	M. Titov
His Wife	Mlle Gorokhova
1st Courtier (Friends of the Prince)	M. Litavkin
2nd Courtier (Friends of the Prince)	M. Goulyaev
3rd Courtier (Friends of the Prince)	M. Ershov
Herald	M. Zaitsev
Messenger	M. Alekseyev
1st Peasant Girl . . .	Mlle Stanislavskaya
2nd Peasant Girl . . .	Mlle Karpakova II[2]
3rd Peasant Girl . . .	Mlle Nikolayeva II
4th Peasant Girl . . .	Mlle Petrova

Ladies and Gentlemen of the Court, Guests, Pages, Village Girls and Youths, Servants, Swans, and Cygnets

So far as I am aware, there exists no detailed eye-witness account of the *première* of the Reisinger production, but there are two interesting drawings engraved on wood, which appeared in the Russian magazine, *Vsemirnaya Illustratsia* (*World Illustration*). These represent the second and fourth acts of the ballet; there is also a photograph of Sobeschanskaya as Odette.

[1] Pelagia Mikhailovna.

[2] Sister of the above.

D. I. Leshkov in a monograph devoted to the centenary of the Bolshoy Theatre, Moscow, quotes this contemporary notice, without unfortunately giving the source. "Reisinger's imagination was very poor and the majority of the dances were weak and lacking in interest; the swimming swans were represented by rows of *corps de ballet* who stretched bands of tulle across the stage to suggest water, above which were seen the heads of the dancers intended to represent swans."

The reception accorded the ballet was no more than polite, not to say indifferent. The fact is the choreography was mediocre, some settings and costumes undistinguished, and the production scamped, while the orchestra was conducted by Ryabov, an experienced conductor of ballet music whose acquaintance with scores, however, was limited to the compositions of Minkus and Pugni. On examining Tchaikovsky's music for *Swan Lake*, he observed that never in all his life had he seen so complicated a score. The truth is the ballet public of that day expected and desired no more than lively dances to light and tuneful melodies. Hence, unable to appreciate Tchaikovsky's completely different conception of music for ballet, raised to the dignity of a symphonic work, they saw only a new and unusual type of performance which to them appeared displeasing and boring. One contemporary critic, however, Hermann G. Laroche, praised the merits of Tchaikovsky's work, for he predicted that, given new scenery and other choreography, the work would attain an interest surpassing even that of the charming score with which the composer had endowed it.

Nearly three years after the original failure of the ballet, *Swan Lake* was revived on the 13th July, 1880, again at Moscow, with new choreography by Olaf Hansen, who later became *maître de ballet* and *professeur de danse* at the Opera, Paris. This new version was produced for Hansen's benefit, the role of Odette being taken by a promising pupil called Kalmikova.

The dances in this production were arranged thus: Act I. Waltz. Scène de Seduction, Pas de Deux, Pas de Guirlandes. Act II. Appearance of Odette, Appearance of the Swans, Scène Dansante, Adage, Pas de Deux. Act III. Danse Hongroise, Danse Napolitaine, Danse Russe, Danse Espagnole, Mazurka. Act IV. Games and Pastimes of the Swans, Return of Odette, Farewells.

In 1882, on October 28th, the ballet was again revived in a new version by Hansen. The principal change, according to the programme, however, would appear to have been the replacing of the "*Danse Russe*" with a new number entitled "*Cosmopolitana*," danced not by a ballerina, but by another promising

PELAGIA MIKHAILOVNA KARPAKOVA

The creator of the role of Odette in the first production of "Swan Lake," Bolshoy Theatre, Moscow, 1877. Here, however, she is shown in another role.

A. O. SOBESCHANSKAYA AS ODETTE
Reisinger Production, Moscow, 1877

pupil called Lydia Geiten. From then onwards little or nothing is heard of *Swan Lake* until the "nineties."

The great success of Tchaikovsky's later ballets, *The Sleeping Beauty* (1890), and *Casse Noisette* (1892), inspired the directorate of the St. Petersburg Imperial Theatres with the idea of reviving *Swan Lake*. When I. A. Vsevolozhsky discussed this project with Petipa and sought his views on the possible causes of the failure of the Moscow production, the *maître de ballet* observed that he could not conceive that Tchaikovsky's music had been at fault, and that the weakness must lie elsewhere, either in the choreography or in some vital defect of production.

It was decided to send to Moscow for the score of the ballet. As soon as Petipa had studied it in relation to the theme, he realised its possibilities. It is likely that, pressed for time, he decided to make a beginning with Act II only, that is, the lakeside scene, and, having sketched out the sequence of dances and mimed scenes, he entrusted his assistant, Lev Ivanov, with the onerous task of giving material form to his suggestions.

Tchaikovsky was delighted at the prospect of his first ballet being revived, but almost at the beginning of the rehearsals, the composer died, on the 6th November, 1893. In view of the composer's immense popularity, the Government felt called upon to pay public tribute to Tchaikovsky's achievements and a memorial performance was planned to be given at the Maryinsky Theatre, the final date being February 17th, 1894.

Petipa, entrusted with the choreographic section of the programme, decided to include Ivanov's second act of *Swan Lake*, which, already well advanced, was hurried forward and quickly completed, and presented as something composed specially for the occasion. Ivanov's choreography with Pierina Legnani as Odette, achieved a decided success. The *St. Petersburg Gazette* observed: "the production reflects great honour on L. Ivanov. The *adage* is a complete choreographic poem."

Of the ballerina, the historian A. A. Pleschayev wrote: "The principal role was allotted to Legnani, who was truly a Swan Queen. What continuity, what plasticity, what velvety soft movements! What tenderness and execution! The ballerina's success was immense."[1]

Before leaving this chapter it should be mentioned that there is another version of the events leading up to the revival of *Swan Lake*. When it was resolved to honour Tchaikovsky's memory by a performance of one of his ballets, the directorate of the Imperial Theatres, St. Petersburg, were in some doubt as to what to choose, since both *The Sleeping Beauty* and *Casse-Noisette*

[1] *Nash Balet.*

to her will. He respectfully enquires as to whom she has chosen for his bride.

"I have selected no one," she replies, "since I wish you to choose your bride yourself. To-morrow I am giving a big ball, at which the nobility and their daughters will be present. You must choose from among those maidens the one that pleases you the most, and she shall be your bride."

Siegfried, seeing that the matter is not quite so serious as he had feared, answers that he will carry out his mother's wishes.

"I have said my say," declares the Princess, "and now I shall depart. Make merry and do not allow this matter to weigh upon you." She exits.

When she has retired, the Prince's friends surround him and he imparts to them the depressing news.

"This means an end to our merry-making," he laments, "and farewell to my freedom."

"The actual event is still some way off," observes Benno, trying to soothe him. "It belongs to the future. And, since the immediate prospect is pleasing, why not let us enjoy ourselves while we may."

"You speak truly," smiles the Prince.

So the feasting is resumed. The peasants dance in groups or apart. The respected Wolfgang, having again indulged in wine, begins to dance himself, but in so ridiculous a manner as to arouse derision. His dancing at an end, Wolfgang begins to plague the peasant girls with his attentions, but they mock the tutor and flee from him. One of the girls has a particular attraction for him and, having declared his passion, he tries to kiss her, but the pert girl eludes his grasp, and, as always happens in ballets, he kisses her swain instead. Wolfgang's bewildered air provokes general laughter.

Night begins to fall and the scene grows darker. One of the guests suggests a dance while holding wine-cups in their hands. They assent to his proposal.

A flock of swans is seen flying in the distance.

"Do you think they are too difficult to hit?" says Benno, pointing to the swans and trying to incite the Prince.

"Of course not," the Prince replies. "I should hit the target for sure. Bring me my cross-bow."

"Nay, do not heed him," reproves Wolfgang, "the hour is late and it is time to retire."

The Prince's expression seems to imply assent. But, as soon as the pacified old man withdraws, Siegfried summons a servant, calls for his cross-bow, and hurries away with Benno in the direction of the flight of swans.

POSTER OF FIRST PERFORMANCE OF "SWAN LAKE," 1877

With choreography by Reisinger, and Karpakova as Odette

grandfather took care of me, for he dearly loved my mother. Indeed, he was so distraught at her death and wept so much, that from his tears was formed this lake, into whose depths he descended and hid me away from all the world. Now, of late, he began to spoil me and gave me full liberty to enjoy myself. So by day my friends and I become transformed into swans and, joyfully cleaving the air with our breasts, we soar almost as high as the sky. And at dusk we dance and play near the old man. But my stepmother does not leave either my friends or myself in peace. (*At this moment the hoot of an owl is heard.*)

"Listen! That is a voice of ill omen," cried Odette, looking about her in alarm. "Look! There she is!"

On the ruins appears a gigantic owl with gleaming eyes.

"She would have killed me long ago," continues Odette, "only my grandfather watches her closely and will not allow her to work her wicked will. When I marry, the witch will lose the power to harm me. Until then, this crown alone protects me from her evil wiles. That is all. My story is soon told."

"Oh, forgive me, my beautiful one," pleads the bewildered Prince, falling on his knees.

From the ruins emerge a stream of young girls and children who hasten towards the young huntsman, saying that thanks to his foolish pastime he nearly robbed them of their dearest friend.

The Prince and Benno are overwhelmed with despair.

"That is enough," says Odette to her friends. "You see that he is good and sorry, and that he feels pity for me."

Quickly the Prince takes his cross-bow and, breaking it, casts it away, saying:

"I swear that henceforth my hand shall never more be raised to slay any living bird."

"Calm yourself, Sir Knight, all is forgotten; and now come and share in our pleasures."

Dancing begins in which the Prince and Benno take part. The swans and the cygnets form beautiful groups or dance apart. The Prince is continually at Odette's side. During the dancing he falls madly in love with her and implores her not to reject him (*Pas d'action*). Odette laughs as though to express her doubt of his sincerity.

"You do not believe me!" cries the Prince. "Oh, cold and cruel Odette!"

"I dare not believe you, noble knight, retorts Odette. "I fear that you are simply deceived by your own imagination. To-morrow at the ball that is to be given by your mother, you will see many beautiful young girls. You will fall in love with one of them and soon forget me."

"O never, I swear it on my knightly honour."

"Very well then, listen. I shall not conceal from you that I, too, love you. But I am filled with a foreboding that the evil witch may contrive some misfortune for you that will wreck our happiness."

"I defy the whole world," challenges Siegfried. "You shall ever be my one and only true love, and naught that the witch may do shall avail."

"Very well, to-morrow shall decide our fate. Either you will never see me again or else I shall lay my crown at your feet. But enough, it is time to depart, dawn is approaching. Farewell till to-morrow."

Odette and her friends vanish into the ruins. The sky is flushed with the roseate hue of sunrise. Over the lake glides a flock of swans. Above them hovers a gigantic owl.

(*Curtain.*)

ACT THREE

Scene. A magnificent hall in the Princess's castle. Everything is prepared for the festival.

Old Wolfgang is giving his final orders to the servants. The Master of Ceremonies receives and places the guests.

A herald announces the arrival of the Princess and of Prince Siegfried, who enter, accompanied by their courtiers, pages, and dwarfs. The noble couple bow graciously to the guests, then take the seats of honour which have been prepared for them. The Master of Ceremonies goes to the Princess and receives the signal for the dances to begin. Guests of both sexes compose different groups. The dwarfs begin to dance. The sound of a trumpet announces the arrival of a new guest. The Master of Ceremonies goes forward to greet him and a herald announces their names to the Princess.

Enter the aged Baron von Stein with his wife and young daughter. They bow respectfully to their hosts, and the daughter, at the Prince's invitation, takes part in the dancing. Once more the trumpet sounds, and the Master of Ceremonies again performs his office. New guests arrive.

The Master of Ceremonies seats the older people, while the young girls are invited by the Princess to dance. After several such arrivals, the Princess summons her son to her side and asks him who among the guests has produced a favourable impression upon him. The Prince sadly replies: "So far, there is no one who appeals to me, mother."

CHAPTER III

PETER ILYICH TCHAIKOVSKY AND THE MUSIC OF "SWAN LAKE".

PETER ILYICH TCHAIKOVSKY was born at Votkinsk in the province of Vaytka, on May 7th, 1840. Only two Russian composers, Mikhail Glinka and Anton Rubinstein, had begun to achieve reputations at the time of Tchaikovsky's birth. Italian and French opera were popular, but music by Russian composers was not only unknown to foreigners, but almost unknown to Russians themselves.

Peter was the second son of Lieut.-Col. Ilya Petrovich Tchaikovsky (1795–1880), chief inspector of the Kamsko-Votkinsk mines and metallurgical works. He married three times; having a daughter by his first wife, Maria Karlovna Keiser; and five sons and two daughters by his second wife, Alexandra Andreyevna Assière, the grand-daughter of a French *emigré* who had fled to Russia to escape the Revolution. The Colonel married a third time in 1865.

The Colonel was a gentlemen of pleasant manners, of sunny and credulous disposition; the family was well-to-do and hospitable. A prominent figure in local affairs he lived in a large house with a dozen servants. His second wife, an accomplished linguist, played the piano well and sang agreeably; there was also an orchestrion with a supply of barrels scored with selections from classical composers such as Mozart, Rossini, Donizetti, and Bellini.

Peter's education was confided to a French governess, in whose care he remained for four years. He appears to have been a difficult child, although not without a certain charm, with a passion for music, which presumably he inherited from his mother, and an abnormal sensitivity to sounds and rhythms. In the daytime snatches of melody sang in his brain, and at night he often found it difficult to sleep for the same reason. After a year his parents engaged a young woman to give him lessons in the rudiments of music, but it would appear that her attainments were limited, since the pupil soon outstripped the teacher.

In February, 1848, Tchaikovsky's father resigned his position at Votkinsk in the hope of obtaining an important post at Moscow, a hope which proved abortive. The family moved to St. Petersburg when Peter was sent to a boarding school, but the environment proved distasteful to the young boy and he became unwell and lazy. Since his ill health persisted, a doctor ordered him to have complete rest for six months. Before this period was up, the Colonel secured a post as manager to a group of factories situated in Perm, and the family moved again, this time to Alapeyevsk. As soon as they had settled in their new home, a new governess, N. P. Petrova, was found for Peter, under whom he made good progress.

Almost a year later, it was decided to make a lawyer of the boy. Accordingly, in September, 1850, his mother took him to St. Petersburg. He passed his matriculation early in October and was entered for a two-year course at the School of Jurisprudence. When, however, the time came to part with his mother, just a week after passing his examination, he was seized with a frenzy of despair at the thought of being left alone.

But, before his mother returned to Alapayevsk, she had taken him to hear a performance of Glinka's opera, *A Life for the Tsar*, which made a great impression upon him. Contrary to expectation, the boy did well at his new school. In the summer of 1851 he went for a holiday and began to resume his study of music. He continued to make good progress in his general education, forming many friendships and maintaining a pleasant exterior, although in the secrecy of his room he was sometimes seized with bouts of melancholia.

Then, in June, 1854, his mother caught the cholera and died, an event which had a shattering effect upon her son, whose affection for her was of an almost morbid intensity. His father also caught the fever, but recovered, then moved to Oranienbaum. In endeavour to banish the haunting memory of his beloved mother, Peter turned to music. He composed a waltz which constitutes his first original composition. On his return to St. Petersburg he began to increase his musical studies; he took lessons in singing and frequently attended concerts and performances of opera.

The next year, in response to his son's insistent entreaties, his father made arrangements for him to receive private tuition in music from R. V. Kindinger, a well-known teacher. Later the Colonel asked the tutor whether Peter should devote himself entirely to music. The professor replied that while his pupil showed ability, he could not so far discover any signs of real genius. As a result of this verdict, Peter was told to concentrate upon his law studies, in the hope of obtaining a post in the Ministry of Justice.

Now the Colonel went to live with his elder brother, a change which resulted in his son's making new acquaintances, among them a Neapolitan teacher of singing called Piccioli, an old man of seventy made up to resemble a young man, an odd character who might have stepped from a tale by Hoffmann. The strange pair became firm friends and Peter acquired all kinds of information relating to various aspects of music.

On May 13th, 1859, Peter successfully passed his final examination and was awarded a diploma entitling him to rank of government clerk. He was attached to the Ministry of Justice and less than a year later he became senior assistant to the chief clerk. His career seemed assured and he spent his evenings in a round of theatre-going—opera, ballet, and plays—and social pursuits alternated with intervals of serious study of music. He liked best fantastic ballets or ballets set in a fairy world. His father seems to have divined his son's true vocation, for he encouraged him to develop his knowledge of music.

In the summer of 1861 Tchaikovsky had the offer to go to Western Europe as an interpreter to an acquaintance travelling on business. He accepted and so passed through Germany, Belgium, England, and Paris. At the last-named he revelled in an orgy of concerts and operas, but had the misfortune to quarrel with his employer and so returned to St. Petersburg alone. There he again applied himself to the study of musical theory by attending the classes sponsored by the Russian Musical Society, an organisation which presently founded the St. Petersburg Conservatoire of Music, with Anton Rubinstein as principal, assisted by a distinguished group of teachers. Tchaikovsky was enthusiastic and excited by the classes offered. No sooner had he completed his work at the Ministry than he hurried off to learn at the Conservatoire or practise at home.

He was much sought after as an accompanist. Failing to secure a government appointment he coveted and had worked for, he used this as an excuse to devote himself to a musical career. He was then twenty-three years old, but the prospects were far from bright. His father was in financial difficulties, and could only grant him a small allowance, board, and a room. But in that small room furnished simply with a bed and writing-table, he set to work to achieve a reputation as composer.

His first attempts at composition and orchestration were in the nature of exercises rather than inspired works. His teacher, Rubinstein, wished him to take the works of Mendelssohn and Schumann as his models, but, as a result of attending the concerts organized by the Russian Musical Society, he was drawn far more towards the works of such unorthodox masters of orchestral colour, as Glinka, Berlioz, and Wagner. One of Tchaikovsky's first successful compositions was a group of peasant dances styled "Dances of the Serving Maids," which had

PETER ILYICH TCHAIKOVSKY

From a photograph taken in 1879

TCHAIKOVSKY: LEBEDINOE OZERO ("SWAN LAKE")

Title-page of first piano score, arranged by N. Kashkin, as published by P. Jurgenson, Moscow

the good fortune to be conducted by Johann Strauss the younger at one of his concerts. Peter next composed a String Quartet in B flat major and an Overture in F major. Then he worked at an examination cantata setting for Schiller's *Ode to Joy*, which composition earned him his diploma and a silver medal.

A little previous to this, Tchaikovsky received an invitation from Nicholas Rubinstein (Anton's brother) to teach the theory of composition at the Moscow Conservatoire of Music. Accepting the post, Tchaikovsky arrived in that city on January 18th, 1866. He quickly became friends with the other Rubinstein, who, unlike his austere brother, was fond of wine, women, and cards. Tchaikovsky began to make many new friends, among them V. P. Begichev, Intendant of the Imperial Opera, Moscow.

At this period Tchaikovsky appears to have been a hypersensitive neurasthenic, caused partly by his being overworked and partly by his being obsessed by an inferiority complex. He worked at a symphony to be called *Winter Reveries*, and composed an *Overture based on the Danish National Hymn*, in celebration of the marriage of the Tsarevich to Princess Dagmar of Denmark. The symphony, which received a polite reception at St. Petersburg, was an undoubted success in Moscow, perhaps because the composer had begun to achieve a measure of local celebrity, although the fact remains that sixteen years were to elapse before it was played again.

Next, Tchaikovsky had the idea of writing an opera based on Ostrovsky's play, *The Voyevoda*, for which the dramatist was to supply the libretto. This opera was eventually produced on February 11th, 1869. It achieved success at the *première*, but, as a result of adverse criticism, lasted for five performances only. Then he worked at another opera, *Undine*, suggested by Zhukovsky's poem of the same name. Some excerpts were played at Moscow in 1870, but, since they failed to please, the composer later destroyed the score, saving only three numbers, one of which, an *adage*, was introduced into the score of *Swan Lake*.

Early in June, 1868, Tchaikovsky, in company with K. N. de Lazari, V. Shilovsky, and the young man's guardian, Vladimir Begichev, went on a tour of Western Europe, which included visits to Berlin and Paris. The composer returned to Moscow at the beginning of September. Later that month he went to the Bolshoy Theatre to hear some opera performances by an Italian company and fell in love with the prima donna, Desirée Artôt, but, although she led him to believe that she would wed him, she married a Spanish baritone the following year. The profound mortification produced on the composer by this unexpected news can be imagined.

The composer, Balakirev, becoming temporarily resident in Moscow, grew friendly with Tchaikovsky and having himself composed an overture for Shakespeare's *King Lear*, suggested that his friend should write a similar score for *Romeo and Juliet*. This work was composed and performed at Moscow on March 16th, 1870. The piece failed to please, although to-day it is a popular feature of concert programmes. Early that same month, Tchaikovsky began working on a third opera, *The Oprichnik*. But as the composition moved slowly, he conceived the plan of composing a four-act ballet on Perrault's *Cendrillon*, an idea which unfortunately he abandoned.

On March 28th, 1871, the first all-Tchaikovsky concert was given at Moscow and with success. In June the composer took a holiday and went to stay with his sister at Kamenka, for whose children he composed a little ballet for them to dance to; it was called *The Lake of the Swans*.

He returned to the Conservatoire in a state of acute depression. He longed to give up teaching and devote himself to composition, but he could not afford to lose his salary as teacher. He also wished to live alone and presently found a modest apartment. Then Shilovsky suggested that he should go on a visit to Berlin, Paris, and Nice. He did so accompanied by his young friend. From Nice they went to Genoa, Venice, and Vienna. On his return Tchaikovsky worked hard at composition. He completed *The Oprichnik* and a Festival Cantata which had been commissioned by the St. Petersburg Conservatoire. Then he went to Kamenka and set to work on his Second Symphony, but, feeling exhausted, he decided to go on holiday and travelled to Kiev and thence to Usovo, where he worked steadily at his symphony. He returned to Moscow late in August, 1872. In December he was preoccupied with the question as to whether he should marry.

On February 7th, 1873, the Second Symphony was performed at Moscow and received with enthusiasm. In March he was invited to compose the incidental music for *Snegourochka*. In June he was off again on holiday in Germany, Switzerland, and Paris, returning to Moscow in August. The following year he wrote his Second String Quartet. Next followed his incidental music for *The Tempest*, which, given in Moscow on December 19th, pleased greatly. On April 24th, 1874, *The Oprichnik* had its *première* at the Maryinsky Theatre; but, although it had an enthusiastic reception, the critics were divided as to its merits.

Tchaikosvky became depressed and doubtful of his ability as a composer. Finally, he decided to write an opera on a comic theme, *Vakula the Smith*; it was completed in one month, when the composer orchestrated it and sent it to St. Petersburg. He than left for Usovo (June, 1875), where he wished to work at two compositions: his Third Symphony and a ballet called *Swan Lake*, which had been commissioned by the directorate of the Imperial Theatres. He moved to Kamenka where he completed the symphony and began work on the ballet.

It is of interest to consider a photograph of the composer taken in 1879. He has a fine large head crowned with thick black hair brushed back, thin eyebrows, and moustache and clipped rounded beard fringing the jaw from ear to ear. He has a broad brow, straight nose, and rather sensual lips. His eyes, which were blue, have a half guarded, half wistful expression.

Towards the end of 1876 Tchaikovsky was asked to arrange some of his small pieces for violin and piano. This commission came from a certain Nadezhda Filaretovna von Meck, a wealthy widow some nine years older than himself, who greatly admired the composer and longed to further his work. She was well educated; and her father having been a great lover of music who played the violin for hours on end for his own amusement, his daughter had inherited his taste. She offered Tchaikovsky an allowance thus enabling him to devote all his attention to composition. Although they never met, they carried on a correspondence for some fourteen years. In short, Mme von Meck, with her constant encouragement and helpful counsel, took the place of the composer's beloved mother. Did they never meet because the patron felt that the man might differ sharply from the musician? In one letter to him, she observes, "The more you fascinate me, the more I shrink from knowing you." But the gifted composer was ill suited for normal relationships. A strange neurotic being, he preferred the society of men to that of women. Sometimes such relationships were carried to a questionable degree of intimacy.

At this time Tchaikovsky met Antonina Ivanovna Milyukina, a pretty girl of twenty-eight, a former student at the Conservatoire, who loved the composer to distraction and hinted at suicide if her passion were not returned. The composer, fearful of the consequences that might ensue if he refused to see her, and faced with the alternatives of either allowing her to become his mistress or of marrying her, chose the latter. The marriage took place at Moscow on July 18th, 1877, after which the couple left for St. Petersburg. Alas, his wife proved physically repugnant to him.

He parted from her only to resume his platonic relations with Mme von Meck, who sent him money to enable him to flee to the Caucasus, where he could rest and ponder upon his unhappy situation. At the last minute, however, he changed his mind and went to Kamenka, where he began to orchestrate his Fourth Symphony and resumed work on another contemplated opera, *Eugène Onegin*. But presently, he felt that he could not postpone any longer the dreaded return to Moscow where his wife had taken rooms. Their reunion was not a success. He became so demented through worry that one evening he walked into the icy waters of the Moskva, hoping to catch pneumonia. When this failed he induced a friend to send a telegram recalling him to St. Petersburg. On his arrival there he became seriously ill and remained in a state of coma for two whole days. The doctor told him that he must renounce his present manner of living, a divorce was imperative.

In October Tchaikovsky left for Western Europe wishing to flee the gossip that had been aroused by his marriage and generally strange behaviour. The quietness of Switzerland proved a balm to his tortured nerves. There he received a letter from Mme von Meck with the welcome news that she had decided to make him an annual allowance of seven hundred pounds. From Switzerland he passed to Paris, thence to Florence, Rome, Venice, Vienna and San Remo. In Paris, Tchaikovsky heard Delibes' music for *Sylvia* and Bizet's *Carmen*, both of which charmed him greatly.

After six months' sojourn in Europe, Tchaikovsky returned to Russia, going to Kamenka to stay with the Davidovs. He did not wish to return to Moscow for fear of meeting his wife. So Mme von Meck came to his aid by inviting him to spend a few weeks on her estate at Braïlov, as she would be absent. He accepted and delighted in the rest and attention afforded him. While there, he received a letter from his wife consenting to a divorce. When, however, she was asked to complete the necessary legal formalities, she declined to do so.

About this time, Tchaikovsky received a letter from Mme von Meck enquiring about his manner of composition. His answer is revealing of his methods. He wrote that he possessed the wonderful gift of being able to compose anywhere and at any time of the day; with him it was a creative process which could even function in one part of his brain, while he was apparently occupied with other matters, and each melodic idea embodied its own harmony and rhythm. He composed as emotion moved him, and it was an enchanting and exhilarating occupation; then came the difficult part, the need to discipline inspiration to the requirements of form.

During March, 1881, Tchaikovsky received a letter from his friend and publisher, Jürgenson, with the surprising information that the composer's wife had taken to herself a lover and even had a child by him. Tchaikovsky, therefore, was in a position to institute divorce proceedings, but he refrained from doing so, perhaps for fear that she might retaliate in a manner which would affect his now constantly increasing reputation. He therefore continued to contribute to her support until the very day of his death.

But it is beyond the scope of this essay to discuss in detail Tchaikovsky's career, to accompany him upon all his various journeys to Europe and America, when he conducted his own works at foreign capitals like Prague, Paris, and London, and at New York, Baltimore, and Washington, nor is there space to describe the reception accorded his works or to give his impressions of the many distinguished composers and musicians whose acquaintance he made.

Tchaikovsky achieved an immense body of work, which included ten operas, six symphonies, three piano concertos, a violin concerto, three ballets (*Swan Lake, The Sleeping Beauty,* and *Casse-Noisette*), incidental music for several plays and operas, and a considerable number of songs and piano pieces.

He died at St. Petersburg on November 6th, 1893. The previous August he had completed the composition of his Sixth Symphony (*Pathétique*), which was performed by the Russian Musical Society on October 28th at a concert conducted by the composer. It was this composition in which he took the most pride, a confidence which has been vindicated by the high opinion of distinguished critics.

On November 2nd, he felt indisposed, but declined to consult a doctor. Feeling thirsty, he poured out a glass of water which he was warned was unboiled and hence suspect in view of the then prevalence of cholera at St. Petersburg. He became rapidly worse, appeared to rally and feel better, then, on November 5th, sank into a coma from which he never recovered consciousness.

It will be remembered that it was in the summer of 1875 that Tchaikovsky was invited by the directorate of the Imperial Theatres, Moscow, to compose a ballet to be called *Swan Lake*; the fee offered was 800 roubles, about eighty pounds at that period. He worked at the ballet while staying with the Davidovs at Kamenka, incorporating in it the music of the little ballet of the same name which he had composed four years earlier to amuse his sister's children, and the theme of the love duet for Undine and Hulbrand in the final act of his destroyed opera, *Undine*, which became Odette's *variation* in the *pas de deux* (Odette and Siegfried) in Scene II; it is the melody marked *andante non troppo*. The first two acts of *Swan Lake* were roughed out by

August 26th. On April 4th, 1876, a preliminary rehearsal of numbers from Act I was held at the Bolshoy Theatre. The following day the composer left for Glebova, where he completed the score on the 22nd of the same month.

The original order of the various numbers comprised in the four scenes is given in the piano score published in 1949 by the Tchaikovsky Foundation, New York, which the reader is recommended to consult. Although, in general plan, the ballet follows Russian ballet tradition: *ensembles* for the *corps de ballet*, *variations* and *pas de deux* for the ballerina and *premier danseur*, and a series of character dances such as the "Danse Hongroise" (Csardas), "Danse Espagnole," "Danse Napolitaine," and "Mazurka," which occur in Scene III, not to mention a number for dwarfs, so characteristic of Russian court traditions—the music is symphonic in approach and invested with a colourful orchestration, very different from the tinkling rhythms of Minkus and Pugni. Indeed, Reisinger, the choreographer for the new ballet, considered some of the numbers completely undanceable! Such a view is sufficient comment on the strangeness, the revolutionary nature of Tchaikovsky's conception of music for ballet. Unfortunately for the success of the ballet, Tchaikovsky's score, so far as ballet in Russia was concerned, was too much in advance of its time.

Apart from the processional marches (Scenes I and III), the lively "Peasants' Dance" (Scene I), and the character dances (Scene III), the music, especially that of Scenes II and IV is charged with a brooding melancholy, a sweet sadness, which wonderfully conveys the poignant situation of the enchanted swan-maidens who may resume human form only during the hours of darkness to dawn. The score of *Swan Lake* may not be great music, nor even profound music, but it does depict in terms of moving lyricism and poetry the love idyll and tragic end of Prince Siegfried and Odette, that beautiful maiden so mysteriously and so fantastically transformed from a swan seen a moment before gliding over the limpid waters of the lake.

Again, music is used to intimate something of the nature and qualities of certain of the characters. Tchaikovsky, like Adolphe Adam in *Giselle*, makes use of *Leitmotiv*, that is, the association of a particular melodic theme or phrase with a certain character or incident. Mention has already been made of Odette's theme, that haunting oboe solo with its poignant melody, now exultant, now despairing, but there is a certain rhythmic pattern for Siegfried, while Rothbart is characterized by another rhythm infused with a mood of foreboding and always blended with Odette's theme.

Note, too, Tchaikovsky's genius for the creation of atmosphere. What contrast could be greater than the romantic wistful mood of the lakeside episode and the pomp and scintillating brilliance of the ballroom scene? Observe, again, how Tchaikovsky uses music to differentiate between Siegfried's tender love for Odette and his mounting ecstatic infatuation for the glamorous Odile, with her arch glances and seductive wiles, who swiftly has him in her toils. Finally, how superb is the composer's music in its purely *dancing* qualities; it has a flow, a surge, and a lilt which seem to bear the dancer on waves of rhythmic melody. Tchaikovsky has been justly acclaimed as the greatest composer of ballet music in the classical tradition.

CHAPTER IV

THE MYTH OF THE SWAN MAIDEN

THE myth of the Swan-Maiden is one of the oldest and most beautiful legends in the world, and it reappears in slightly different forms in the literatures of almost all countries, both Occidental and Oriental. The root of the legend is the metamorphosis of a human being, generally a woman, into a bird—a swan, a goose, or a duck—or *vice versa*. The magical change is effected by the use of a potent talisman, such as the donning of a garment, for instance, a shift fashioned of feathers; and, more rarely, by the putting on of the skin of a quadruped, a silken robe, a girdle, a chain, or a ring. The bird-form most frequently encountered is the swan, doubtless on account of its unusual grace and beauty when seen gliding on the surface of water.

The *apsaras*, derived from *ap*, water, and *saras*, from *so*, to go, who are the houris of the Vedic heaven, are said to have been visualised by the Hindus of old, who, seeing fleecy clouds passing over the blue waters of heaven, regarded these shapes as divine swans, which they resembled in form, and endowed them with the special property of being able to descend to earth at will, when they cast off their feather-dresses, to become changed into beautiful maidens bathing in a pool. Sometimes, a swan-maiden would be wooed by a mortal, who married her and with whom she lived happily, until, yearning for her celestial home, she again put on her feather-dress and soared upwards to the mysterious region which lies beyond the sky.

Scandinavian mythology (for instance *Volundarkvitha*, the tale of Volund-Weyland the Smith) contains many stories and references to swan-maidens and swan-wives. In one of these tales, a young man sees three swans alight on a sea-shore. They take off their feather-dresses or bird-shifts and hide in the grass, change into beautiful maidens, and enter and bathe in the water, after which they take up their bird-shifts, put them on, and fly away in the shape of swans.

This same young man watches for the arrival of the swans, and, on another occasion, seizes the shift of the youngest swan, who kneels before him and entreats him to restore the garment to her. But he refuses, takes her to his home, and marries her. Seven years later he shows her the shift which he had kept

ALEXANDRE BENOIS' "O" FOR "OZERO" (LAKE)

From his "Alphabet in Pictures"

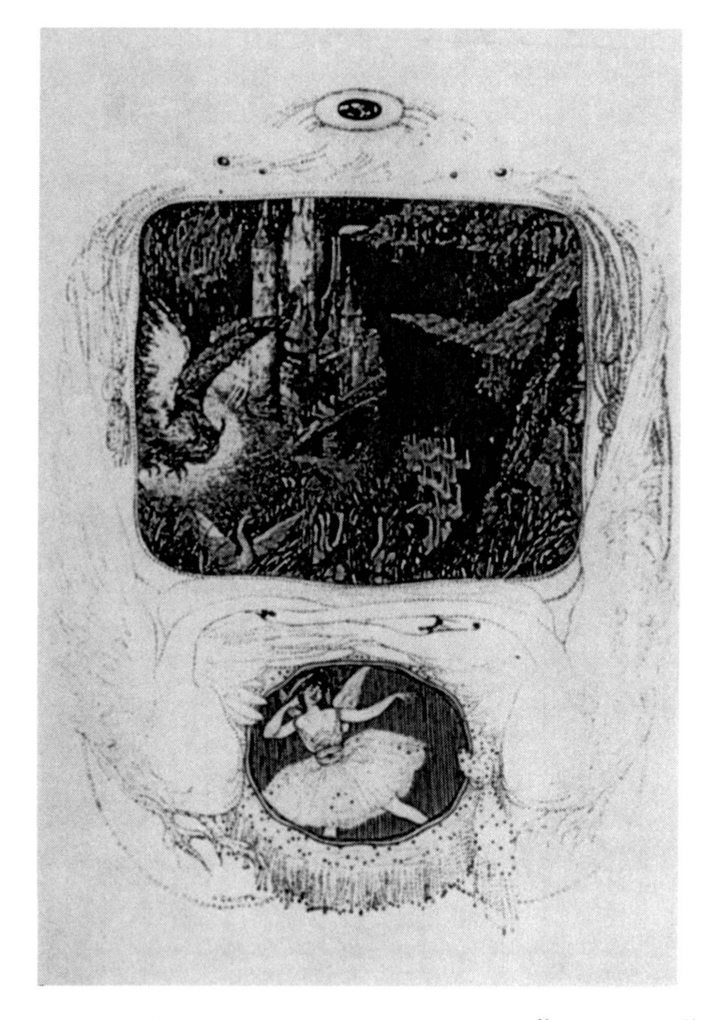

LEON BAKST, DESIGN FOR A PROGRAMME FOR "SWAN LAKE"

From the magazine "Le Toison d'Or'" No. 1., 1906

hidden, but no sooner does she see the garment than she seizes it and, transformed into a swan, flies away through the open window.

The swan-maiden myth is the basis of one of the tales of *The Thousand and One Nights*, the story of Hassan of Bassorah. Hassan, an idle youth, is kidnapped by a crafty magician who forces the boy to journey with him to the foot of a high mountain, when Hassan is sewn up into a skin. A vulture flies down, carries off his prize, and deposits it at the mountain-top. Then the boy cuts the stitches, emerges from the skin, and searches for some pieces of wood, which the magician requires for a particular enchantment, and throws them down to his master. The magician picks up the wood and goes off, leaving the boy to his fate.

Hassan, however, finds his way to a palace inhabited by bird-maidens, with whom he dwells like a brother. Later, called away at their father's behest, they entrust their home to Hassan with the solemn injunction that he must never open a certain door. But, consumed with curiosity, he unlocks the forbidden door and discovers within a wonderful pavilion with a splendid bathing-pool, which is frequently visited by ten birds, each of whom lets fall a feather garment and emerges as a beautiful maiden. Hassan falls in love with one of them, and when the seven maidens return, confesses his disobedience and entreats their aid. He is advised to watch for the return of the bird-maidens and to contrive to steal the feather-dress of his love, and never let it fall into her hands again. He secures the feather-dress and marries the maiden of his choice, but some years later his wife manages to regain possession of the dress, which she immediately dons and flies away. Hassan sets out in quest of his wife and after many adventures succeeds in recovering her.

This story appears to be based in part on the very early Hindu legend of the *apsara* Urvasi, which is described in the *Satapatha-Brahmana*. Urvasi, in love with Pururavas, agrees to marry him on condition that he shall never look upon her naked. But certain supernatural beings, who have missed their playmate, contrive that Pururavas shall break his promise, so that Urvasi shall rejoin them. Pururavas goes in search of his beloved and discovers his wife and her companions swimming on a lotus lake in the guise of water-birds. They change into human form and Pururavas entreats Urvasi to return to him. At first she declines but afterwards relents and the couple are re-united.

There are references to the swan-myth in the mythology of antique Hellas. The ancient Greeks regarded the swan as the bird particularly associated with the Muses, for when Apollo was born at Delos, this happy event was celebrated by flights of circling swans, a romantic conception of fleecy clouds circling about a rising sun.

Consider also the legend of Cycnus, a son of Apollo by Thyria or Hyria, the daughter of Amphinomus. Cycnus, endowed with unusual beauty, aroused the love of many, but repulsed every suitor. One only, called Phylius, persisted in his advances. Cycnus, moved by so constant an affection, resolved to submit Phylius's devotion to a searching test, by imposing upon him three labours: to kill a lion unaided by weapons; to capture some man-eating vultures; and with his hands alone to lead a bull to the altar of Zeus. Phylius performed all three tasks. But when he declined to give Cycnus a bull he had received as a prize, the latter, enraged at Phylius's refusal, threw himself into Lake Canopa and perished. His mother, overcome with grief at her son's death, sacrificed her life in the same way. Apollo caused the two victims to be changed into swans. Another version of this story is related by Ovid in his *Metamorphoses*, where he declares that the Cycnean lake was formed from Hyria's dissolving into tears on the death of her son.

In Slav literature there is a charming version of the swan-myth in the epic called *Sweet Mikhail Ivanovich the Rover*.[1] This is the theme. Prince Vladimir gives a great feast to his nobles, at the conclusion of which he sends three of his most valiant knights on separate missions. Mikhail the Rover is sent to the black horde on Podolia to collect the tribute many years overdue—twelve swans, twelve white falcons, and a writing of submission. When the horde refuses, Mikhail attacks them so fiercely that they yield the tribute and the knight departs.

On his way home along the coast he amuses himself by loosing his bow at swans and geese. At last he prepares to turn inland and, as he gives a farewell glance at the blue sky, he remarks a beautiful swan, her white feathers shot with gold. Swiftly he fits an arrow to his bowstring and pulls on his bow, when the swan cries out: "Ai! Mikhail Ivanovich the Rover, shoot not the white swan, else ill-fortune will doom thee for evermore!"

So saying, the swan takes wing, flies to the shore, and changes into a beautiful maiden. Mikhail goes to her and would kiss "her sugar mouth," but she warns him that she is an infidel and unworthy. If, however, he will take her to the holy city of Kiev, where she can be received into the Church of God, then she will marry him if he desires and he may kiss her as often as he wills. So they set out.

[1] Hapgood (I. F.), *The Epic Songs of Russia*, New York, 1886, pp. 214–231.

There is a South German legend which has certain similarities with the epic of *Mikhail the Rover*. "A Hessian forester once saw a beautiful swan floating on a lovely lake. Charmed with its beauty, he prepared to shoot it, when it exclaimed: 'Shoot not, or it will cost you your life!'" As he persisted in taking aim, the swan was suddenly transformed into a lovely girl, who swam towards him and told him that she was bewitched, but could be freed if he would say an "Our Father" every Sunday for her during a twelvemonth, and not allude to what he had seen in conversation with his friends. He promised, but failed to keep silence, and lost her.

A final example will serve to conclude this brief study of the swan-myth. This illustration, derived from Celtic folk-lore, is *The Legend of the Children of Lir*. King Lir married Finguala, by whom he had three boys and a daughter known as Fionnula. But when Finguala died, Lir married the wicked Arife, who, jealous of her step-children, transformed them into swans, doomed to float over the lakes and weirs of Ireland for centuries, until the Irish became Christians, the sound of the first Mass-bell in the island to be the signal for their release from their swan-form.

This legend inspired Thomas Moore to write the following lines:

> Silent, O Moyle, be the roar of thy water
> While murmuring mournfully Lir's lonely daughter
> Tells the night-star her tale of woes.
> When shall the "Swan" her death-note singing
> Sleep with wings in darkness furled?
> When will heaven, its sweet "bell" ringing
> Call my spirit from the stormy world?

It is very interesting to study these several diverse examples of the swan-myth in relation to the original scenario for *Swan Lake*, because, while no single one of them provides inspiration for the whole ballet, it can hardly be pure coincidence that so many dramatic scenes in the ballet are the counterpart of similar episodes in the folk-lore and literature of several countries at quite different epochs.

The episode of the huntsman about to shoot a swan which changes into a beautiful maiden is to be found in both Russian and South German folk-lore. Odette's story of her persecution by a wicked stepmother which results in her being transformed into a swan, resembles the Tale of Fionnula, although in the scenario of the ballet it is not Odette's stepmother, but her grandfather, who is responsible for the metamorphosis, which is presumably employed as a device for her protection. Again, Odette's declaration that the lake on which she floats in her swan-guise was formed from the tears shed by her grandfather, appears to originate from Ovid's account of the death of Hyria. Finally, the tragic ending of the fourth act, resulting in the dual suicide of Odette and Siegfried, would seem to be derived from the same legend of Cycnus.

SETTING FOR "SWAN LAKE," ACT ONE, SCENE II (FORMER ACT TWO), 1895

As designed by Bocharov for first complete production with choreography by M. I. Petipa and L. Ivanov. Presented at the Maryinsky Theatre, St. Petersburg

SETTING FOR "SWAN LAKE," ACT TWO (FORMER ACT THREE), 1895

As designed by Levogt for first complete production with choreography by M. I. Petipa and L. Ivanov. Presented at the Maryinsky Theatre, St. Petersburg

CHAPTER V

FIRST COMPLETE PRODUCTION OF "SWAN LAKE" (PETIPA-IVANOV VERSION)

IT is possible that the success of an isolated act of *Swan Lake* came as a great surprise to Petipa, who, never backward at seizing an opportunity, promptly decided that he should be associated with it. When, therefore, this second act or first lakeside scene was given as part of a Gala Performance, the new programme revealed the name of Petipa printed beside that of Ivanov, who are styled joint producers. Petipa then resolved to revise the whole ballet and he set to work in earnest at re-shaping it to accord with the taste of the time and the known views of the directorate of the St. Petersburg Imperial Theatres.

In the following chapter I give a translation of the script as adapted by Petipa, which it is of interest to compare with the original scenario. It will be observed that whereas the latter consists of four acts, Petipa divides the piece so that it falls into three acts,[1] the first having two scenes, subdivided into several episodes. Petipa's principal changes in the original synopsis occur in Act II (former Act III) and Act III (former Act IV). In the former he eliminated the scene in which at the moment of Siegfried's betrayal by Odile, Rothbart reveals his true nature by changing into a terrifying owl. The final act was lengthened by the addition of new dances; but the scene of storm and flood, regarded as too melodramatic for the more fastidious taste of the Petersburg public, was omitted, the expressive storm music being used to accompany Rothbart's endeavours to separate Odette from Siegfried.

The music was also edited by Petipa in collaboration with the ballet conductor, Riccardo Drigo. In Act II (former Act III) more prominence was given to the character dances, as a result of which the psychological drama of the struggle between the real and the ideal, so vividly depicted in Tchaikovsky's score, was greatly diminished. Odile was given a brilliant *variation* which was danced to the music of *L'Espiègle* (Op. 72, No. 12), a work from a series of piano pieces by Tchaikovsky (Op. 72) published in 1893. The additional music required for the lengthened

[1] This division now obtains at the Kirov (formerly Maryinsky) Theatre, Leningrad.

Act III (former Act IV) was selected from the collection mentioned and consisted of *Valse bluette* (Op. 72, No. 11), and *A Little of Chopin* (Op. 72, No. 15). Drigo also revised the whole of the orchestration of the last act, and was responsible for editing the entire score. But, instead of concentrating upon the development of the inherent symphonic nature of Tchaikovsky's composition, Drigo sought to make the score lighter in texture and more attractive to the general public. This editing detracted from the essentially theatrical style of the orchestration.

Petipa cast the ballet, divided the action as stated, and allotted the composition of a large proportion of the choreography to Ivanov. As we know, the latter had already composed Act I, Scene II (former Act II); he was now given Act III (former Act IV), and a few numbers in Act II (former Act III), while Petipa assigned to himself Act I, Scene I, and the greater part of Act II (former Act III). In short, Ivanov was given the task of evolving a lyrical form of choreography to accord with Tchaikovsky's symphonic score, to seek an emotional dance symbol which would reflect the emotional qualities of the music. Note how in both these scenes the choreography is conceived as an entity in which the ballerina takes a contributory part, sometimes dancing alone, sometimes dancing with her sister swans, but never dominating the scene, with the *corps de ballet* fulfilling the minor role of a background to the ballerina. Each dancer makes a vital contribution to the whole.

As regards the scenes for which Petipa was responsible; Act I, Scene I, differed little in plan from the original Moscow version. Although the action of the ballet passes in Germany, the style of the dance was French rather than German. Petipa, who was a past master at the devising of dance festivals, provided a waltz for the peasants and introduced a rather difficult but showy *pas de trois* for two *danseuses* and a cavalier, which is pure classical ballet rather than peasant in style. During the *ensemble*, while the peasant girls danced, their swains formed groups and leaped on stools. During the finale Prince Siegfried commanded ribbons to be given to the girls, and a tall pole, to which long ribbons were attached, was brought in, when the pole was held vertical and the girls stretched the ribbons in different directions, thus an appropriate suggestion of Maypole dancing was created.

The act concluded with an *ensemble* by the Prince and his companions, who danced holding cups of wine, a kind of danced drinking-song which, if not boisterous, did not lack vigour. But the dance was devised to a two-beat rhythm, although the music was written in Polonaise time.

In the second act, Petipa composed the *Dance of the Would-Be*

Brides, who wore full-length dresses with long trains, the dance was rather dull; next, a pseudo-*Spanish Dance* for two couples; and a *Mazurka Noble*, full of spirit and character; and a *Grand Pas d'Action* for Odile and Siegfried, which was planned on the traditional lines of a *grand pas de deux*, divided into *pas de deux*, *variation* for cavalier, *variation* for ballerina, and *coda*. Since Legnani was the ballerina, the *pas* was designed to exploit her technical virtuosity.

The opening of this act, which Tchaikovsky had conceived as a ball to which the guests came masked and which would have enabled Odile to come dressed as Odette the Swan Queen, but with her features masked, thus deluding Siegfried into believing that she was his true love until she raised her mask, and proved the contrary—all the wonderful dramatic possibilities of this scene were ignored and confused, and the drama so vividly painted by Tchaikovsky passed unnoticed, obscured by the emphasis on sorcery, further stressed by the flashes of lightning and the unexpected cloud of smoke shot with flame.

The other two dances, *Danse Venetienne* and *Csardas*, were both composed by Ivanov. The first dance, which was undistinguished, bore no relation to Venice, musically considered, since the melody was the popular Neapolitan folk-song, *Santa Lucia*; the *Csardas*, lively, and infused with temperament, was devised for two soloists and an *ensemble*.

In planning the complete ballet, it is clear that Petipa was greatly influenced by the design and mood of Tchaikovsky's music, which he studied by listening intently to repeated playing of the piano score. This is proved by the references contained in the Petipa Archives housed in the Bakrushin State Theatrical Museum at Moscow. Among the scribbled annotations I give those quoted by Yuri Bakrushin in his essay:[1]

"*Hear the music for the Brides (waltz, it seems).*"

"*Hear* pas de deux, *which, I think, was* pas d'action *in Moscow, and out of which I shall make a* pas de quatre, *in order to decide whether I shall introduce Johannsen and others.*"

"*There is a scene and a dance with a tutor and some female dancers. He waltzes intently* pas de menuet. *Then a female dancer takes him and makes him waltz.*"

"*Go to Gerdt's class.*"[2]

Then we have sketches of groups and the positions to be taken by the *corps de ballet* and soloists, and there are suggestions for Act II. The last, for Act III, is concerned with Odette's entrance and the waltz of the swan-maidens. On this sheet there is a

[1] *Tchaikovsky's Ballets and their Stage History.*

[2] Petipa frequently watched Gerdt's classes to seek inspiration for dances for male dancers.

margina lnote by Petipa: "*Entrance of Mlle Legnani. She falls into the arms of Mlle Kulichevskaya. General movement with suggestion of alarm, as though posing the question: 'What has happened to her?' A story. Entrance of M. Gerdt.*" By the side of the sketch for the waltz is another note: "*Here I finished composing. There must be* 16 *more bars before the end, which should be completed with a group.*"

M. Bakrushin also records the existence of a large envelope bearing the number 158473, inscribed: "*Notes on Act I of The Swan Lake, which I have composed, and synopsis of the ballet.*" This envelope is now empty except for a rough general plan of the whole ballet. This evidence suggests that Acts I and III were worked out in some detail. Act I has the note mentioned above, while Act II is limited to a mere enumeration of the dances. On the other side of this plan is a rough draft of a letter: "*A thousand apologies for being late. The reason is I do not know your address.*" M. Bakrushin poses a question and suggests an answer. "To whom is this letter addressed? Perhaps to Ivanov when plans were to be sent to him."[1]

The complete *Swan Lake*, as conceived by Petipa and Ivanov, was planned to be produced during the autumn of 1894, but, on the 20th October, the Emperor Alexander III died, and all theatre performances were discontinued until early in 1895, when the prescribed period of Court mourning came to an end. The ballet in its entirety had its first performance at the Maryinsky Theatre on January 27th.

The cast was as follows:

Princess-Mother	Mme Cecchetti
Princess Siegfried, her son	M. Gerdt
Benno, his friend	M. Oblakov I.
Wolfgang, tutor to the Prince	M. Gillert
Odette, the swan princess	Mlle Legnani
Von Rothbart, an evil geni	M. Bulgakov
Odile, his daughter, who resembles Odette	Mlle Legnani
Master of Ceremonies	M. Voronkov I.
Herald	M. Sosnovski

The principal dances were placed in the several acts as follows:

ACT ONE, SCENE I.

1. *Pas de Trois* (Mlles Preobrazhenskaya, Rikhlyakova I, and M. Kyaksht).
2. *Valse champêtre.*
3. Dance to the clinking of goblets.

[1] *Op. cit.*

SETTING FOR "SWAN LAKE," ACT THREE (FORMER ACT FOUR), 1895

As designed by Levogt for first complete production with choreography by M. I. Petipa and L. I. Ivanov. Presented at the Maryinsky Theatre, St. Petersburg

LEV IVANOVICH IVANOV

From Pleschayev's "Nash Balet"

ACT ONE, SCENE II.

1. *Scene dansante* (Mlle Legnani and M. Gerdt).
2. *Entrée des Cygnes.*
3. *Grand Pas des Cygnes.*
   (*a*) *Valse.*
   (*b*) *Adage.*
   (*c*) *Variation.*
   (*d*) *Coda* and *Final.*

ACT TWO.

1. *Valse des Fiancées.*
2. *Pas Espagnol* (Mlles Skorsuk, Obukhova, MM. Shirayev, Litavkin).
3. *Danse Venitienne.*
4. *Pas Hongrois.*
5. *Mazurka.*
6. *Pas d'action* (Mlle Legnani, MM. Gerdt, Bulgakov).

ACT THREE.

1. *Valse des Cygnes.*
2. *Scène dansante* (Mlle Legnani, MM. Gerdt, Bulgakov).

Skalkovsky, reviewing the performance, observed: "*Swan Lake* afforded Legnani a wide field of action. The *Grand Pas des Cygnes*, already given last season at the Tchaikovsky Memorial Performance, again had the greatest success. Each of the ballerina's attitudes seemed more beautiful than the last.

"In the *pas d'action* of the second act Legnani again displayed her excellent technique in wonderfully daring and beautiful groups. Particularly effective were those *renversés* which the ballerina executed in the course of her *variation;* the votaries of Terpsichore considered this *pas* to be the equal of a whole ballet.

"The majority of the spectators preferred the character dances just as the general public are more impressed by gypsy songs than by Schumann's melodies. There are plenty of character dances in *Swan Lake.*

"The second act (former third act) opens with character dances. The choreography of the Venetian Dance and Hungarian Dance is by M. Ivanov, that of the Spanish Dance and the Mazurka by M. Petipa. There is a wealth of taste and novelty in these *pas* and they were excellently rendered by our Spanish girls from

Kolomna[1] and our Hungarians from the Five Points.[2] The costumes for the Venetian Dance and the Csardas were beautiful, but the former would undoubtedly gain by being danced by a soloist. . . .

"The entire production of *Swan Lake* is a very lavish one. The settings of the second act (former third act) by M. Levogt are very beautiful, that for the last act, the swan lake, is by M. Bocharov. The apotheosis is likewise lovely. The music of the ballet is very melodious, but it contains an excess of waltzes."[3]

Of Legnani, Pleschayev wrote: "We must accord fitting honours to the talent of Legnani. She is the queen of *ballerine*, astounding us by the caressing beauty of her dances, by the plasticity of her poses, and by the grace with which she is endowed. The explanation of Legnani's success lies in the exceptional charm and simplicity of her execution. Legnani is not a good mime and her merit resides in that she does not attempt to mime what is beyond her powers. She simply dances with feeling, endeavouring to interpret in her own way the touching moments in the music."[4]

Khudekov observed: "Legnani was the supreme ideal of plastic movement. She had none of those abrupt movements so often to be encountered in Italian *danseuses*. Her movements were graceful, plastic, feminine, but she was unable to make her movements expressive,[5] to invest them with an inner meaning, and that is why she never appeared at the Paris Opera. . . .

"Legnani, although herself unconscious of it, assimilated from the Russian dancers their refined style and graceful stage manners.

"Her best role was that of Odette in *Swan Lake*. In the first act of that ballet Legnani was a being transformed, unrecognisable as the normally impassive Legnani. In the *Grand Pas des Cygnes*, the danseuse evoked a charming image of a dancing swan. Legnani seemed to live through those moments so impregnated with poetic melancholy. Each one of her graceful movements was invested with languor. In this role Legnani attained the height of artistry."[6]

[1] A suburb of St. Petersburg inhabited at that period by the lower middle class. Kolomna has been immortalised by Puskhin in his poem *Domik v Kolomne* (*A Little House at Kolomna*).

[2] A part of St. Petersburg close to the Haymarket Square (*Sennaya Ploshad*), at which five streets meet, forming five corners. In Skalkovsky's time, Five Points was inhabited by small dressmakers, poor artists, petty officials, and other humble folk. Five Points is mentioned in Dostoyevsky's novels; for instance, in *Crime and Punishment*, Marmeladov is run over by a carriage passing that district.

[3] *In the World of the Theatre* (Russian text), p. 211.

[4] *Op. cit.*

[1] Tikhomirov, former *premier danseur* at the Bolshoy Theatre, who saw Legnani's interpretation of Odette at the *première* of the Petipa-Ivanov production, has recalled that the movements of Legnani's arms and back attained a remarkable swan-like quality.

[6] *Istoriya Tanzev*. Vol. IV., pp. 133-134

CHAPTER VI

THE BOOK OF "SWAN LAKE" AS ADAPTED BY MARIUS PETIPA

ACT ONE

SCENE I. *A park fronting a castle.*

I. Benno and his friends await the arrival of Prince Siegfried, preparatory to celebrating with him his coming-of-age. Enter Prince Siegfried accompanied by his tutor Wolfgang. The festival begins. Village girls and youths arrive to congratulate the Prince who offers wine to the youths and favours of coloured ribbon to the girls. Wolfgang, already slightly tipsy, gives effect to his pupil's commands. Peasant dances.

II. Enter retainers who announce the arrival of the Princess-Mother. This news interrupts the carousing. The dances cease and the servants hasten to put away the tables and conceal evidence of the merry-making. The young people and Wolfgang try to appear quite sober.

Enter the Princess preceded by the ladies in her suite. Siegfried goes towards his mother in dutiful welcome. She lightly upbraids him for attempting to deceive her, saying that she is well aware that he had just been carousing. However, she has not come to interfere with his enjoying himself in the company of his friends, but to remind him that he has entered upon his last day of bachelorhood and that he must be affianced on the morrow. When the Prince enquires to whom he is to be betrothed, the Princess replies that this will be decided at to-morrow's ball, to which she has invited the presence of all young girls eligible to become her daughter-in-law and his wife. From these maidens he himself will choose the one that pleases him the most. Then, having given permission for the interrupted merry-making to proceed, the Princess departs.

III. The Prince is moody. He is saddened at the thought of ending his bachelorhood. Benno persuades him not to spoil the present by reflections on the future. Siegfried signs for the celebrations to continue. The merry-making and dances are resumed. Wolfgang, now quite tipsy, makes everyone laugh with his participation in the dances.

IV. Night begins to fall. One more farewell dance and it will be time to depart. Dance with wine-cups.

V. Overhead flies a flock of swans. The young people have no thought for sleep. The sight of the swans inspires them with the thought to end the day by shooting at them. Benno knows where the swans rest for the night. Having left behind the drunken Wolfgang, Siegfried and his young companions depart.

Scene II. A wild and rocky landscape. In the background a lake. To the right, on the bank, a ruined chapel. Moonlight.

I. Over the surface of the lake glides a flock of white swans, led by one bearing a crown upon its head.

II. Enter Benno accompanied by several friends in the Prince's suite. Sighting the swans, they prepare to shoot them, but the flock glides out of sight. Benno, having dispatched his companions to inform the Prince that the swans have been discovered, remains alone. The swans, now transformed into beautiful young girls, surround Benno, who, spellbound by this magical transformation, is powerless against their charms. His friends return, heralding the arrival of the Prince. At the sight of the newcomers the swan-maidens fall back. The young men prepare to shoot them. Enter the Prince who also takes aim. But now the ruins become illumined with a magic radiance and Odette appears, beseeching their pity.

III. Siegfried, astonished by her beauty, forbids his friends to shoot. Odette expresses her gratitude and tells him that she is the Princess Odette and that her maidens are the unhappy victims of an evil geni who has bewitched them. They are doomed to become swans; but at night, in the precincts of these ruins, they are permitted to return to human form. Their master keeps watch over them in the guise of an owl. His terrible spell will continue until someone falls completely in love with her and for ever, and the man who would free her from this spell must never have plighted his troth with any other woman. Siegfried listens to Odette with delight. Meanwhile the owl flies near them, changes into an evil geni, appears among the ruins, and, having listened to their conversation, vanishes from sight. Siegfried is filled with horror at the thought that he might have killed Odette when she was in her swan-form. In a burst of indignation at his stupidity, he breaks his bow and flings it from him. Odette soothes the young Prince.

IV. Odette summons her friends and they try to distract his thoughts with dances. Siegfried, more and more enraptured by the beauty of the Princess Odette, offers to free her from enchantment. Since he has never pledged himself to any woman he can rescue her from the owl's enchantment. He will kill him and secure Odette's release. She replies that this cannot be. The downfall of the evil geni can only be achieved when some

SETTINGS FOR "SWAN LAKE," AS PRESENTED AT BOLSHOY THEATRE, MOSCOW, 1901

(Above) *Golovin: Design for Act One, Scene I*
(Below) *Korovin: Setting for Act One, Scene II*

SOME SETTINGS FOR "SWAN LAKE"

(Above) *Golovin: Setting for Act Two, Bolshoy Theatre, Moscow*, 1901
(Below) *Setting for Act Two, Bolshoy Theatre, Moscow*, 1921

madman will sacrifice his life out of love for her. Siegfried is even willing to do this. He would be glad to die for her sake. Odette does not doubt his love or that he has never plighted his troth to another, but, on the morrow, a whole bevy of lovely damsels will come to his mother's ball and he will be forced to choose one of them as his bride. Siegfried answers that he will wait until Odette comes to the ball. Odette, overjoyed, replies that this is impossible since at that hour she will still be in her swan-form and can only fly near the castle. The Prince swears that he will never be unfaithful to her. Odette, touched by the youth's passion, accepts his word, but warns him that the evil geni will do all in his power to contrive that he shall betroth himself to another girl. Siegfried solemnly promises that no spell shall deprive him of Odette.

V. The light of dawn appears. Odette bids her lover farewell and then she and her friends vanish into the ruins. The scene lightens.

Over the surface of the lake glides a flock of swans and above them, heavily flapping its wings, flies the giant owl.

ACT TWO

A magnificent hall. Everything is prepared for the festival.

I. The Master of Ceremonies gives the final orders to the servants. He receives and places the guests as they arrive. Enter the Princess and Siegfried, preceded by the whole Court. Procession of the would-be Brides and their parents. Waltz of the would-be Brides.

II. The Princess-Mother asks her son which maiden pleases him the most. Siegfried considers them all to be beautiful but sees none to whom he could pledge eternal love.

III. Trumpets announce the arrival of new guests. Enter Von Rothbart and his daughter, Odile. Siegfried, struck by her resemblance to Odette, greets her with delight. Odette, in her swan-form, appears at a window, to warn her beloved against the machinations of the evil geni. But Siegfried, infatuated by the newcomer's beauty, pays no heed and has eyes for Odile alone. The dances are resumed.

IV. Siegfried's choice is made. Convinced that Odette and Odile are one and the same, he chooses Odile as his bride. Triumphant, Von Rothbart takes his daughter's hand and gives it to the young man, who swears before the company that she is his eternal love. At this moment Siegfried sees Odette at the window in her swan-form. He realises that he has been tricked, but it is too late; he has pledged his word. Rothbart and Odile vanish. Odette must remain for ever in the power of the evil geni who appears above her in the window. The Prince, heartbroken, in an outburst of despair, hurries out. General confusion.

ACT THREE

A desolate landscape near the swan-lake. In the distance, the enchanted ruins. Rocks. Night.

I. Swan-maidens are anxiously awaiting the return of Odette. To while away the time, they seek distraction in dancing.

II. In runs Odette. The swan-maidens joyfully greet her, only to be filled with despair on learning that Siegfried has forsworn himself. Everything is at an end. The evil geni has triumphed and there is no salvation for poor Odette. She is doomed to remain for ever the victim of enchantment. It would be better while she is in her human form for her to perish in the waters of the lake, rather than go on living without Siegfried. Her friends attempt to console her, but in vain.

III. In runs Siegfried. He seeks Odette in order to fall at her feet and implores her forgiveness for his unwitting betrayal of her trust in him. He loves her alone and only pledged himself to Odile, in the belief that she was Odette. The latter, at the sight of her beloved, forgets her fears and surrenders herself to the joy of the meeting.

IV. The appearance of the evil geni shatters their momentary joy. Siegfried must fulfil his oath and marry Odile, while Odette, at the approach of dawn, must be transformed into a swan, this time for good. It is better to die while there is still time. Siegfried swears to die with Odette. The evil geni, alarmed, vanishes from sight. Were Siegfried to sacrifice his life for love of Odette, it would be his ruin. The unhappy girl, having embraced Siegfried for the last time, runs to the top of the ruins, so as to cast herself into the lake from that height. The evil geni, in the form of an owl, soars above her in order to change her into a swan. Siegfried hurries to her side and together with her throws himself into the lake. The owl falls headlong—dead.

Apotheosis.[1]

[1] This was designed by M. I. Bocharov. Odette and Siegfried voyage to "the world of eternal happiness" in a golden barque drawn by a swan with a gold crown on its head.

CHAPTER VII

LEV IVANOV

LEV IVANOVICH IVANOV was born in 1834. He is said to have been the natural son of Tia Adamova. He was only eleven months old when his mother placed him in a foundling hospital, from which she reclaimed him on November 25th, 1837. He appears to have been brought up in a merchant's family until the age of eight, then sent to boarding school for two years, after which he was entered as a pupil in the Imperial School of Ballet, St. Petersburg.

He was placed in the class conducted by Pimenov. Later he studied with Gredlu and Frédéric, then passed to the class taught by Jean Petipa. While still a pupil Ivanov danced with Muravieva in *La Péri*, and with Fanny Elssler in *Catarina*, *Esmeralda*, and *La Filleule des Fées*. He early revealed a phenomenal gift for music which, however, did not please his teachers. It is said that he had only to hear a melody once, to be able to play it from memory, a faculty which attracted the attention of the director of a music society. He thought Ivanov a musical genius, but failed to wean him from the School of Ballet.

In 1852 Ivanov completed his training and was appointed dancer at an annual salary of 360 roubles. Jules Perrot, then *maître de ballet*, did not care for Russian dancers and kept him in the *corps de ballet*, from which he did not emerge until two years later. This change was initiated by the ballerina T. P. Smirnova, who suggested that Ivanov should partner her in a *pas de deux* in *La Fille mal gardée*, in connection with a benefit performance. Ivanov accepted and his début was so successful that Perrot began to give him minor roles and even to compose some dances expressly for him. In 1858 Ivanov's salary was raised to 600 r., and the same year he was appointed a teacher of dancing in the School of Ballet at an additional salary of 300 r. In 1859 he married Vera Lyadova.

When Marius Petipa succeeded Perrot as principal *maître de ballet*, Ivanov filled the post of *premier danseur* and mime. His best performances were in the following ballets: *Faust*, *Esmeralda*, *Catarina*—all by Perrot; *Fiammetta* by Saint-Léon; *Satanella; La Fille du Pharaon* and *La Bayadère*—both by M. Petipa. Ivanov danced with many famous ballerine and interpreted the most diverse roles. But, in addition to classical ballet roles, he was excellent at character parts, especially in the rendering of Italian and Spanish dances.

In 1860 Ivanov was accorded a new one-year's contract by which he received an annual salary of 834 r. as dancer, 300 r. as teacher, and a fee of 5 r. for each performance. Two years later this performance fee was doubled. In 1863 he received a salary of 1140 r., 400 r. as teacher, and a fee of 10 r. per performance. In 1870 he was granted a pension of 1140 r., plus 400 r. as teacher, and 15 r. per performance. Ivanov showed his appreciation of the pension granted him by giving his services for two years without fee, receiving only 400 r. as teacher and 10 r. per performance.

In 1875 he re-married, his second wife being Varvara Ivanova whose theatrical name was Malchugina. In 1882 the chief *régisseur* of the Maryinsky Theatre, A. Bogdanov, retired, and Ivanov was appointed to his post with a salary of 5000 r., with an additional 1000 r. in respect of his teaching activities. A year later, in recognition of his outstanding services, Ivanov received the Gold Medal with the Stanislaus ribbon.

In 1885 he was appointed second *maître de ballet*. Petipa, who was growing old, for he was then sixty-three, needed an assistant, and he naturally preferred to choose a colleague, with whose character and qualities he was acquainted, rather than engage someone from abroad who might prove a rival. But Petipa did not fail to impress upon his new assistant that he would always be acting under his instructions. It was only when Petipa was overwhelmed with work or taken ill, that he called upon Ivanov to deputise for him. And even when Ivanov had composed the dance or ballet required, it was still incumbent upon him to submit his work for the approval of his principal, who asserted his authority by editing or altering it, which corrections Ivanov dutifully accepted, although sometimes chagrined by the unceremonious treatment of his work.

Ivanov's first production was a revival of *La Fille mal gardée*, which both maintained the tradition of Dauberval, the eighteenth century choreographer, and reflected Perrot's ideal of the expressive dance. Ivanov produced a number of ballets, for instance: *The Wilful Wife* (1885), *The Haarlem Tulip* (1887), *The Enchanted Forest*, *The Beauty of Seville*, *Casse-Noisette* (1892), *The Magic Flute* (Drigo, 1893), *Flora's Awakening* (1893), *The Mikado's Daughter*, *Marco Bomba*, *Camargo*, *Swan Lake* (1894–5), *Cinderella*, *Acis and Galathea*, *The Trials of Damis* (1900). The majority of these works were produced in collaboration with Petipa, but, according to Borisoglebovsky, this partnership was not born of the necessity for Petipa's help, but from an enforced collaboration which resulted from Ivanov's being Petipa's subordinate, a relation which also imposed Petipa's name on the posters and programmes as joint producer. It is further asserted that Petipa interfered in Ivanov's work simply in order to have the right to style himself producer. Whether this is true or false, it cannot be denied that for many years the choreography of *Swan Lake* was attributed solely to Petipa, without a word of acknowledgement to Ivanov. The reason why the choreography of *Casse-Noisette* was ascribed entirely to Ivanov resulted from the simple fact that Petipa was ill at the time the ballet was composed.

In 1891 Ivanov was awarded the Order of Stanislaus, 3rd Class. In 1893 he received the Order of Anne, 3rd Class. In 1899, on attaining his jubilee, he was given a benefit, the ballet performed being *Esmeralda*. In 1900 he asked to be appointed assistant to A. V. Shirayev. The following year he received the Order of Stanislaus, 2nd Class.

As a teacher he contributed much to the excellent technical training of the Maryinsky company, among his pupils being E. I. Sokolova, A. F. Vergina, E. O. Vazem, M. N. Gorshenkova, V. A. Nikitina, K. M. Kulichevskaya, and O. I. Preobrazhenskaya.

Some idea of Ivanov's appearance may be gleaned from the photograph of him reproduced in this book. As to his character, he was easy-going, good-tempered, and always accommodating; he was modest in regard to his own achievements and never asserted himself; móreover, his natural abhorrence of anything in the nature of 'scenes' induced him to accept things as they came, rather than make exertions to change them.

Let us deal briefly with two of his best-known choreographic works: *Casse-Noisette* (1892) and *Swan Lake* (1894–5). The theme of *Casse-Noisette* was chosen by the director of the Imperial Theatres, I. A. Vsevelozshsky. When Tchaikovsky received from Petipa the scenario with a complete programme of the type of dances required and their length, he was disappointed, and approached the task of composition with extreme reluctance and doubt of his ability to make a success of it. He derived no inspiration from a study of the theme.

Tchaikovsky's first act is treated on symphonic lines, the distinctive qualities of the several characters being conveyed in expressive music, while the scenes with Drosselmeyer and the War with the Mice are impressionistic. The second act is a *divertissement* in which the ethnographical character of the dances is suggested in terms of music. The most interesting numbers from the dance aspect are the *Danse Chinoise*, the *Buffoon's Dance*, the *ensemble Dance of the Snowflakes*, and the *Pas de Deux*. The *Danse Chinoise*, with its nodding head, sideways movement of the arms, and upward-pointed fingers, is obviously inspired by that phase of Chinoiserie so popular during the eighteenth century and reflected in the porcelain, tapestry, and stage costumes of the period. But the dance has not been really well performed in London since its interpolation in Diaghilev's presentation of *The Sleeping Princess* (1921). The *Buffoons' Dance* has not so far been seen in this country, for the original conception comprised both soloist and groups of dancers, who danced an almost acrobatic version of Russian folk dance steps.

The *Snowflakes ensemble* was a very successful attempt to present in dance form a snowstorm in which we see the flakes—represented by dancers in long white ballet dresses—float and whirl, finally to drift softly down to earth. According to contemporary accounts, the patterns and figures of the composition were remarkable for their poetry and invention. Consider, too, the beauty of the *Pas de Deux* in which the *adage* not only follows but also expresses the melodic line of the music. In the *ensemble* and the *Pas de Deux* we see the lyrical and elegiac approach so soon to attain the heights of poetic composition in the second and fourth scenes of *Swan Lake*.

I have not had an opportunity of reading Ivanov's *Diary*, in which he set down with frankness his inmost thoughts. My knowledge of it is limited to extracts quoted by various Soviet writers on Ballet, particularly Yuri Slonimsky. But it is clear that Ivanov was a dreamer and idealist obliged, through force of circumstances, to be a sort of ballet man-of-all-work, carrying out every kind of task, often distasteful, when he was pining to make the dance more and more expressive. He often ponders on the future of his pupils, and, although his natural shyness makes him reticent in public, in the secrecy of his *Diary*, he becomes forthright. "I am always surprised and astonished at your indifferent and careless attention towards your Art. You do not evince the slightest interest in your profession. You are not artists but automata. At rehearsal you are lazy and unwilling to strive, and you do not give your mind to your work. You are just the same at an actual performance. For these reasons our joint labours suffer."

His impatience with the lackadaisical attitude of his dancers and of their indifference to the Dance as an Art, irritated him beyond measure, and this disillusionment and sorrow are reflected in his work from 1892 to 1895, the period during which he created *Casse-Noisette* and the two lyrical acts of *Swan Lake*. Shirayev, in his *Memoirs*, describing the Ivanov of this period, observes:

"He would suddenly produce so inventive and strikingly original a combination of movements and staging of dances, that we could not understand whence he had derived them, so much of the work was new and hitherto unseen."

It would appear that in *Swan Lake*, fortune having accorded Ivanov a theme exactly suited to his taste and genius, he decided for once to go his own way. The gaiety and glitter characteristic of Petipa's work are replaced by a melancholy lyricism, sometimes infused with a dark presage of impending disaster. Ivanov's deep love of music immediately appreciated and responded to the poetry and expressiveness of Tchaikovsky's score, and he wished his choreography to be rooted in and flower from that music, not to be a purely literal interpretation of its rhythm and pattern.

This new conception of Ballet, in which the choreography would not only reflect the rhythms of the music but also give visual expression in terms of movement to its mood and emotional core, was a most important contribution to the development of Russian Ballet. This conception of ballet as a fusion of music and dance initiated by Jules Perrot, and so lovingly developed and extended by Ivanov, both in his *variations* and *ensembles*, later inspired certain choreographic ideals of Michel Fokine.

It is of interest to compare Petipa's manner of composition with that of Ivanov. Petipa had a precise and orderly mind, and the planning of the scenario, the arrangement of the music, and the selection of the costumes and settings were for him the principal stages in the production of a new ballet. Ivanov, on the contrary, set little store by plans; his work began only in the rehearsal room, where he listened to the music and sought to transmute its mood and message into choreography. Petipa could compose an excellent dance to indifferent music; Ivanov could achieve nothing with music that failed to move him.

Whether he derived inspiration from his early association with Perrot, or whether it came from his idealist nature, Ivanov worked in the tradition of the Romantic Ballet. *Swan Lake* resembles *La Sylphide* and *Giselle* in that it is based upon a romantic conception leading to an emotional conflict, which springs from a mortal man's love for a fantastic being, the balance swinging between a love returned and a love frustrated.

But *Swan Lake* marks both the pinnacle and the close of Ivanov's achievement. After its presentation, he fell back into his old mood of subservience and accepted the inevitable daily humiliations, and thus the choreographic ambitions so dear to his heart declined and withered. He sought solace in the bottle. Nevertheless, conscientious as ever, he worked unceasingly at production and teaching; but he was an embittered man. He died, as he had wished, "in harness," for while he was preparing a new production of *Sylvia* he was seized with periods of intense fatigue. He became ill and passed away in December, 1901, his version of that ballet, like so many of his personal dreams, remaining unachieved.

But although Ivanov had vanished from the scene to which he had contributed as much poetic beauty as can be compressed into a few short hours, his ideals inspired a gifted young choreographer called Michel Fokine, who carried on and developed Ivanov's conception of the lyrical ballet. A short time before his death, Ivanov wrote in his *Diary* some lines addressed to his pupils, the rising generation of dancers. His exhortation constitutes both a fine gospel and a noble epitaph on his own life as artist. That last earnest wish may be summarised thus: "May you ever be blessed with the spirit and strength not to regard your profession merely as a means of livelihood, but as an Art to which you are resolved to dedicate your very soul."

SOME COSTUMES FOR "SWAN LAKE"

(Above left) *Ponomaryev Costume for Odile*, 1892
(Above right) *Ponomaryev Costume for Swan-Maiden*, 1892
(Below left) *Golovin: Costume for Spanish Dance*, 1902
(Below right) *Golovin: Costume for Spanish Dance*, 1902

"SWAN LAKE," PETIPA-IVANOV PRODUCTION. ST. PETERSBURG, 1895.
CHARACTER DANCES FROM ACT TWO. COSTUMES BY PONOMARYEV

(1) *Mazurka* (*Kshesinskaya I, Kshesinsky I*)
(2) *Pas Espagnol* (*Shirayev Matveyeva III*)
(3) *Danse Venetienne* (*Tsalissor Pantaleyev*)
(4) *Pas Hongrois* (*G. Bekefi, Petipa I*)

CHAPTER VIII

SOME SETTINGS FOR "SWAN LAKE"

THE four settings for the four acts of the first Reisinger production of *Swan Lake* were contributed, according to the programme, by the following designers: H. Shangin (Act I), K. Valts (Acts II and IV), and H. Groppius (Act III). I have not been able to discover any details respecting Shangin, but Groppius was the name of a purveyor of settings to the Imperial Theatres at Moscow, and therefore he was presumably less a designer than an agent for a firm in Vienna, then the main centre for such products, which supplied settings from their range of stock scenes ready for use. Valts was a designer-machinist attached to the Bolshoy Theatre, long associated with the stage, who wrote an interesting autobiography called *Sixty-Five Years in the Theatre* (Pub. Academia, Leningrad, 1928). So far as the writer is aware, the only existing records of the scenic aspect of the Reisinger production are to be found in the two drawings, engraved on wood, which appeared in the *Vsemirnaya Illustratsiya (Illustrated World)*.

If the illustration facing page 21 be examined, it must be admitted that Valts has very skilfully given effect to the scene of action imagined by the scenarists, which, it will be remembered, called for "a wild and mountainous countryside bounded on all sides by forest. In the distance, a lake, on the bank of which, to the audience's right, is a half-ruined stone building resembling a chapel. It is night and the moon is shining." The single tree in the left centre, with the wing formed by a cluster of serried tree-trunks, conveys clearly the suggestion of forest, while the leafy branches are kept high to form a natural arch and at the same time permit a clear view of the lake and allow the moonlight to filter through, thus affording contrasting patches of light and shadow in the foreground and dancing area. The ruins at the right ingeniously serve as a screen to mask the metamorphosis of the swans into young women, for the swans are shown gliding across the surface of the lake, to pass beyond the ruins and disappear from view; and then from the entrance archway of the building there emerge the charming forms of young girls, freed for a short span from their dread enchantment. The whole setting has the half-mystical, half-romantic air which is so essential to the mood of this ballet.

It is vital to the success of this scene that when the curtain rises the spectator should be able to see the swans gliding slowly and gracefully over the surface of the lake from his left to his right. Similarly, at the end of the scene, when Odette leaves Siegfried at the imperious summons of Rothbart, for the approach of dawn heralds Odette's return to swan-form, and vanishes from sight into the forest bordering the lake, the spectator should see a moment later the swans gliding over the lake in the reverse direction from which they entered. In the latest revival by the Sadler's Wells Ballet, the swans are not seen and so the whole point of the ballet is lost. This omission is excused on the ground that the sight of the swans gliding over the water arouses ill-timed hilarity rather than produces a dramatic atmosphere. If obviously poorly designed outlines of swans are used, and they are drawn over a guide wire which has become bent or knotted, so that the swans advance by a series of spasmodic leaps and sometimes fall flat on their sides, naturally the result tends to be humorous, but the fault lies not with the effect but with the manner in which it is carried out. If the swans be well designed, their bases mounted on rubber-tired wheels and drawn over rails, the effect can be charming. Perhaps it is unnecessary to observe that the swans should face one way, and not some look one way, and some another, as they were in another production. Swans do not normally travel in reverse.

Valts's setting for Act II was also used for Act IV, only the branches of the trees, which were evidently practicable, were made to snap off during the storm, and there was a special cloth for the simulation of the wind-lashed waters of the lake. Tchaikovsky often discussed the action of the ballet with Valts, and enlisted his aid in the closing episode of the last act. After the thunderstorm, when the lake overflows its banks, Valts planned at the composer's request a realistic whirlwind in which the branches of trees were broken off and fell into the lake, to be swept away by the foaming waters. The storm was succeeded by an apotheosis in which the trees were lit up by the rising sun just as the curtain began to fall. All these effects were achieved to Tchaikovsky's complete satisfaction.

Valts's settings then, which we may reasonably assume to be the outcome of many talks with Tchaikovsky, afford future designers a sound basis for the period and style-atmosphere of the ballet. As the reader will observe on reading the original scenario, there is no definite indication as to period or season of the year. Tchaikovsky himself placed the ballet "in the age of chivalry," which implies the Middle Ages. This is confirmed by the costumes of Siegfried and Benno in the wood-engraving to which reference has already been made, also Odette addresses Prince Siegfried as "noble knight."

The amount of foliage on the trees suggests late summer or early autumn, and the whole of the action occupies two days, for we first meet the Prince when he is celebrating his coming-of-age, which presumably takes place in the late afternoon. The festivities over, the Prince, excited by the sight of a flock of swans passing overhead, decides to go hunting that same evening. It is while searching for the swans that he encounters the mysterious Odette and her disenchanted friends. The ball in the great hall takes place the day following, because when his mother visits him during his coming-of-age festivities, she informs him that she has arranged for a ball to be held on the morrow, to which the most eligible daughters have been invited, and from whom he must choose his bride. The ball would presumably take place after the second meal which, in the Middle Ages, was partaken at from five to seven in the houses or castles of the nobility. It is during the ball that Siegfried is duped by Odile's resemblance to Odette and tricked into asking her to be his wife. When the deception is unmasked, Siegfried, horror-stricken, rushes out to find Odette and beseech forgiveness for his error. In the last scene, which occurs on the night of the ball, he finds Odette, and the dual sacrifice restores the two lovers to each other.

The reader will doubtless be curious as to the appearance of the settings for the Petipa-Ivanov production. This was first presented in its entirety at the Maryinsky Theatre, St. Petersburg, in 1895. The first two scenes were designed by Bocharov, and the last two by Levogt.

The first scene is not particularly attractive and has something of the air of a Victorian pseudo-Gothic grammar-school set in a sub-tropical garden on the *côte d'azur*. The second scene is attractive and the ruined monastery more delicate than the massive structure imagined by Valts. The third scene, with its excess of pierced screens, is over-elaborate and too ecclesiastical in design and decoration; and suggests the interior of a Gothic cathedral rather than the great hall of a castle. The final scene strikes a note of savage grandeur in keeping with the sombre action, while the flat-topped rocky knolls to the right afford a natural eminence from which Siegfried may leap down into the lake below.

Of the four scenes, the third appears to cause designers the most difficulty, possibly because some are uncertain as to what is implied by the term "great hall." In the Middle Ages the "great hall" was the principal room in a nobleman's castle. While the hall was occasionally square or round, it was usually a large rectangular room placed between the inner ward and outer ward, with the lord's private apartments leading off at one end, and the kitchen and buttery at the other end. In plan the hall was a long parallelogram, the roof supported by one or two rows of semi-circular arches supported upon cylindrical columns. The building was constructed of hewn stone and lighted by arched windows, at first of white window-glass, but later of glass stained red, blue, and green, and often depicting good deeds or the principles of knightly conduct. The actual walls were generally concealed by hangings or tapestry representing tournaments, battles, or scenes of the chase. Between the windows were suspended swords and lances, and shields and banners of heraldic device. In winter the great hall was warmed by log fires and lighted at dusk by torches in sconces or crude chandeliers suspended by chains depending from the roof.

When *Swan Lake* was revived at Moscow in 1901, with new choreography by A. A. Gorsky, the Intendant of the Moscow Imperial Theatres, V. A. Teliakovsky, made a sharp break with tradition by inviting distinguished painters, as opposed to professional designers for the theatre, to collaborate in decorating theatrical productions. The designers of the settings for *Swan Lake* were A. Y. Golovin, K. A. Korovin, and Baron Klodt. The newspaper critics passed severe strictures upon the settings. One writer, for instance, compared the castle in Act I to a factory or a huge granary. If the reader will examine Golovin's settings for the first and third scenes, it must be admitted that they are far more Russian than German in feeling. The great hall scene has even a suggestion of one of the chambers in the Kreml. On the other hand, Korovin's design for the lake-side episode is pleasing.

Some idea of the course taken over the years by the settings for various productions may be gathered from a study of the specimen designs reproduced in this book. Some settings are over elaborate, some too fantastic, such as Hurry's designs for scenes two and three; others, like the setting for the great hall in the Lopukhov production of 1946, with its Carolinian architecture and Elizabethan statues in niches, seem to have strayed far from the ideals of the Middle Ages. But since Tchaikovsky's score, with its successful attempt to paint in terms of music the age of chivalry, dominates the whole ballet and inspires its choreography, it is essential that the settings should likewise conjure up that romantic period, with due regard for appropriate mood and authenticity of architectural style and decoration.

CHAPTER IX

SOME COSTUMES FOR "SWAN LAKE"

IF the documentation regarding the settings for the original Reisinger production is limited, it is even slighter in relation to the costumes. So far as I am aware, there exist only the figures to be observed in the wood-engravings of the lake-side scene, that is to say, the characters Siegfried and Benno, and a group of the swan-maidens temporarily restored to their human form.

The Prince and Benno wear, as one would expect, cap, doublet, and hose, the latter striped in the fashion particularly common to German taste. The maidens wear short, low-necked tunics reaching only half down the thigh, with wings at the shoulders; their hair is dressed in the pompadour style which was the mode in the late nineteenth century, with some tresses flowing over the shoulders.

There exists no photograph or representation of Karpakova as Odette, but there is a photograph of Sobeshchanskaya in the role and perhaps it may fairly be assumed that her costume was at least similar, if not the same, as that worn by Karpakova. It consists of tights, shoes, and a simple white ballet-skirt reaching to just below the knee; the sleeves are slightly puffed, and there appear to be wings at the shoulders. The hair is dressed with ringlets, the style fashionable during the eighteen-seventies, and is decorated with a miniature crown.

We are a little more fortunate in documentation respecting the Petipa-Ivanov production, in the shape of contemporary photographs of some of the characters which are reproduced facing page 65. Prince Siegfried, as interpreted by Pavel Gerdt, wears plumed cap, doublet, and parti-coloured hose. The doublet is decorated with a quatrefoil design, and is scalloped at the lowest edge; on his breast is a small appliqued shield decorated with an heraldic swan—perhaps an allusion to the Knight of the Swan —which seems a little previous since he has not yet encountered Odette. His waist is girded with a knightly belt supporting on the left side a wallet, and on the right a dagger. Note the long hair and beard and moustache which hardly accords with a youth who has just attained his majority.

Rothbart, as interpreted by Bulgakov, wears a fur-edged surcoat over armour, while on his cap is set a figure of an owl, like the crests borne on their helmets by knights at jousts or in battle.

The swan-maidens wear a short, tiered ballet-skirt, ending just above the knee; the bodice and short over-skirt are decorated with a design in outline suggested by the formation of a swan's breast and wing feathers, while a few ropes of pearls adorn the bosom. There is a touch of swansdown at the waist, epaulets of the same material, and skull caps also of swansdown. The hair is worn in the same contemporary style with a few tresses allowed to fall over the shoulders. Viewed in the cold light of an untouched photograph, the costume is far from becoming, although it may have appeared differently when viewed under stage conditions.

Legnani's costume as Odette appears to have varied little from that designed for the swan-maidens, except that she wore a crown; it is not quite clear whether the same swansdown cap was worn or a few feathers. The coiffure follows the fashion of the day, without any tresses at the back.

The reader who is acquainted with present-day full length revivals of *Swan Lake* may like to see the costumes worn by the four character dances which occur in the ball scene as presented in the Petipa-Ivanov production of 1895. Photographs of the principals in the Polish Mazurka, Spanish Dance, Venetian Dance, and Hungarian Csardas will be found facing page 57. Except for the male dancer in the Venetian dance, the costumes have little relation to the Middle Ages.

Viewing the changes in costume for the principal characters over the years, that for Prince Siegfried has remained basically the same: doublet and hose, the sleeves of the doublet puffed or slashed to reveal material of another colour. Sometimes the doublet has the skirts widely pleated, sometimes it is decorated with sequins. Again the doublet is sometimes cut to reveal a broad shield-shaped expanse of undershirt. The collar also exhibits many variations, from being low and open at the neck, to high like the collar of a Russian caftan. Head-dresses, too, differ considerably, from a plumed cap or hat to a simple circlet of gold with or without a central jewel from which springs an ostrich plume or osprey feather. There have also been costumes with the close-fitting doublet which ends at the navel to meet the top of the tights, which, to the writer, always suggests an acrobat rather than a knightly personage. The governing principle is to design a costume which is historically correct, whatever the degree of simplification, which sets off the dancer's figure and does not impede the movements of the limbs or body;

which confers grace and nobility; and finally, which suggests without ostentation that the wearer is a nobleman of high rank.

Similarly, the costume for Odette is founded on the ballet-skirt, generally ending just above the knee. The shape of the skirt and the number of petticoats may vary in accordance with the prevailing fashion. There is a frequent tendency to introduce a short over-skirt of feathers arranged to suggest a swan's wings, the remaining expanse being left plain or decorated with bands of swansdown. Sometimes the shoulders are left bare, the bodice supported by flesh-coloured straps, sometimes the strap is covered with swansdown or feather trimming. The objection to the swansdown straps is that it both spoils the shoulder line in *port de bras* and suggests that the dancer is committing the elementary fault of hunching her shoulders. The arrangement of the feather-trimmed strap worn by Ulanova is an interesting example of how to use the strap without detracting from the shoulder line. The colour of Odette's dress is invariably white, indicative of her virginal character and of her other life as a swan.

According to the late Agrippina Vaganova, Legnani, as Odette, wore a crown on her head. The same informant declared that the ballerina, Vera Trefilova, introduced the familiar headdress composed of two feathers, one placed on either side of the brow.

One of the most charming conceptions for Odette's costume is that designed by Leslie Hurry for Margot Fonteyn in the production by the Sadler's Wells Ballet. The bodice is in the form of a swan's wings and is shaped to follow the contour of the breasts, while the surface is faintly shaded to suggest the pattern of the wing feathers. The bodice follows the century-old tradition of the Romantic Ballet of being "off the shoulders" so that the lovely line of the arm and shoulder is retained in all its purity. The head-dress is a delightful conception, a narrow white headband with a small wing covering each ear, while a miniature swan floats on the jet-like surface of the dancer's hair.

CHAPTER X

ALEXANDER GORSKI

ALEXANDER ALEXEYEVICH GORSKI was born near St. Petersburg on August 6th, 1871. His father earned his livelihood as a book-keeper in a commercial house, but his chief interests in life were painting, embroidery, and the breeding of silkworms. When the son was eight years old his parents wished to send him to a School of Commerce. To this end his mother went to St. Petersburg in the summer of 1879, accompanied by her son and daughter, hoping to place the latter at the Imperial School of Ballet, through a friend of hers, O. B. Adams, who was attached to the school as inspectress. The mother first entered her son at the School of Commerce, and then went to the School of Ballet, where her daughter was accepted as a pupil. As they were leaving, her friend said: "What about the boy?" His mother replied that she had already entered Sasha for the School of Commerce. "Rubbish!" said the inspectress, and took the boy to see the director. She returned with the news that the boy had also been accepted. The parents, feeling it unwise to oppose the dictates of fortune, decided to let matters take their course.

In 1880 Gorski joined the School of Ballet as a paying pupil. He was placed in the junior class conducted by Platon K. Karsavin, father of the famous ballerina. The boy's application and diligence were such that a year later he was transferred to the category of non-paying pupils and so received his choreographic and general education free. From Karsavin, Gorski passed to the care of N. I. Volkov, an exacting but cultured teacher, finally to be transferred to the senior class taught by Marius Petipa himself, then at the height of his fame.

On 31st May, 1899, Gorski graduated and became a member of the *corps de ballet*. He was soon promoted *coryphé* (second class), then *coryphé* (first class), and in six years attained to the rank of solo dancer (second class). After taking many minor roles he was accorded the leading male role in *La Fille mal gardée*, and then in *The Magic Flute*. He danced classical ballet roles such as Aquilon in *Flora's Awakening*, and also character numbers such as Satyr in the opera *Tannhäuser*, and the Danse Chinoise in *Casse-Noisette*, showing that he was very versatile. Apart from the

"DANSE VENETIENNE": "SWAN LAKE," GORSKI PRODUCTION

ALEXANDER GORSKI

SOME CHARACTERS FROM "SWAN LAKE"

(Above left) *Bulgakov as Von Rothbart, Maryinsky Theatre, St. Petersburg,* 1895
(Above right) *P. A. Gerdt as Siegfried, Maryinsky Theatre, St. Petersburg,* 1894–5
(Below left) *P. Legnani as Odette, Maryinsky Theatre, St. Petersburg,* 1894–5
(Below right) *A. A. Giuri as Odette, Bolshoy Theatre, Moscow,* 1903

dance aspect of his studies, he did all he could to improve his general education by attending evening classes, by reading, and by studying foreign languages.

In 1895 Gorski became a friend of the dancer V. I. Stepanov, who was trying to evolve a practical system of dance notation. The next year Gorski was appointed teacher of dancing to the class of P. A. Gerdt, later becoming his assistant. When Stepanov died in 1897, Gorski felt it his duty to carry on his friend's work, and on his recommendation the Stepanov system of dance notation became a recognised subject in the school studies, Gorski being appointed to teach it.

At the end of 1898 the directorate of the Moscow Theatres desired to present Petipa's *Sleeping Beauty*,[1] which had not yet been seen there. Doubtless on the advice of Petipa himself, Gorski was entrusted with the production, and his arrival in Moscow coincided with the foundation of the Moscow Art Theatre. Returning to St. Petersburg, Gorski produced at the Mikhailovsky Theatre on April 11th, 1899, a one-act ballet called *Clorinda, Queen of the Mountain Fairies*, music by Ernst Keller, as an examination performance for the St. Petersburg School of Ballet. Later in the year he again visited Moscow to stage Petipa's production of *Raymonda* (music by Glazunov), in which he collaborated with the Moscow choreographer, I. I. Clustine.

On September 1st, 1900, Gorski was nominated *premier danseur* of the St. Petersburg Ballet, but on the 9th he was transferred to the Moscow Theatres as *régisseur* to the ballet company. He himself regarded this post as purely temporary, but in actual fact Gorski was to remain in the old capital for good. He came to the city at a time of a great renaissance of the arts. The Mæcenas Mamontov was founding his Opera Theatre with the youthful Chaliapin; the Moscow Art Theatre was beginning its productions destined to bring it world-wide fame; there were art exhibitions of paintings by Korovin, Levitan, and Vrubel; and literary circles sprang into being at which the works of Gorki and Chekov were read and discussed—only the world of ballet seemed to take no part in all this artistic activity.

The reason for this, as the historian Yuri Bakrushin[2] points out, were not hard to seek. The Moscow ballet company could boast no choreographer of distinction, while, as soon as an artist of the ballet showed promise, he or she was transferred to St. Petersburg. The repertory was poor and often the theatre was only a third full when ballet was given. Yet the School of Ballet continued to produce year after year a fresh reserve of

[1] It is said that Ivanov composed the "Vision Scene" in that ballet but never received credit for it.

[2] *Alexander Alexeyevich Gorski.*

young and talented dancers, who only needed a leader to inspire and direct them.

Gorski was next invited to revive Petipa's *Don Quichotte*, which he resolved to produce not in accordance with established practice but more on the lines advocated by the Moscow Art Theatre, which proclaimed the new theory of unity of artistic conception. Gorski commissioned the painters Korovin and Golovin to design the settings and costumes. The new production was achieved in eighteen months and first performed at Moscow on December 6th, 1900. As Karsavina tells us in her charming reminiscences, *Theatre Street*, "our ballet stood bewildered at this breaking away from the state tradition of quasi-realistic scenery, of accepted canons of costumes." The *corps de ballet* no longer took a passive or purely decorative part in the ballet, but became an integral part of the whole composition, while the groups were assymetric as opposed to the usual symmetrical groups and masses.

Reports of the decisive success achieved by Gorski reached St. Petersburg, sending ballet-lovers hot-foot to Moscow to see the wonder for themselves. One of these, Alexander Benois,[1] records his impression of the new production in blunt terms which permit of no misconception. "There had been rumours that the Moscow production of the old ballet *Don Quichotte* was a masterpiece, and that its producer, the ballet-master Gorski, had revealed new horizons. This proved to be untrue, Gorski's new version was vitiated by the abhorrent lack of organisation that is typical of amateur performances. His 'novelties' consisted of making the crowds on the stage bustle and move about fitfully and aimlessly. As regards the action, the dramatic possibilities and the dancers themselves were depressed to a uniformly commonplace tint. *Don Quichotte* had never been an adornment to the Imperial stage, now it had become something unworthy of it and almost disreputable."

In 1901 Gorski revived *Swan Lake*, retaining much of the Petipa-Ivanov choreography, but revising the first and third scenes to afford greater contrast with the lyricism of the second and fourth scenes. This same year Gorski produced seven ballets, including his own version of *The Humpbacked Horse*, which had a particular attraction for him, in view of its opportunities for mimetic dance.

In 1902 Gorski was appointed *maître de ballet* to the Moscow Theatres and his *Don Quichotte* was transferred to St. Petersburg at the Maryinsky Theatre. In the summer, he went to Paris accompanied by the painter Korovin, to study some of its medieval buildings with a view to gaining inspiration for a new ballet called *Gudule's Daughter*, based, like Perrot's *Esmeralda*, on Hugo's novel *Nôtre Dame de Paris*. The new ballet was produced on November 24th, but had a mixed reception owing to its markedly realistic tendencies. The principal role of Esmeralda was assigned to a young dancer called Sophia Fedorova, whose dramatic interpretation aroused great interest. Dispirited by the reception accorded his ballet, Gorski produced nothing new for more than a year, when he devised a ballet called *Le Poisson d'Or*, based on Pushkin's fairy tale; this work also failed to achieve complete success.

At the end of 1904 Gorski taught regularly at the Moscow School of Ballet, giving lessons in mime and *plastique* to the senior students and instruction in academic technique to the junior pupils. According to M. Bakrushin,[2] Gorski was responsible for substituting the piano as an accompaniment for class exercises in place of the traditional violin. His teaching was designed to develop individual creative ability.

At the end of 1905, Gorski revived Petipa's famous old ballet, *La Fille du Pharaon*, trying to *suggest* the style and atmosphere of ancient Egypt, rather than attempt to convey it by realistically painted settings. Fedorova achieved a success as Khita the slave, while the roles of Pharaoh and the King of Nubia were taken by Sidorov and Mordkin respectively. All three were pupils of Gorski. The revival aroused such interest that Pavlova herself came from St. Petersburg to dance the role of Aspicia, thus creating a precedent which soon became a regular practice.

In 1906 Gorski produced new editions of *Swan Lake* and of *Don Quichotte*. The next year he devised a *divertissement* called *Etudes* in which he successfully achieved the evocation of mood, and at the end of 1908 he revived *Raymonda*, which achieved considerable success, repeated by his production, on January 10th, 1909, of *Salammbo*, based on Flaubert's novel.

In 1911 Gorski revived *Giselle*, transferring the period of the first act from the Middle Ages to the early nineteenth century, to contrast the realism of the first act with the fantastic quality of the second act. During that year he went to London to produce *The Dance Dream* at the Alhambra Theatre in connection with the Coronation festivities. In January 1912 he revived in Moscow Perrot's ballet *Le Corsaire*, and later produced for the Maryinsky a new version of *The Humpbacked Horse*. In 1915 he produced a new ballet, *Eunice and Petronius*, inspired by Sienkiewicz's novel, *Quo Vadis?*, which aroused considerable controversy. The following year he devised a ballet to Glazunov's *Fifth Symphony* and revived another of Petipa's ballets, *La Bayadère*.

[1] *Reminiscences of the Russian Ballet.* [2] *Alexander Alexeyevich Gorski.*

The year 1918 was marked by the Russian Revolution, which interrupted Gorski's activities, resumed on its first anniversary by his production of *Stenka Razin.* In 1920 he produced a new edition of *Swan Lake*, in which he collaborated with Nemirovich-Danchenko, one of the founders of the Moscow Art Theatre. In 1921 Gorski revived *Casse-Noisette*, retaining some of Ivanov's dances, and creating new numbers of particular brilliance.

Apart from his choreographic activities, Gorski served on several administrative bodies connected with the ballet and devoted much thought to improving the standard of training for the ballet. In 1922 he again revived *Swan Lake* and at the end of the year devised a ballet to Mozart's *Les Petits Riens*. In 1923 he staged at the New Theatre, Moscow, a children's ballet called *Immortal Flowers*, and the season 1923–4 saw his ballet *Venusberg* arranged to Wagner's music from *Tannhäuser*. Gorski appeared to be a man of inexhaustible energy, but in the autumn of 1924 he had a nervous breakdown while conducting a rehearsal at the Bolshoy Theatre. He never recovered and died on September 20th.

The Moscow Ballet company deeply mourned his passing. Apart from his qualities as teacher and choreographer, Gorski was not only a well-educated man, but he could paint, write, act, and play a musical instrument. He took a lively interest in all his artists, in whom he tried to develop a sense of style and appreciation of mood. Only those who are acquainted with his productions can judge of his merits as choreographer, but it is clear that his original ballets were small in number, only some half-dozen as opposed to well over twice that number of revivals, not to mention at least five versions of *Swan Lake*. Gorski never ceased to urge the necessity to develop creative initiative, always maintaining that new choreographers were vital to the art of ballet, without whom it would perish.

CHAPTER XI

THE CHARACTERS IN "SWAN LAKE"

THERE are only seven characters in *Swan Lake*: four male and three female. These differ considerably in importance and may be divided into three groups: primary, secondary, and tertiary.

There is only one principal role, the dual character of Odette-Odile, so that the ballet follows the prototype of *La Sylphide* and its successor, *Giselle*, by concentrating the supreme interest in the ballerina. Similarly *Swan Lake* follows the tradition of *Giselle* in that the action not only oscillates between the two poles of the material world and the world of phantoms, but also between the conflicting forces of good and evil.

There is one secondary role, that of Prince Siegfried.

Finally, there are the four subsidiary roles of Benno, Rothbart, Wolfgang, and the Princess Mother.

As I have observed elsewhere, while the writers of *scenarii* for ballets often describe the action in some detail, they frequently are singularly reticent when it comes to no less vitally important questions of the appearance and qualities of the actual characters; so that the dancer called upon to interpret a role must either imitate to the best of her ability a previous interpretation with which she is familiar, or model herself on what is presumed to be the traditional rendering of the character, or else apply herself to a study of the role in question, with a view to forming her own conception, within the confines of the traditional mime and choreographic script. For this reason, it may be of interest to speculate upon the several characters in *Swan Lake*. Consider first the role of Odette-Odile. It is a dual character, a Jekyll and Hyde role, in which the ballerina must assume for two scenes the role of the chaste Odette, and in one other scene the part of the evil Odile. In brief, she must appeal to the most noble qualities of human nature in the one case, and to the baser elements in the other instance. It will be convenient to examine the two halves of the dual role separately.

Odette, as we know from the script, is a strange, enchanted, composite being; a swan from dawn to dusk, a woman from dusk to dawn. As a swan she wears a small crown on her head; as a woman, she wears a jewelled crown. As a swan she leads the flock, and as a woman she is clearly regarded by her sister swan-maidens as their leader. These signs betoken her rank. One may, therefore, conceive Odette as a young and beautiful woman, with an air of refinement and nobility. And since a swan has dark velvety eyes set in a head covered with white down, one might expect these traits to be preserved in the woman as dark eyes in a pale face. One must also expect a swan-maiden, doomed to so strange a fate, to radiate a certain mystery appropriate to so enigmatic a personality.

Is Odette dark or fair? Karpakova, the first of the line, was not dark; on the other hand, Legnani, the first Odette of the Petipa-Ivanov production, was a brunette. I have seen Odettes of every shade from dark to fair, but there is no doubt that dark hair not only best sets off pale features and contrasts well with the traditional white dress, but emphasises that air of mystery and wistfulness which is essential to the character.

In interpreting the role of Odette it is a cardinal point for the ballerina to remember that in all her meetings with Siegfried, she is in her guise as woman. It is true that Ivanov has conceived many of her steps and gestures in a bird idiom, but in my view these are intended merely to hint at Odette's dual nature, at her shifting life between woman and swan, and to remind us that her irrevocable return to her other existence is only a few hours away.

Those suggestions of fluttering wings, of nestling the head in the downy socket of the wing, of preening, might reasonably be stressed on Odette's first entrance, since, although her physical metamorphosis is complete, her actual nature is perhaps still in a state of transition. But, with the development of the action, the suggestion of bird behaviour should gradually be lightened to a mere trace, as she becomes more and more feminine, a quality heightened by the awakening of her love for Siegfried, a tenderness which grows under his gaze and at his touch, to return, at the close of the second scene, to a mood of despair at the poignant thought of being parted from her lover, perhaps for ever, when Rothbart summons her to resume her life as an enchanted swan now emphasised by her resumption of bird behaviour.

Odile, we are told, is the daughter of Rothbart the magician, but since he makes her assume the likeness of Odette, the expression "daughter" is more a convenient figure of speech for what is clearly a familiar spirit. That such was the authors' intention is corroborated by the fact that Skalkovsky, describing a performance of *Swan Lake* at the Maryinsky Theatre in 1899, records that immediately after Siegfried asked Odile—believing her to be Odette—for her hand in marriage, the great hall went dark and Odile changed into an owl.

Odile, then, like the wraith of Giselle, when admitted to the evil sisterhood of wilis, is not a living woman, but a phantom, a chimera fashioned by black arts of which Rothbart is master, and for the express purpose of tricking Siegfried into breaking his oath to Odette, an oath which, if kept, would eventually free her from Rothbart's enchantment. The problem for the ballerina is to convey by some new phantom quality in her dancing, by some suggestion of the unreal, that Odile is a creature from another world, a seductive misty vision which would vanish if breathed upon. The ballerina must attempt the difficult task of conveying the impression that while to all outward appearance she is Odette, one feels that she is someone else, that her seeming loving tenderness is assumed and false, a view confirmed when, having Siegfried fast in her toils, her tenderness and sweetness give place to her true character, which is shallow and vicious.

The chief of the secondary roles and the principal male character is that of Prince Siegfried. We know that he is a young prince who has just attained his majority. It is fair to conceive him as a handsome, well-proportioned young man, whose gentle birth is revealed in his charming manners and noble bearing. He is usually represented as clean-shaven, but the first interpreter of the role of Siegfried in the Petipa-Ivanov production, Pavel Gerdt, wore both moustache and pointed beard, as may be observed in the contemporary photograph.

What is the character of Siegfried? So far as the first scene is concerned, he is unlike most young men of his age in that he evinces little interest in the opposite sex. Assuming the village girls to be beneath his notice, although even kings have not been above chucking a pretty wench under the chin, or more, it may be observed that he does not even bestow a glance in the direction of the high-born maids of honour who attend his mother. His leisure hours appear to be divided between the chase and in drinking with his companions, young men of his own age.

In the latter pursuit he bears no resemblance to our own Prince Hal, who sought entertainment among the lower orders, in the more diverting and more worldly-wise company to be encountered in the common alehouses. Siegfried has more of the coldness and diffidence of the character of Charles XII of Sweden when a youth. It is therefore always something of a surprise to see in the second scene an apparent misogynist's falling in love with Odette, at his first sight of her. Are we to suppose that Siegfried, personifying a familiar aspect of romanticism, had formed a mental picture of an ideal woman with whom he was spiritually in love and who to his astonishment is suddenly revealed to him in material form in the person of the mysterious Odette.

One interpreter of the role of Siegfried has designated it a prince of cardboard, a character which cannot be infused with warm life. It is true that the part can be, and generally is, presented purely as cavalier role, apart from his *pas seul* in the ballroom scene; but I venture to maintain that the Prince *can* be made to live. Actually, Siegfried moves in two worlds, the realistic world of the court, his own everyday existence, which is depicted in scenes one and three, and the world of fantasy, dominated by the enchanted swan-maidens, which is presented in scenes two and four.

Few interpreters of Siegfried attempt to suggest these two contrasting spheres. One would expect Siegfried to adopt a formal demeanour in his own world, as though he were discharging an irksome duty imposed upon him by virtue of his birth and position, for which he assumes an appropriate mask of princely dignity and graciousness, a position in which, paradoxically enough, he is the centre of all eyes, yet feels strangely alone, as though surrounded by an invisible barrier.

At the lakeside, in the friendly surroundings of lush glades and leafy trees, untrammelled by court ceremonial, he has a new sense of freedom and for a brief period can be himself and live his own life. Here, then, one would expect Siegfried to exhibit a natural manner.

The interpreter of Siegfried, like that of Albrecht, needs to be both graceful and manly, a fine mime with a sensitive appreciation of style-atmosphere, and an excellent *danseur classique*, for although the major part of the role is concerned with miming and with partnering the ballerina, in the third scene he is called upon to execute a difficult *pas seul*. It may be added that the success of the *pas de deux* both of Odette and Siegfried, and of Odile and Siegfried, depend not only on Siegfried's ability as cavalier, but also on the two partners maintaining a sense of interplay and interest in each other. In short, it is not merely a question of Siegfried's supporting and presenting the ballerina, but of maintaining a perceptible emotional link between them, which in turn is communicated no less clearly to the audience. The spectator must share in Siegfried's wonderment at the first appearance of Odette, his growing admiration, his sympathy for her fate, the dawn of his love, and so on to his supreme sacrifice,

[*Photo: Roger Wood*

"SWAN LAKE," ACT ONE, SCENE I, PEASANTS' DANCE. SADLER'S WELLS BALLET PRODUCTION

Settings and costumes by Leslie Hurry, Royal Opera, Covent Garden, 1950

"SWAN LAKE," ACT ONE, SCENE II. SADLER'S WELLS BALLET PRODUCTION

[*Photo: Tunbridge-Sedgwick*

his act of contrition for the pain he has inflicted upon Odette for having allowed himself to be tricked by her counterfeit, Odile.

The role of Benno resembles in some degree that of Wilfrid in *Giselle*, for although Benno is not a squire but a friend of the Prince he is in constant attendance on Siegfried, ready to come to his aid or wait on his bidding as his lord may require. It is strange that Siegfried's friend should be accorded so Italian a name.

Rothbart is an evil enchanter whose like is so often to be encountered in mediaeval romances, a character resembling Archimago in Spenser's *Faerie Queene*, and with the same power to assume diverse forms. Here, however, Rothbart alternates only between Owl and Knight. It is perhaps unnecessary to add that Rothbart is merely the German for Redbeard. Can the name have been suggested by Barbarossa, the surname of Frederick I of Germany, who sleeps in Thuringia, a district already familiar to us as the scene of action of *Giselle*?

In the Petipa-Ivanov version Rothbart was presented as a man in the early forties, with long hair trimmed to nape level, eyebrows set at an angle of forty-five degrees, a moustache with the ends pointed and upturned in a fashion popular in Germany at the beginning of the present century, a fringe of whisker along the jaw, with a narrow beard falling over the chest in two long points. The character of Rothbart must be invested with a dominating personality, at once mysterious and evil.

Wolfgang the tutor is presented as greybeard who is beginning to feel the weight of his years. His countenance and actions suggest that he is addicted to the bottle. Since, in nineteenth-century Russia, most tutors engaged to teach the children of well-to-do families were *emigrés*, the attribution of insobriety is perhaps the reflection of a popular joke at the foreigner's expense, unless it was inspired by actual experience. It is curious how tutors in ballet are so often represented thus. In *The Sleeping Beauty*, Gallison, tutor to Prince Desiré, is shown in his cups in the picnic scene in the forest. But in the production of *Swan Lake* by the International Ballet, Wolfgang has been given a different interpretation by Algeranoff. He depicts the tutor as a kind of Erasmus, an austere scholarly figure, which in some ways is more appropriate, although it is difficult to believe that he would so far forget himself as to flirt with the village maidens.

The Princess Mother must clearly be a lady approaching fifty. She will obviously exhibit the dignity and graciousness consonant with her exalted position. Upon the interpretation of this role depends the prestige of the court of which she is queen, for it stands or falls by her. It is not sufficient to wear a rich costume and a crown, her manner must accord with her position. The average portrait of the character suggests a radiant elder sister to Siegfried rather than his mother, whose health is possibly not too robust, since she is so anxious to see her son make a fitting match, that she may die content in the knowledge that the traditions of their noble line will be worthily upheld.

CHAPTER XII

THE ANATOMY OF "SWAN LAKE"

FOLLOWING the plan of my previous study of the ballet *Giselle*, I have placed after this chapter a choreographic script of all four acts of *Swan Lake*. I have taken as my authority the several productions of *Swan Lake* staged in this country by the late Nicholas Sergeyev, which revivals were based on his stenochoreographic records of the traditional version presented at the Maryinsky Theatre, St. Petersburg.

In the difficult work of compilation I have had the expert advice and assistance of several friends. Mary Skeaping, formerly *maîtresse de ballet* of the Sadler's Wells Ballet, Covent Garden, recorded Act I, Scene I, with the exception of the *Pas de Trois*, which was notated by Molly Lake, a former member of the Markova-Dolin Ballet and now director of the Continental Ballet. Miss Lake has also described Act I, Scene II, with the exception of the *Coda*, which was set down by Miss Skeaping. The latter also recorded Act II, with the exception of some sections which were notated by Gerd Larsen and Harold Turner, so long associated with the Sadler's Wells Ballet. Act III was recorded by Peggy van Praagh, *maîtresse de ballet* of the Sadler's Wells Theatre Ballet, and Gerd Larsen. The whole has been edited by Mary Skeaping. I do not give the relation of the steps to the music as this script is not intended as a basis for performance, but solely for the use of the ballet-goer, who is expected to study it in conjunction with an actual performance or with his recollection of a performance.

Viewed from a technical aspect, *Swan Lake* is composed of two elements—dancing and mime. In Acts I (Scene I) and II the action consists of short mimed scenes preceding or following dancing. Act I, Scene II, exhibits the same characteristics, but here Odette's dancing is so infused with a mimetic quality that the mime constitutes an integral part of her dancing. Act III is mainly pure dancing, sometimes embodying a mimetic quality.

An examination of the choreographic structure shows that the choreographers have been content to make use of a comparatively limited number of movements, steps and poses, most of them well known to students of classical ballet. It is a characteristic of the greatest choreographers to aim at using *a few steps well,* their effect depending on the artistry with which they combined, and the manner in which they are embellished with attractive movements of the arms, head, neck, and torso. For instance, Fokine's "*La Mort du Cygne*," which Anna Pavlova made famous the world over, is largely built up on one step only—the *pas de bourrée*. The elements used in *Swan Lake* may roughly be classed thus:

Movements: *développé, retiré, rond de jambe, grand rond de jambe.*
Poses: *arabesque, attitude.*
Beating steps: *cabriole, entrechat, petit battement.*
Cutting steps: *coupé.*
Gliding steps: *chassé, glissade, pas de basque, pas de bourrée.*
Hopping steps: *ballonné. temps levé.*
Raising steps: *relevé.*
Springing steps (horizontal): *échappé, grand jeté, petit jeté.*
Springing steps (vertical): *sissonne.*
Turning steps: *petit tour, pirouette, renversé.*
Whipping step: *fouetté.*

There are a few other steps such as the *pas de gavotte*, *pas de cheval*, *pas de mazurka*, *pas de valse*, and *temps de flèche*, but these are used in special instances only.

The *arabesque* position plays a very important part in the choreographic design, sometimes the *abaresque* is *à terre*, but generally *en l'air*. The *arabesque* position, travelled by a series of *temps levés*, with the arms front and back or both forward, or in crossed fifth position *en bas* with head inclined towards the breast or towards the extended front arm, has something of the manner of a swan gliding over the surface of water. The *arabesque* position is of such frequent occurence that it almost fulfils the role of the swans' *Leitmotiv*. Another effective step is the *pas de bourrée* in fifth position *sur les pointes sur place*, with arms extended at the sides and undulating in the manner of a bird flapping its wings.

The tracks or linear ground patterns along which the dancers move are mainly straight lines, sometimes at right-angles to the audience, that is passing from 4—1, 3—2, or reverse directions; sometimes parallel to the audience, that is, passing from 2—1, 3—4, or 6—8, or the reverse directions; or along the diagonals 3—1, 4—2, or the reverse directions.

The four scenes can be detailed thus:

ACT ONE, SCENE ONE

Short mimed scene (Siegfried and Benno).

Entrée of Peasants.

Pas de Trois.

Mimed scene (Princess Mother, Siegfried; then Siegfried, Benno).

Humorous Mimed scene (Tutor and Peasant Girl).
Ensemble for Peasant Girls and Youths.
Short mimed scene.

ACT ONE, SCENE TWO

Mimed scene (Benno and huntsmen searching for swans).
Mimed scene (Siegfried enters, desires to be alone, sees swan's metamorphosis into girl).
Mimed scene (Odette explains cause of her enchantment and manner in which she can be released from it).
Entrée of Swan-maidens.
Mimed scene (Benno and huntsmen are about to shoot at swan-maidens when Siegfried enters and bids them put up their weapons).
Ensemble for Swan-maidens (Waltz).
Pas de Deux (Odette and Siegfried, sometimes accompanied by the Swan-maidens).
Pas de Quatre.
Dance of Two Leaders of Swan Maidens.
Odette's variation.
Coda.

ACT TWO

Entrée of Princess-Mother and Siegfried, with suite.
Dance of the Would-Be Brides.
Entrée of Odile and Rothbart.
Danse Espagnole.
Csardas.
Danse Venetienne (omitted in Sadler's Wells Ballet production).
Mazurka.
Pas de Deux (Odile and Siegfried).
Mimed scene (Siegfried, Rothbart, Princess-Mother; Siegfried, Rothbart, Odile).

ACT THREE

Entrée of Swan-maidens and their Leaders.
Mimed scene (Leaders and Swan-maidens).
Entrée of Odette.
Mimed scene (Odette and Leaders).
Pas de Deux (Odette and Siegfried).
Mimed scene (Odette, Siegfried, and Rothbart).
Finale.

Act I, Scene I, presents the world of every day, although here restricted to court life. The action passes in the castle grounds, and serves to introduce the noble characters who live in the adjacent castle, the chief dance interest is the rousing Peasants' Dance.

Act I, Scene II, transports us to the world of fantasy, where the dancing is infused with lyricism, yet tinged with an ineffable strain of sadness. There are two beautifully composed *adages* for Odette, and the *ensembles* have a rare expressiveness which can rise to the height of pure poetry. Note, too, how the dancing of the *corps de ballet* is an integral part of the choreographic picture; the corps sometimes dancing apart, sometimes dancing with the principals absent, sometimes dancing with them, but always making an essential and vital contribution both to the choreographic design and to the romantic mood of this act.

Act II is largely an excuse for presenting the traditional series of character dances.

Act III returns us to the world of fantasy and ends with dramatic double suicide of Odette and Siegfried, the latter's devoted sacrifice procuring the lovers' reunion in another happier sphere.

The mimed scenes, in general, consist of short episodes, the meaning of which is doubtless sufficiently plain to the average ballet-goer. The only mimed scene which might present difficulty to the spectator occurs in Act I (Scene II), the episode where Odette explains how the lake came into existence, how she became enchanted, and how the spell may be broken.

Act II contains an unusual mimed episode involving three persons, one passive, two active. I refer to Odile's attempt to captivate Siegfried. We see her stepping towards Rothbart. As she stands posed *en arabesque*, holding on to his shoulder and right hand, he suggests the imparting of secret advice, first by touching his lips with his left forefinger, then slightly raising the finger in the air. Odile inclines her head in acknowledgement and looks over at her shoulder at Siegfried, who stands a little away, lost in admiration of her beauty.

In ballet there are two kinds of mime, the Italian school, a vocabulary of stylized gesture of the hands and arms which has its origin in the days of antique Greece and Rome, and the freer, natural style evolved by Michel Fokine, who required that the whole body should be expressive. In *Swan Lake* the miming is of course in the Italian tradition. Something of its principles may be gleaned from an examination of a few typical scenes.

1. *The Princess-Mother shows her disapproval of Siegfried's boon companions.* To convey this, she mimes: I pray you—these companions—have not. That is, she places both finger-tips to her breast, clasps her hands in entreaty, points to Siegfried, extends her arms towards his companions, then, turning her hands palms

downwards, crosses and uncrosses them in a horizontal plane. All negative actions are achieved by first presenting the required phrase of mime in *positive* form, then negativing it by the crossing and uncrossing of the extended hands.

2. *The Princess-Mother expresses the hope that Siegfried has not been drinking.* To convey this, she mimes: You—drink—not? That is, she points her right hand at Siegfried, carries her open hand to her lips as though it held a goblet, then, giving the gesture of negation, gazes at him in enquiry.

3. *Siegfried sees the swan change into a girl whose face is beautiful.* The beauty of another person is always indicated by lightly passing one's hand in a circular movement about one's face.

4. *When Siegfried asks Odette why she appears frightened, she replies that she is afraid he is going to shoot her.* To convey this, she mimes: You—me—shoot—not? That is, she points to Siegfried with her right hand, places both finger-tips to her breast, lifts both hands shoulder high as though holding and aiming a cross bow, draws back the right hand as though about to shoot, then makes the gesture of negation.

5. *Rothbart asks the Prince to swear that he will marry Odile.* To convey this, he mimes: You—swear—to marry—Odile. That is, he points with his right hand to Siegfried, then raises it with the index finger extended vertically upwards, at the same time gazing upwards, then touches the ring finger of his left hand with the index finger of his right, and extends his right hand towards Odile.

6. *Odette declares that she is doomed to die.* To convey this, she mimes: I—here—must die. That is, she places both finger-tips to her breast, points to the ground, then raises her arms above her head, clenching the fists, crosses her wrists, lowers her arms straight in front of her, then, just as the arms fall vertically downwards, she unclenches her hands and sharply separates them. Death is conveyed by a gesture of strength which is suddenly snapped in two.

The most enchanting and most complete of the four scenes is the second, the first lakeside scene, for which reason it is often given apart, for the sake of its homogeneity and the several beautiful *ensembles* and *variations* which it contains. I think Tchaikovsky felt the mood of this scene very deeply, and expressed in the music his own sad thoughts and the frustration of some of his own cherished ambitions. The no less sensitive Ivanov responded with equal force to the haunting melodies, which inspired him to achieve his greatest work. The second scene is a masterpiece of composition which will ever hold a high place in the annals of choreography.

CHAPTER XIII

SIMPLIFIED CHOREOGRAPHIC SCRIPT OF "SWAN LAKE"
ACT ONE, SCENE ONE

WHEN the curtain rises, six men in hunting-dress (Prompt side) and six peasant youths (O.P. side) are seen strolling to and fro, and talking. Benno is at centre. At 2 there is a small table loaded with a flagon of wine, and goblets; nearby is a rustic bench. Enter the Tutor at 3, whom Benno greets centre stage. Tutor crosses to table. The huntsmen look off-stage at 3, and, espying the Prince arriving, inform their companions. Siegfried enters at 3, shakes hands with Benno and one of the huntsmen, and bids them take a stoup of wine at the table at 2, while he and Benno walk to 1.

Six peasant girls[1] enter at 3, each holding in right hand a posy of flowers, and dance diagonally across stage facing 1, in two lines of three. The step used is: *Temps levé* L.F., *chassé* R.F., *pas de bourrée dessous*, repeat to other side, three *emboîtés* forward. Curtsey. Repeat *temps levé–chassé–pas de bourrée dessous* to each side and curtsey, handing posies to Prince. They then go to R. and stand at 8.

Enter the solo dancers of the *Pas de Trois*, in this instance two girls and a youth, the girls on either side of the youth. Travelling from side to side and diagonally down-stage to face Siegfried at 1, they do: *temps levé* L.F., *chassé* R.F., *pas de bourrée dessous*, quick *pas de bourrée sur place*, changing feet (youth does first step but two small *pas de bourrée dessous* with *épaulement* instead of the *pas de bourrée sur place*). Repeat all to other side. *Chassé–temps levé* R.F., to R. in 1st *arabesque*, *coupé–ballonné* and *petits tours* to 1. The girls curtsey and youth bows to Prince, when they go past 8 up-stage so that they arrive at 3 in time to commence the *Pas de Trois*.

Meanwhile six new peasant girls enter at 3, each holding a posy of flowers as before, and do four *pas de basque* beginning with R.F. travelling in the formation of two lines of three towards 1. Curtsey to Prince, offer him their posies and do eight *pas de basque* in circle 2–6–3–2–4 and join other peasant youths and girls on O.P. side.

The Prince hands all the flowers to Benno, and with him

[1] For alternative entry of peasant girls see *Appendix* A, page 158.

[*Photo: Roger Wood*

"SWAN LAKE," ACT ONE, SCENE II, SADLER'S WELLS BALLET PRODUCTION

Settings and costumes by Leslie Hurry, Royal Opera, Covent Garden, 1950
Triangular wedge formation

[*Photo: Roger Wood*

"SWAN LAKE," ACT ONE, SCENE II, SADLER'S WELLS BALLET PRODUCTION

Settings and costumes by Leslie Hurry, Royal Opera, Covent Garden, 1950

crosses stage to 2, when Benno deposits the flowers on the table, while Siegfried takes a cup of wine and talks with his friends.

Pas de Trois.

Commence at 3 two village girls and man (G., M., G.), the leading girl does the first solo.

I. *Temps levé* on L.F., *développé à la 2de* with R. leg, *chassé* on to R.F. and *pas de bourrée dessous* towards R. Repeat the whole three times in all, travelling in straight line across back to 8, then Man lifts 1st Girl in *temps levé en arabesque* on R.F., 2nd Girl does same *temps levé* without lift.

Repeat the whole travelling to L. to 2 (2nd Girl is lifted on this side).

II. All three dancers do *pas de bourrée—grand jeté en tournant* to R., travelling up-stage towards centre. First Girl does pose on R.F. in 3rd *arabesque* to 8, then same to 6 on L.F., while 2nd Girl does preparation and *double tour en dehors* with Man, then all three step forward in 5th pos., R.F. front. Repeat all this on other side with 1st Girl doing the *pirouette*.

III. In circle round stage to R., led by 1st Girl: *Pas de bourrée* and *jeté élancé* to *arabesque*, first on to R.F., then on to L.F., on to R.F. again, on to L.F. again. This brings them to straight line across back, leading girl near 3. They now do eight *temps levés* in 3rd *arabesque* on R.F. travelling to 1.

Repeat the whole of Step II taking circle to L., and *temps levé* to 2.

IV. Repeat Step I once across front to 8, but, in place of lifted *arabesque*, 1st Girl exits with *temps levé* in *arabesque* on R.F., while 2nd Girl does *pirouette en dehors* and is caught by Man; she ends with both arms over her head, hands turned palms out.

V. 2nd Girl and man travelling back towards 3: Lift in 1st *arabesque* on R.F., *glissade* back to L., repeat lift in *arabesque* and *glissade* back to L., preparation (*bourrée* in 5th) *pirouette en dehors*, caught as in No. 3. Repeat all.

VI. Girl to R., Man to L. Girl does *chassé* R., *coupé dessous* L., *fouetté battu* to back R. Man does same opposite side. They repeat this step four times in all, alternate sides. On 2nd, 3rd and 4th times they begin with *coupé dessous* before *chassé*.

Both now travel in circle to L. (girl leading) with series of *pas de bourrée–temps levé* in 3rd *arabesque*, L.R.L.R.

They now repeat first part of step (*chassé–coupé–fouetté battu*, etc.) but only twice and this time Girl starts L., Man R., Girl then does *temps levé* in 1st *arabesque* on L. towards 3, and runs to 3, while man goes to 1. On each *cadenza* girl does series of *petits tours* on point towards 1 for count of six, on count of seven she does *posé–double tour en dehors* without preparation and is caught by man as before, on count of eight.

These two dancers exit.

1st Girl's Solo.

First girl enters at 3 on introduction to her solo. She runs to centre and stands in 5th pos., R.F. front and facing 2.

I. *Relevé–retiré devant* on L., arms across to supporting leg, close front, *relevé–retiré derrière* on R.F., arms to supporting leg, close back *retiré–relevé devant* on L.F., arms as before, close front and *entrechat six*. Repeat four times in all, alternate sides, ending R.F. front in 5th position facing 2.

II. *Relevé–retiré derrière* on R.F. close 5th pos. back, *relevé–retiré passé en avant* on R.F., *demi-plié* on R.F., keeping L.F. *sur le cou-de-pied devant*, *relevé* again on R.F. opening L. leg to *éffacé*, make sharp *retiré* movement with L.F. and open again to *éffacé*, without dropping off R. point, at the same time L. hand makes a movement to the lips then out (synchronising with movement of L. leg) close in 5th pos., L.F. front. Repeat step three times in all alternate sides, then *temps levé* in *arabesque* on L.F. and run to 2.

III. Travelling back to 4 facing 2: Polka *sur les pointes* back R., stretching R. arm forward in *arabesque* position, same L. but finish this polka in 5th pos., *demi-plié*, R.F. front, arms 5th *en bas*, eight *changements sur les pointes* turning to R., taking arms to 5th *en haut*. Repeat three and a half times in all, the last time omit the *changements* and do *temps levé* in *arabesque* on L.F. to 3 and run to 3.

IV. Travelling from 3–1: *Assemblé* over R., *temps levé* on R.F. making *développé* to *arabesque* with L.F., L. arm up, palm turned back, head inclined to R., looking to raised hand, *chassé croisé* L., and *pas de chat* R., arms 4th *en haut* (L. hand high). Repeat four times in all.

Coda. Travelling back to 3, *pas de bourrée* and *temps levé* in 3rd *arabesque*, five times in all starting R., then pose on L.F., R.F. *pointe tendue croisé devant.*

Six *posé* turns *en dehors* on L.F. to 1, three or four *petits tours sur les pointes* and standing on L.F., R. *pointe tendue croisé derrière*, arms 4th pos. *en haut* (R. arm high).

Man's Solo.

Start at 2, L. leg *pointe tendue croisé derrière*, L. arm extended in *arabesque* to 2.

I. *Pas de bourrée, grand jeté en tournant* with L.F., *pas de bourrée* (L.R.L.) towards 1 and *cabriole croisé derrière* on L.F. Repeat four times in all, L.R.L.R., travelling each time right across stage.

At 4th time omit the *pas de bourrée* and *cabriole croisé*, substituting *chassé* on R. towards centre and *pas de bourrée dessous* to 5th pos., L.F. front.

II. Two *entrechats quatre* (L.F. front), one *entrechat six* and *double tour en l'air* to R. Repeat this four times in all.

Note.—This step is sometimes executed thus: two *entrechats quatre* and two *entrechats six*; two *entrechats quatre* and *double tour en l'air*. Repeated twice only.

III. *Sissonne croisée en avant ouverte* on to L.F. to 1 (R. arm forward in *arabesque*) *assemblé derrière* R. Repeat on to R. to 2, preparation and *pirouette en dehors* to R.F. close front. Repeat two *sissonnes* and *assemblé*, then *temps levé en arabesque* on L.F. and run to 2.

IV. Round stage to R.: series of twelve *coupés jetés en tournant* ending centre, quick preparation, *pirouette en dehors*, end with *double tour en l'air* and drop down to knee.

2nd Girl's Solo.

Enter at 3 before music and stand centre on R.F., L.F. *pointe tendue*, arms in *demi-seconde* pos.

I. Eight little *jetés sur les pointes*, turning to R., starting *jeté* back on to L., then *jeté* forward on to R.F. Repeat these two *jetés* eight times, arms make little swinging movement on each *jeté* towards supporting leg, head follows arms, bring L.F. over tiny *bourrée devant* and *dégagé* R.F. to side, R. arm across body down to extended leg. Repeat this *bourrée* and *dégagé* four times in all, alternate sides.

This step is repeated four times in all, always commencing same side. Last time omit the *pas de bourrée* and do *temps levé* in *arabesque* on L.F. and run to 2.

II. Travelling back from 2 to 4, *dégagé* R.F. *pointe tendue croisé devant demi-plié* on L.F., hands crossed low in front, body bow to extended R.F. *Relevé* on L.F. and *développé* R.F. to 1st *arabesque*, quick little *bourrée sur les pointes* towards 4, turning head and shoulders to 4 and taking arms to 5th pos. *en haut*. Repeat four times in all.

III. This step travels back from 4–2, and is a Russian folk step done on point. With the weight always on the R. point, the L.F. does a series of *retirés derrière* with a *demi-plié* on the R.F. on each *retiré*, the L.F. drops from the *retiré* on to the point each time, so that during entire step neither foot is off the point. For the first eight *retirés*, the body faces 4, both hands in front making a little circling movement inwards with wrists on each *demi-plié*, the hands and head passing from low to high. For the next eight *retirés* the dancer faces 5, taking her head to 2, and her arms from 5th *en bas* to 5th *en haut* and opening them to *demi-seconde* pos.; repeat four more *retirés* facing 4 as 1st eight. *Soutenu sur les pointes* to L. and run to centre and stand in 5th pos. R.F. front, facing 2.

IV.[1] Two *soubresauts sur les pointes*, hop on L. point raising R.F. to high *retiré devant* and, opening arms to *demi-seconde*, palms upwards (again as Russian character movement), step R. point, step under L. point and close in 5th pos., L.F. front facing 1 (these last three movements are similar to a *pas de bourrée*), repeat step three times in all, *temps levé en arabesque* on L.F. and run to 3.

Coda. Four *posé* turns *en dehors* on L.F. and three *petits tours sur les pointes* finishing at 1, taking R.F. back to deep 4th *croisé*, arms extended back, body forward, head inclined to R., looking forward.

Coda of Pas de Trois.

I. Enter 1st Girl at 3 and runs to centre for count of five introduction, she then goes straight into six *demi-contretemps*, *fouetté sauté* to 1st *arabesque*, alternate sides, starting with L.F., then *temps levé en arabesque* on L.F. and runs to 2.

II. Circle round stage to R., with series of six *sauts de basque en tournant*, *temps levé en arabesque* on L.F. and exit at 2.

III. Man enters at 3 with *demi-contretemps, assemblé—entrechat six* three times, travelling to 1. *Chassé—temps levé* in 1st *arabesque* on R.F. *Pas de bourrée—grand jeté en tournant* back to 3, three times. He meets 2nd Girl who enters at 3, she does *temps levé* on L.F. and *développé* with R.F. to 2nd, *pas de bourrée* under the 4th pos. L.F. front, *pirouette en dehors* ending with *développé a la 2de* executed four times in all, very fast and brilliant towards 8, then *bourrée sur les pointes* towards 2, Man walking behind her and fall over Man's knee to L., arms 5th *en haut*.

IV. Re-enter 1st Girl at 3 with series of *demi-contretemps–entrechat cinq élancé* (four times in all to 1) then four *entrechats six sur place*, *temps levé en arabesque* on L.F. and run to join Man and 2nd Girl at 2.

V. All three together in line facing 2 and travelling to 4: *pas de bourrée–grand jeté en tournant* R., man then stands still while 1st Girl (who is on his R.) runs behind him and does *jeté élancé* to *arabesque* on her L.F. and 2nd Girl passes in front of him stepping out wide on her R.F., then stepping round on to her L. point *en attitude*, holding his extended R. arm with both hands (she is behind his arm), girls have now changed places, 1st Girl is on L., and 2nd Girl on R. Repeat all this four times in all.

VI. In straight line at back, *pas de bourrée* and *temps levé* in 3rd

[1] For an alternative version of 2nd Girl's Fourth Step, see *Appendix A*, page 158.

arabesque four times, R.L.R.L., then *pas de bourrée* and *jeté élancé* to 2nd *arabesque* four times travelling to 5 (R.L.R.L.). Girl on L. (2nd Girl) now does preparation and *pirouette en dehors* in front of Man who catches her in *retiré*, both arms up, palms out, while 1st Girl walks round behind Man, 1st Girl now does *pirouette en dehors* in front of Man and is put down in front of him on her R. knee, facing 1, arms crossed over breast, while 2nd Girl walks behind Man and takes up pose *en attitude* on her R. point, holding his L. shoulder with her R. hand.

The Tutor walks over to O.P. side to converse and joke with the peasants, then, looking off-stage at 3, sees the Princess Mother approaching. He hurries down-stage and warns the Prince and his companions to conceal the flagon of wine and goblets.

Enter at 3, four Court Ladies who walk in a small circle clockwise, ending in a diagonal line 3–1 up-stage. The Prince, perturbed at the news of his mother's arrival, goes to them. They curtsey. He asks them why they have come. They indicate the approach of the Princess Mother, who enters at 3.

Siegfried goes to greet her, leads her down-stage by his L. hand, when the following mimed scene takes place. Princess Mother walks round to L. up-stage, looking disdainfully at Benno and his companions in hunting-dress, then she faces the the Prince and says: "I pray you—these companions—have—not! You—drink—not?" Siegfried affirms: "I—drink—not." Continuing, the Princess Mother says: "I—command—you—to marry," then she walks up-stage and, indicating the castle in the distance, turns to the Prince and observes: "The castle—ball—1–2–3–4—beautiful—court ladies—you—to marry—one." The Prince answers: "I—love—not." The Princess Mother advances towards Siegfried but he crossed over near 2, where he is met by Benno. Siegfried is depressed at the command that he must marry. The Princess Mother follows him, raises one hand in a peremptory gesture to remind him of his duty, and looks coldly at Benno. Prince goes back towards 1, where Princess Mother follows him. She makes a gesture of entreaty and places her R. hand on his R. shoulder; Siegfried faces her and bows his head in submission. The Princess Mother walks to L. up-stage with a slightly more gracious manner to her son's companions. She turns round and, facing him, raises her R. hand in a gesture which suggests "Remember." The Prince goes towards 3, kisses the hand of his mother, and escorts her to 3 where she exits, followed by the four Court Ladies who curtsey to the Prince in passing. Siegfried returns to centre-stage, looking very distracted. Benno goes to him, bids him leave the future to itself and forget his troubles in a cup of wine. The Tutor walks round stage, exchanging salutations with the peasants, looks off-stage at the departing Princess Mother, and makes a gesture of relief at her exit.

Now the Tutor is seized with an idea to show some of the peasant girls how they used to dance when he was a youth. He asks the Prince's permission to dance with one of the village maidens. Siegfried bids him choose a partner. He walks among the peasants, beckons to one that pleases his taste, and conducts her to centre-stage.

They face 5 holding hands, the girl on his R., R.F. *pointe tendue éffacé*, close in 5th pos. front. *Pas de bourrée dessous*. Repeat to other side. They face each other holding R. hands in 5th *en haut*, making a "window." *Balancé* towards and away from each other in same position, then four *pas de basque*, making semi-circle to R. (Girl passes up-stage of Tutor). Repeat "window" and *balancés*. Then Girl does eight *pas de basque* in an "S" pattern passing up-stage of Tutor, then down-stage towards 1, then to 4. She then runs to centre where Tutor has been attempting to execute, not too successfully, *pas de basque sur place*. Girl curtseys, Tutor bows, each stepping L. Repeat curtsey and bow, each stepping R. Repeat "window" and *balancés*. Then Girl suddenly seizes Tutor about the waist and whirls him round with little runs *sur place* and suddenly releases him, so that he totters towards 2 and falls down. Girl now dances by herself. Travelling to 6 and facing 5, she does: small *cabriole* to side with L.F., *chassé–pas de bourrée dessous*, three times in all, three *petits jetés derrière sur place*. Repeat to other side, but making only two *petits jetés derrière* at end, with the third taken *en avant* on R.F. to 1. Travelling back to 3 facing 1, she does: *pas de bourrée couru–fouetté–cabriole*–two *petits jetés en arrière*, R.F. and L.F., then *jeté en avant* on R.F. in 2nd *arabesque* to 1, do this three times in all, then, on diagonal 3–1, five *soutenus en tournant* and stand in pose on R.F., L.F. *pointe tendue* to side, R. arm in half 5th *en haut*, L. arm in half 5th *en avant*. Girl curtseys to Prince who has come forward from table, then she goes back to rejoin the other peasants who are standing about in groups, watching (O.P. side). Benno goes to the Prince at centre down-stage and suggests that he should invite the peasants to present their dance. He accepts the suggestion and the peasants, both youths and girls, all run into the centre of the stage in groups of three, one youth between two girls, one arm around the waist of each. The formation is as follows:

G—Y—G G—Y—G
G—Y—G G—Y—G
G—Y—G G—Y—G

Peasant Dance (for twelve Girls and six Youths).

I. Holding inside hand of each girl, youth turns round with the girls, doing *balancés sur place*, girls doing four *pas de basque*, inside girl passing under arch made by the holding of hands and making one circle to R., outside girl making one circle to L., end facing 5. They leave go of hands, then youth puts out both his hands, girls put their hands on his and both turn *en dedans* under arm *sur place*. Repeat all this step.

II. Youths now face 7, girls 5; girls do three *pas de basque* commencing R.F. and, travelling down-stage, stamp feet. Youths do same towards 7, only they turn and face 5 on the stamp of the foot. Repeat, girls going up-stage, youths coming down. Repeat the whole step, end with two centre lines of girls turning round *sur place* three times with *balancé* movement of feet, the two outside lines of girls do four *pas de basque* round youths, making one whole turn. Youths go out to the side, girls now in four lines:

* * * *
* * * *
* * * *

III. *Pas de bourrée en avant* and *en arrière croisée*, exaggerated body movement backwards with opposite arm to raised leg extended in high *arabesque* front, lean forward in *arabesque* on *pas de bourrée en arrière*. Repeat the *pas de bourrée en avant* and *en arrière*. All the dancers do this step *croisé* to 1, *chassé–temps levé* four times round themselves, turning to R. Repeat the *pas de bourrée en avant* and *en arrière*, repeat the *chassé–temps levé* four times *dos à dos* (back to back) to form two lines.

* *
* *
* *
* *
* *
* *

IV. Commencing with outside feet, *jeté devant*, *jeté derrière sur place* six times, outside arm half 5th *en avant*, inside arm half 5th *en haut*, look to wings. *Pas de bourrée en avant*, *pas de bourrée en arrière*, twice, *coupé–fouetté derrière* arms open to low 2nd pos., sway body on *bourrées*, this step travels slightly towards wings. Repeat travelling back towards centre. *Point outside feet *éffacé*, *plié* on inside feet, inside arm at waist, outside arm up towards corner, and make a little circular movement of the wrist.* Do this three times.

V. Girls do *chassé–temps levé* in 1st *arabesque*, *pas de chat* twice, going out to wings and *chassé–temps levé* four times, *dos à dos* with next girl in line. Youths do *chassé–temps levé* in 1st *arabesque*, *chassé croisé* twice, *chassé–temps levé* four times, *dos à dos*. Repeat this, the girls travelling in, and the youths out.

VI. All together in four lines at right angles to audience do step from * to * in Step IV five times with outside feet, smack thighs on 6th with little jump on two feet, girls do this three times on alternate sides, youths twice only, on last time youths do *chassé–temps levé* on alternate feet three times, travelling in towards girls, ending with one girl on each side of each youth with their hands on youth's shoulder. Youth has one arm round the waist of each girl.

VII. They all do *chassé–temps levé* eight times on alternate feet, following this track:

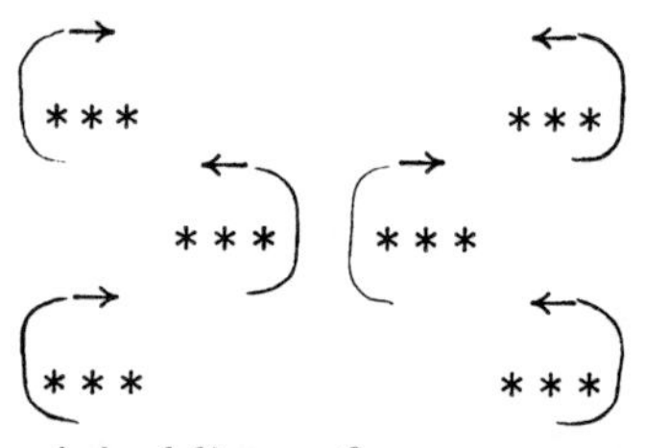

and ending up in original lines of

G—Y—G G—Y—G
G—Y—G G—Y—G
G—Y—G G—Y—G

VIII. Youths kneel on one knee, girls repeat Step VI on inside feet, boys clap hands on 2, 3, 5 and 6, looking to inside girl. Then girls do their step on outside feet looking back over shoulder at the youth, the youth now claps in same rhythms as before, but looks at outside girl. Repeat this on both sides.

IX. Youths rise from knee and the girls link arms through youths' arms. In formation as at end of Step VII the sides cross stage from 8–6 with *chassé–temps levé*, *pas de chat* twice, then, making a little circle, they run round bending forward towards centre of circle in a huddle. Repeat back to own side of stage.

X. All do from * to * in Step IV twelve times pointing R.F.

XI. Eight *pas de basque* backwards facing 5 and commencing to R.

XII. Coming down-stage, step forward on R.F., jump, raising L. leg high in front, allowing knee to bend, holding hands and

[*Photo: Tunbridge-Sedgwick*

"SWAN LAKE," ACT TWO, SADLER'S WELLS BALLET PRODUCTION

Settings and costumes by Leslie Hurry, New Theatre, 1943. *Rothbart (Nigel Desmond) instructs Odile (Fonteyn) how to captivate Siegfried (Helpmann)*

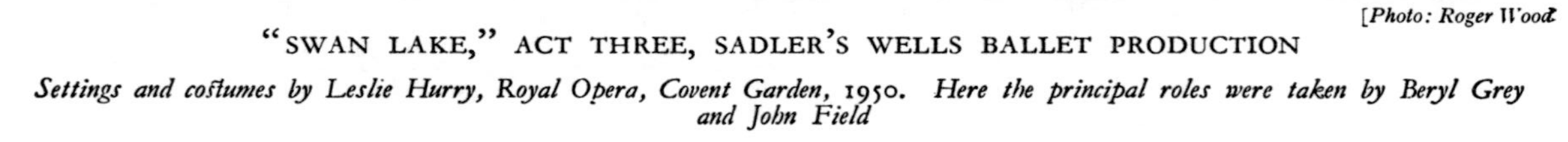

[Photo: Roger Wood

"SWAN LAKE," ACT THREE, SADLER'S WELLS BALLET PRODUCTION

Settings and costumes by Leslie Hurry, Royal Opera, Covent Garden, 1950. Here the principal roles were taken by Beryl Grey and John Field

swinging arms forward and up, bringing them down again and stepping on L.F. Do this four times.

XIII. Youths bow, girls curtsey to R. and L. *Outside* girl and youth waltz turning *sur place*, *inside* girl waltzing round them, coming first inside then outwards towards wings. Girls all skip in big circle holding hands and travelling clockwise. They break up into pairs and do *pas de basque* off at 3, not turning.

Towards the end of the dance the light begins to wane and the Prince's friends in hunting costume go off-stage at 6 and re-enter bearing lighted torches. As soon as the peasant girls have departed in pairs, Benno perceives a flock of swans passing overhead. Siegfried calls for his crossbow. One of the huntsmen hands his torch to a companion and goes off, to return with the crossbow which he hands to Siegfried, who bids the huntsmen keep the swans in view. They give their torches to the peasant youths who exit with them at 3. Huntsmen then exit at 4. The Prince and Benno mock the Tutor by pretending that they wish him to join them in hunting the swans. The Tutor declines, saying that he wishes to go and sleep. The Prince and Benno go off at 8, while the Tutor crosses to 2 and, lifting up the flagon, clasps it to his heart. Patting it affectionately, he shuffles off the stage in a circle 1–8–4–7–3. The curtain slowly falls on the retreating figure.

CHAPTER XIV

ACT ONE, SCENE I: SOME ASPECTS OF PRODUCTION

BEFORE discussing the action of Act I, it is of interest to consider the setting. The curtain rises on the gardens of Prince Siegfried's castle, and since he is a German princeling, all that is required is a stretch of green sward relieved by trees and flowers; the background is dominated by the towers and crenellated walls of a gothic castle. But, with a view to the introduction of another plane, I suggest that the back cloth be crossed by a raised low-walled walk, broken in the centre by a flight of moss-grown stone steps giving entrance to the garden below.

In Leslie Hurry's setting for the Sadler's Wells Ballet, near the "wings" are fantastic stone edifices, more suited to Walpole's Strawberry Hill, entwined with strange climbing plants which suggest the tropics; there is a castle in the background, but the narrow towers and bulbous domes imply Russia rather than Germany. It is true that *Swan Lake* is a Russian ballet, but the place of action is Germany. If, on the other hand, William Chappell's setting for the same scene, as presented by the International Ballet, be considered, this suggests the quadrangle of a monastery, except that the stone arches are each decorated with a sculptured swan, a device which is scarcely warranted, seeing that the Prince has yet to encounter Odette.

Presumably the time is early afternoon. The Prince, his morning (one imagines) passed in the dispatch of state business and receiving the congratulations of his mother and his counsellors upon attaining his majority, is coming to celebrate the occasion in the company of his boon companions, headed by Benno; Siegfriend's aged tutor is also in attendance.

Usually the only indication of good cheer is a small gothic table on which is placed a flagon of wine and some goblets; beside it is a low form which might have come from a classroom. I venture to suggest that the form might be replaced by an oblong raised dais, supporting a low rail hung with rich damask and decorated with garlands of flowers and leaves; the dais would be cloth-covered and on it would be set a stool and a table, bearing a flagon of wine, goblet and dishes of fruit and cakes. There would be a gap in the rail at the front and down-stage side of the dais with a step to afford entrance.

At the rise of the curtain, nobles would be seen waiting by the dais; on the opposite side would be peasant youths in holiday attire, for the peasantry are to entertain their lord with a series of dances. It is essential that their respective costumes should imply which are nobles and which are peasants. This observation is not so unnecessary as might be thought. The costumes designed by Leslie Hurry for the peasant youths, who wear rich costumes with hanging scalloped sleeves, hardly suggests toilers of the soil or 'rude mechanicals'. The dresses of the nobles must indicate that they are habited ready for the chase, in the belief that the Prince will later so disport himself. The reason for this is a practical one, for the second scene follows the first without interval, hence there is not time to effect a change of costume.

I do not approve the practice of designing a uniform costume for the courtiers, with perhaps a different design for Benno so that he may readily be recognized; nor the planning of another uniform dress for the peasants. This uniformity may make for economy in production and is also certainly effective on the stage as affording a block of colour. Unfortunately, this uniformity carries with it the suggestion of a troupe, thus all individuality is banished. Yet, by varying slightly the shades of a particular colour, and details of decoration, a sense of individuality can be attained without detracting from the general colour effect in the mass.

I visualize the Prince making his entrance across the walk and down the steps to be greeted by Benno, while the rest of the company bow in homage. In most productions the two shake hands. I think it would be more in keeping with mediaeval usage if Siegfried extended his hand and his friend inclined his head and kissed the Prince's hand, or else dropped on one knee and followed the same procedure.

The *Pas de Trois* should, I think, be danced slightly on a diagonal line, so that it is directed simultaneously towards the Prince and to the theatre audience. The same conception applies to all the dances in this act, so that there is a sense of the peasants entertaining their lord. The *Pas de Trois* strengthens this otherwise rather weak act, but it is so academic is style that it seems out of key with the other dances. For this reason this *pas* is sometimes transferred to Act II. When the Girls' *soli* are danced expressively they are invested with a light touch of coquetry, together with a faint suggestion of competing for the young man's admiration. The *Pas de Trois* has a brilliant finale concluding with first one girl, then the other, turning a *pirouette* to be caught by the male dancer, followed by an attractive concluding group.

I suggest that the Princess-Mother and her ladies should enter by the walled walk and depart by the same way.

The scene with the Tutor and the peasant girl is a humorous one, serving as a contrast to the gloom cast upon the company by the Princess-Mother's pronouncement that the Prince must take a wife to himself on the morrow. The humour of the situation lies first in an old man's trying to dance as he was wont to do in the days of his youth; second, in his mannered deportment and the old-fashioned character of his steps; and third, in the contrast between his slow movements and the agile steps of the young girl whom he has chosen for partner. But it always strikes me as incongruous that a peasant girl, shown the steps of a court dance for the first time, should immediately be able to dance them as though to the manner born. Would it not be more logical if at first she appeared a little awkward and ill at ease when attempting an unfamiliar measure?

It would, I think, add to the gaiety of this scene and also stress the suggestion of merrymaking, if the now omitted scene with the maypole were restored.

During the Peasants' Dance the light should gradually begin to fade. Then torches are brought in by retainers and handed to the nobles, who hold them on high as the peasant girls go home by way of the steps and walled walk. It is imperative that the torches should be held vertically upright and not allowed to incline at different angles.

When Benno sights the swans flying overhead, Siegfried indicates his desire to hunt them and calls for his crossbow, which is brought to him. His nobles might then hand the torches to the peasant youths who would go up the steps, lining the wall with torches raised as they peer down at the courtiers going in search of the swans, while the Prince and Benno follow; but the Tutor, pleading sleepiness and the desire to seek his bed, retires by way of the walk.

Quite often the "curtain" devised for this act is weak and ineffective because of the casual manner in which the Prince and Benno make their exit. I suggest that they should walk slowly towards the wings, both looking upwards, while Siegfried slowly raises his hand and traces for Benno the path of the swans flying homeward.

CHAPTER XV

SIMPLIFIED CHOREOGRAPHIC SCRIPT OF "SWAN LAKE"

ACT ONE, SCENE II

THE curtain rises on an empty stage. Huntsmen enter, some singly, some in little groups; they carry crossbows. One of the huntsmen, looking towards 3, espies a file of swans, led by one bearing a tiny crown on its head, gliding from left to right over the surface of the lake, to disappear into the low-lying mist which clings about its banks. The watching huntsman hails Benno and indicates the distant swans. Benno goes to 3 and, having assured himself of the presence of the swans, calls to Prince Siegfried, who enters at 2, asking the reason for the summons. Benno points to 3, indicating that the swans are there, within easy range. Siegfried sees the swans for himself, then bids Benno and the huntsmen retire into the surrounding woods while he remains in the glade. He hesitates a moment and then walks round the stage clockwise to 4, now looks towards 3, makes a gesture of surprise, looks to 5, and then, miming "a beautiful face," he too takes cover by hiding behind a tree on the left at 1.

Enter Odette with run and *pas de chat*, landing in 4th pos. *croisé*, facing 1, her hands crossed at wrists in 5th pos. *en bas*, palms facing body—this position will in future be referred to as "crossed 5th pos. *en bas*." She does *posé* in 1st *arabesque*, R. point dropping to same 4th pos., then makes three little spasmodic movements of her head, upwards, to R., then to L. Repeat *posé arabesque* and head movements once more, which brings her near 1. As Siegfried enters at 1, she does *posé* in *arabesque*, closing *arabesque* in 5th pos. *sur les pointes*, bringing arms to 3rd *arabesque*, elbows and wrists bent, palms towards Siegfried as if protecting herself, and runs[1] in fear across stage to 2. Siegfried asks Odette why she flees from him. She replies that she is frightened. When he asks her why, she replies: "You—me—shoot—not?" Siegfried answers: "I—you—shoot—no. I—you—protect."

Odette expresses her gratitude with a low bow, then sweeps round stage from 2–3–4–1 with a *series of *glissades changés* turning, and *relevé en arabesque* done six times in all, both arms are up

[1] For alternative version of first entrance of Odette, see *Appendix A*, page 158.

alternate sides (the movement is full and flowing). Siegfried attempts to seize her on the last movement at 4, but she darts under his arm and runs to 2. Siegfried asks her what she is doing in such a lonely glade. Odette replies that she is Queen of the Swans, which gives rise to the following conversation in mime:

Siegfried: "I—the Queen—salute. You—a swan—why, why?"

Odette: "You—see—the lake. The lake was formed from my mother's tears. Over there (*pointing to* 3) one—wicked person—me—carried away—and—I—Queen of Swans. But if—one—loves—me—and one—marries—me—I am saved. I—swan—never more."

Siegfried: "I—you—love. I—you—marry. I—swear [it]. The wicked one—where?"

Rothbart, in the guise of an Owl, appears at 3 as Siegfried swears he will marry Odette and then kneels at her feet. Odette runs to 3 and begs Rothbart not to harm Siegfried.

Siegfried: "Wait! I—him—shoot!" (*Runs off at* 1 *for his crossbow.*) He returns with weapon, while Rothbart remains at 3. Siegfried drops on one knee near 1 to take aim, but Odette, running to 3, stands before the Owl, shielding it and bidding Siegfried not to shoot. He lowers his bow as Odette, running to him, does *posé* in 1st *arabesque* on R. point, leaning over him. The Owl vanishes at 3. After a short pause, Odette and Siegfried exit slowly together at 2.

Entrance of Swan-Maidens.

Two swan-maidens appear at 3 travelling *sur les pointes* and using their arms to simulate the beating of wings—four times. They then cross back of stage, followed by rest of *corps de ballet.* The step is *temps levé* in 1st *arabesque* and four *petits jetés devant*, the arms crossed 5th pos. *en bas*, and head brought down. This is repeated fourteen times on alternate sides, the first *temps levé* commencing on R.F., the second on L.F., the third on R.F. and so on. They travel first across towards 4, then back to 6, then to 8, then to 2. (The number of times the stage is crossed is governed by its area and by the number of dancers in the *corps de ballet*, but the leading dancer should finish at 2, with the rest disposed in straight lines across the stage, facing 5.)

The swan-maidens now execute a series of *ports de bras.* Stepping to the "wings" (outwards) they extend their inside feet *pointe tendue* to centre, raising their outside arms as they do so and, lifting their heads to raised arms, they carry their inside hands across to outer shoulders then, continuing, bring them down their bodies to extended feet with a brushing movement as though preening their feathers. Repeat this stepping—inwards, then once more outwards—but taking both arms up and bringing them down, the hands stroking the sides of the body which is curved back, the extended legs being now in *arabesque à terre* to centre. Repeat this second movement inwards (four *ports de bras* in all).* Then *temps levé* in 1st *arabesque* on inside feet, *chassé croisé* and *pas de chat*, arms crossed 5th *en bas*. Repeat from *, the lines cross doing this, those on R. end on L., and *vice versa*; they now repeat the first single-arm *port de bras* preening movements, then cross back with *temps levé* and *pas de chat* as before and again repeat the two single-arm preening *ports de bras*. *Pas de bourrée* in 5th pos. *sur les pointes sur place*, making two *ports de bras* like the beating of wings, all face 5. The swan-maiden at 2 now leads round in circle across front first, the other swan-maidens follow waving their arms, gradually unwinding themselves as they run, until they come into the circle. First swan-maiden runs past 1–4–7 then down centre to 5, the others run behind her until they form a triangular wedge in this manner:

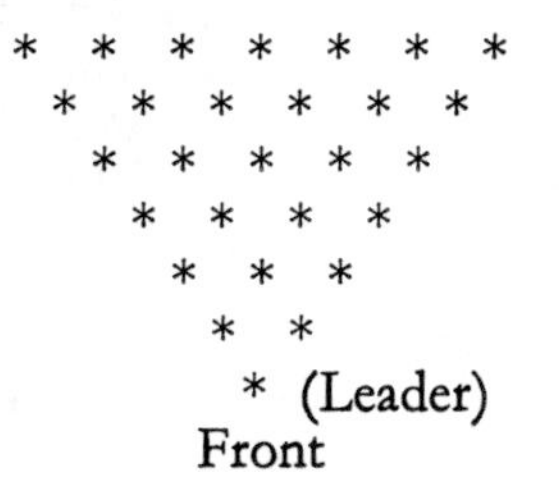

The actual formation depends upon the number of dancers comprising the *corps de ballet*, but the leader is always in front with the rear lines growing progressively wider. As soon as each dancer arrives in position, she commences to "*bourrée*" *sur les pointes sur place*, undulating her arms in the manner of a bird beating its wings. Then all together the swan-maidens do * *chassé–temps levé* on R.F. in 1st arabesque, and a species of *ballotté* on to R.F., opening the L.F. with *développé éffacé* to 2, arms 4th *en avant*, R. arm across body.[1] Repeat from* four times in all to alternate sides, keeping the wedge formation, then repeat the *bourrée sur place* with wing-beating arm movements. Benno comes on at 2, gazes at swan-maidens, kneels down-stage centre, back to audience, then the leading swan-maiden runs in a circle to R. She makes one complete circle ending centre front, during

[1] In the Sadler's Wells production at Covent Garden, this step is done to alternate sides by each row in turn, i.e. first swan-maiden goes to R., the two in next row to L., the three in third row to R., and so on.

which all the swan-maidens follow her, waving their arms up and down as they run, then finish in a circle in pairs, the components of each pair facing each other. Benno is now in the centre of the circle; he lowers his head and shields his face with his arm as the swan-maidens seek to attack him as they weave in and out, later to unwind and form into final huddled group. Each swan-maiden now steps on to her R.F. so that they step alternately towards and away from centre and execute the single arm *port de bras* (preening movement) as at beginning. All step L. and repeat it, then again to R., and again to L. All now do two steps forward, commencing R. and *posé* on R. point in *arabesque*, both arms raised above head, palms outwards; half the swan-maidens will go inwards to form a circle of their own centre, half outwards to form circle at edge of stage; this movement is done four times in all. Then all again run in circle to R., waving their arms, to end huddled together near 6, their R. feet *pointe tendue*[1] back, hands placed at left cheek, palms facing each other, R. shoulders up. The whole pose of the swan-maidens suggests their cowering in fear.

Benno hails huntsmen from all sides of the glade. As they run in, answering his summons, they ask his bidding. He indicates the swan-maidens crouching in fear, and bids the huntsmen fetch their crossbows. They exit to fetch them and promptly return to drop on one knee at 8, Benno at their head, to take aim at the trembling girls. Just as they are about to shoot, the Prince runs on from 2 and, standing in front of Benno with his arms outstretched in a gesture of protection, prevents the huntsmen from shooting. Almost at the same instant, Odette runs on from 3 in a circle to L., ending with *soutenu* down on to her R.F., her L.F. *pointe tendue* to the side, her arms outstretched, standing in front of her companions as though to shield them. She implores the Prince not to shoot her companions. Siegfried turns to his followers and, indicating the swan-maidens, peremptorily orders them not to shoot. They bow in acquiescence and exit slowly between 1 and 4. Odette acknowledges the Prince's gesture with a deep bow, which Siegfried returns, and all the swan-maidens bow in gratitude. Then the Prince and Odette exit together at 2, and the swan-maidens take up their positions in readiness for their waltz.

Waltz[2] *for the Corps de Ballet.* [*There are several versions of this*

[1] Throughout this act all *pointe tendue* positions to 4th pos. back are taken with the working knee *bent*, which brings the working foot closer to the supporting foot, than would otherwise be the case.

[2] For an alternative version of the Waltz by the Swan-maidens, see *Appendix A* page 158.

SOME SETTINGS FOR "SWAN LAKE"

(Above) *Setting for Act Three, Bolshoy Theatre, Moscow*, 1926
(Below) *Setting for Act One, Scene II, Bolshoy Theatre, Moscow*, 1926

dance, the pattern of which is governed by the number of dancers used. The following version is that used by the Markova-Dolin Company, according to records kept by Nicholas Sergeyev, then by Bronislava Nijinska, the strength of the corps de ballet being sixteen, with two swan-maiden leaders, making eighteen dancers in all.]

I. One column of four swan-maidens walks to make a line from 3–2; two columns of four walk down centre; one column walks to make a line from 4–1. Those in centre work toward one another first, then away from one another, those at sides work inwards first, then outwards; step is a series of *balancé* alternately forward and backward on place; if *balancé* forward starts R.F., then R. arm rises outwards, palm outwards, head with it; apex of rise is as L.F. comes across, then, on *balancé* back, R. arm comes down crossing under L. arm low in front, head inclined well to L. shoulder on this movement. If the *balancé* forward and backward is taken as one step this step is done four times in all.

II. Two side lines now run inwards, two centre outwards, they meet with *posé* in 1st *arabesque sur la pointe*; side lines then run out, *posé arabesque* out, centre lines to centre meeting in *posé arabesque* towards one another. Repeat Step II. Repeat Step I, followed by Step II twice, ending in four lines of four swan-maidens evenly spaced and facing 5.

III. *Temps levé rond de jambe en l'air en dedans*, inside feet, same outside, *coupé assemblé devant* and *relevé* in 5th pos., taking arms to 5th pos. *en haut*, hands are in crossed pos. *en bas* on *rond de jambe*. Do this step four times to alternate sides.

IV. *Relevé* in 5th pos. *sur les pointes*, taking arms to 5th *en haut*, facing 5, drop, passing up-stage feet to lunged 4th pos. back *croisé*, same arm as lunged foot, extended forward in *arabesque*, head down to arm. *Relevé* again in 5th pos., facing 5, and drop lunged 4th pos. back *croisé*, but this time on the opposite side with the arms dropping to low *demi-seconde*, palms and head upwards and look back. On these lunges swan-maidens in each column go alternate ways, that is, 1st swan-maiden to R., 2nd to L., 3rd to R., 4th to L., they close in column facing front on *relevé* in 5th pos., then take lunge to opposite side, that is, 1st swan-maiden goes to L., 2nd to R., 3rd to L., 4th to R., close in column again on *relevé* in 5th pos. After these two lunges, *relevé*, etc., which are done three times, the swan-maidens do *temps levé-fouetté* to back, alternate sides, *assemblé* front, and *relevé* in 5th, arms 5th *en haut*, facing 5. Repeat last step to other side.

V. Side lines travel to centre, centre ones travel outwards, side L. line crosses with centre L. line, side R. line crosses with centre R. line. Step is *temps levé* in 1st *arabesque*, *chassé croisé* and *pas de chat*, three times, then three times back other way, this should end with centre clear and two columns of four on each side of stage (or one line of eight on each side). *Port de bras* (as preening of feathers in first entrance of swan-maidens), first with one arm outwards, then with one arm inwards, then with both arms outwards, next with both arms inwards, take both arms over head and bring them sharply down to crossed 5th pos. *en bas*, taking inside feet to *pointe tendue* back.

VI. Entrance of swan-maiden leaders, one at 3, one at 4. They stand with outside feet *pointe tendue croisé* to centre, bringing arms to low 2nd pos. with a wing-like movement. Step on outside feet and *relevé rond de jambe en l'air en dedans* with inside feet, drop *croisé* bringing arm down with leg, *glissade* outward and repeat *rond de jambe en l'air en dedans*. Repeat the *glissade–relevé–rond de jambe en l'air*, step on outside foot to 5 and *posé* on inside feet in *arabesque*, facing 5, both arms up, palms outwards, then three *pas de bourrée–grand jeté en tournant* with outside legs, travelling up-stage, *soutenu* outwards, arms 5th pos. *en haut* and take up first pose. Repeat all step to *posé arabesque*, then in place of *grand jeté*, etc., up-stage, each travels in circle outwards, crossing centre back and ending so that one is at head of column on L., the other at head of column on R.

Step in circle is *temps levé* in 1st *arabesque*, *chassé croisé* and *pas de chat* four times.

VII. * All together, *entrechat trois* to back with inside feet, taking arms up over head and bringing them down close to body in front with preening movement, at the same time body turns to face outside corner, head turns to raised back foot *pas de bourrée*–(=two steps) *posé* inwards on inside foot in 3rd *arabesque*, close it in front. Repeat all this three times in all, after 3rd *posé en arabesque*, one slow turn inwards on point, arms 5th *en haut*. Repeat all from * travelling to wings, hold last pose in 5th pos. *sur les pointes*, then go to group which consists of swan-maidens at back of columns leading to centre back, where they face one another in 1st *arabesque à terre*, the rest behind them in a wide semicircle, all facing centre back and gradually sinking down to deeper and deeper *plié* on supporting leg. Leading swan-maidens sink to ground, sitting with outside legs extended *croisé devant*, hands crossed on extended leg, body right down. From this pose the *corps de ballet* walk out to form two columns at each side and take up pose for opening of *Pas de Deux*.

Pas de Deux : Odette and Siegfried.

The *corps de ballet* is grouped in pairs with a huntsman standing between each pair, his arms round their waists, their heads inclined to his shoulders, their hands clasped against their inner cheeks. They stand in line on either side of stage at wings facing front.

On Introduction, Siegfried enters at 6. He comes to centre and summons Benno, who enters at 8, telling him to seek for Odette among her swan-maidens. Benno obeys, gazing into the faces of the maidens in line from 2–3; Siegfried looks down the line of faces on the opposite side. Benno arrives near 4, facing 5, and hesitates. Siegfried is further forward centre-stage. On last *cadenza*, Odette enters at 3, running behind Benno. She does *arabesque* on her L. point, facing 2, holding his extended arm with both hands, then continues to run until she arrives in front of Siegfried. She pauses in 5th pos. *sur les pointes*, facing 5, her arms 5th pos. *en haut*; he gazes at her entranced. She sinks to ground sitting back on her L. leg, her R. leg extended *pointe tendue, croisé devant* to 2, her body forward, her hands crossed along her extended R. leg, and makes three fluttering movements with her body, arms and head. Siegfried bends over her, taking her R. hand in his R. hand, her L. hand in his L. hand, then raises her to 5th pos. *sur les pointes*, facing 2, her arms 4th *en haut*, R. arm up; held thus, she does *développé croisé devant* to R. on last notes of Introduction.

I. *Fouetté pirouette en dehors* (not holding Siegfried's finger), end in 1st *arabesque*, facing 6, slow *penché* down and up. Walk toward 1, *posé* in 1st *arabesque* on R.F. being caught by Benno who slowly turns her in same pose, one turn, then lowers her gently off point same pose. She steps back to Siegfried, L.R.L., turning to L. as she does it, and *posé* on L. point in *arabesque croisée* to 1, her R. hand held behind in Siegfried's R., *demi-plié* coming off point in same pose, again she steps back to Siegfried, turning to R. on R.F., this time she does *posé* in 1st *arabesque* on her R. point to 1, her L. hand held behind by Siegfried, *demi-plié* in same pose. Again she steps back to Siegfried, turning to L., *posé* on L. point with *retiré* and *développé* to 1st *arabesque*, facing 6.

* *Soutenu sur les pointes* to R., end R. front facing 2, standing just behind Siegfried's extended R. arm, holding it with both hands, *développé* to 4th pos. front *croisé* R.F., take R. hand off Siegfried's shoulder lightly to 4th *en haut*, bringing R. hand back to his arm, when she falls to R. and is caught over Benno's R. knee, her arms in 5th pos. *en haut*; he raises her and returns her gently to Siegfried, she standing on her L.F., R.F. *pointe tendue* back. Repeat all from*, and this time sustain fall over Benno's knee as *corps de ballet* begin to move.

II. This section is danced by the *corps de ballet* only, who move to form a double diagonal line from 1–3; to achieve this they execute a series of *temps levés* in 1st *arabesque*, commencing with *chassé* R. six *temps levés* making one complete turn to R., *coupé chassé* to L., and repeat to other side, front arm in half 5th *en avant* on *arabesque*, opening to full stretch at end.

Swan-maidens in line 2–3 travel up-stage and across back to come to diagonal; swan-maidens in line 1–4 work almost *sur place*. They end by standing 5th pos. *croisé sur les pointes*, arms 5th pos. *en haut*, heads turned to 5, hold for one bar, then drop sharply to *pointe tendue* back on L.F., hands crossed 5th pos. *en bas*. During this, Odette walks slowly with Siegfried towards back, where they stand together until just before the end of this section, when they come forward.

III. Odette and Siegfried centre. Siegfried lifts Odette shoulder high, at the same time she does a *développé* R.F. *à la seconde*, R. arm raised high to the side, elbow straight, L. arm *demi-seconde*, drop and repeat to other side, preparation and two *tours en dehors* on L.F., end with *développé à la seconde* with R.F., arms 4th pos., L. arm up, head turned to R. Lower R.F. to 5th pos., doing *pas de bourrée sur place*. Repeat from beginning, only doing the *développé à la seconde* twice instead of three times.

Odette now moves away from Siegfried, travelling towards 1, with *bourrée sur les pointes*, *demi-plié* on R. point making a *retiré derrière* and making gentle waving movement with arms, body turned slightly to 2. She does this four times then, turning to R., runs back to Siegfried, to repeat this section from the beginning, but omitting *pas de bourrée*, etc., to 1, instead last *pirouette* (which should consist of at least three turns) ends in *arabesque croisée* facing 1, hands stretched in crossed 5th *en bas*, body low. Siegfried then turns Odette slowly on herself to face 2 in 1st *arabesque*, leaning back to R.; she breaks away from him and runs to exit at 3, but, anticipating her flight, he bars her way. She hesitates at 3, facing Siegfried with imploring gesture, then turns to face 1.

IV. *Corps de ballet* still in their double diagonal lines execute a series of small graduated lunges downward in *arabesque croisée*, R. foot back, R. arm forward, head down to R. arm, each lunge is lower than preceding one and slightly spasmodic as though to suggest a sob, then rise to 5th pos. *sur les pointes*, arms in 5th pos. *en haut*. Repeat the whole three times in all, then hold 5th pos. *sur les pointes* before dropping on L.F. to *pointe tendue* back, as before.

During this, Odette travels from 3–1 with six *temps levés* in 3rd *arabesque* on R.F. Siegfried follows in her wake, then lifts her, she does a *retiré devant* with R. leg, L. leg extended *en arabesque*, as she makes a circular movement from L. to R. with body, arms, and head. She repeats the whole three times in all, but on 3rd lift he takes her on to his shoulder, her R.F. with high *retiré* movement *devant*, her hands crossed front, her body and head down, and carries her to 2, where he puts her down.

V. Odette steps on R.F. towards 8. *Posé* turn on L. *en dehors* to face 5, arms opening to 2nd, caught by Siegfried. Steps again on R.F. then round to R. on L. point, ending in *arabesque*, holding Siegfried's outstretched R. arm with both hands, preparation and two *tours en dehors* on L.F. ending in 1st *arabesque penchée*, *pas de bourrée dessous* bringing R.F. to *pointe tendue*, *croisé devant*, arms 4th pos. *en avant*, R. arm across body. Repeat from beginning of this step three times in all, last time do at least triple turn and end softly in 1st *arabesque croisée* leaning slightly to L., Siegfried turns her to R. so that she faces 6 in 1st *arabesque*.

VI. *Corps de ballet* repeat Section II, starting L. and travelling back to original positions in pairs, huntsmen re-enter at wings as at commencement of Adage. During this, Odette goes to 3 and Siegfried to 1; she first faces 3, then turns to face 1 with a gesture towards Siegfried.

VII. Odette runs to Siegfried at 1. She does *posé arabesque* on R.F. facing 1, both arms in 5th pos. *en haut*. Siegfried catches her and, taking both her wrists from behind, he turns her slowly to R. to face 2, folding her arms down to crossed 5th pos. *en bas*; then, lunging back until she leans against him, her R. cheek against his L. cheek, he sways her gently from side to side, bringing her upright, her arms again in 5th pos. *en haut*, she balances against him, then gently hurries away to repeat whole of this section to other side to 2.

VIII. Odette steps to centre on R. point, facing 1, her L.F. in high open *retiré devant*, arms crossed 5th pos. *en bas* and head down. Repeats movement to L., facing 2, extends R. leg to 4th pos. *croisé devant* and does *fouetté pirouette en dehors* to R. (one and a half or two and a half times), arms 5th *en haut*, ending facing her partner in deep back bend, her arms opening to *demi-seconde*; Siegfried half-turns her to R. to face 2 in 1st *arabesque*. Repeat whole of this section.

Corps de ballet now move to form two diagonal lines, facing each other centre back: one line extending from 7–1, the other from 7–2; all stand in 1st *arabesque à terre*, their heads lowered to raised front arm, the swan-maidens are graduated in height from back to front, the two centre back being almost stretched to the ground.

As *corps de ballet* move to this pose, Odette walks round to R.,

Siegfried to L., to meet centre-stage, she standing in 5th pos. *sur les pointes*, facing 2, R.F. front, her arms 4th pos. *en haut*, R. arm up. Siegfried stands behind her, holding her wrists.

Benno enters and stands behind them to their R.

IX. Siegfried turns Odette to R., while she executes *petit battement sur le cou-de-pied devant* with her R.F. as she turns (one turn), opens her R.F. *croisé devant* to 2, one *fouetté pirouette en dehors* supported by man's finger, catch and repeat whole of this section with double *pirouette*; then repeat the whole section a third time with triple *pirouette*. Odette steps on to R., point *sur place* making a high *développé à la seconde* with L. leg, facing 5, her hands held in crossed 5th pos. *en haut* by Siegfried who stands behind her. Benno comes forward and Odette falls backward to R. over his R. knee. Benno, Siegfried and Odette exit. *Corps de ballet* moves back into one line at each side of the stage near wings where they remain until the *Coda*.

Pas de Quatre.

Enter four small swan-maidens[1] in line facing 5, standing near 3, L.F. *pointe tendue* back, hands linked in front. On last beat of Introduction they transfer weight to L.F., taking R.F. up *sur le cou-de-pied devant.*

I. Ten *petits jetés,* alternately *derrière* and *devant,* starting with R.F. and travelling towards 8, stronger *jeté* to small *arabesque* on R.F., *pas de bourrée dessous* ending in 5th pos., L.F. front and *relevé* on R.F., L.F. *sur le cou-de-pied devant, demi-plié* on R.F., keeping L.F. as before. Repeat the whole four times in all to alternate sides, gradually working down-stage.

II. Standing in 5th pos., R.F. front, facing 5, do *entrechat quatre–relevé–retiré passé en arrière,* taking heads away from working feet. Repeat other side then four *échappés changés sur les pointes* making a circle from L. to R. with heads; on 1st *échappé* head goes to L., on 2nd it is down, on 3rd it goes to R., and on last it is again erect. Repeat the whole four times in all, travelling back.

III. Travelling down towards 5: *temps levé* on L.F., *chassé* forward on R.F., *relevé* on R. point in small *arabesque,* taking heads down on *chassé* and up on *relevé.* Repeat this eight times in all on alternate sides, then one small *jeté derrière* on R.F.

IV. Travelling slightly diagonally back to 3: *jeté devant* on L.F., *jeté derrière* on R.F. Repeat these two *jetés* then do *jeté devant* on L.F. and *relevé*–sharp *développé écarté* with R.F., *tombé.* Repeat the

[1] The small swan-maidens are often known as cygnets, but of course they must be young girls.

whole four times in all, but, in place of last *tombé*, take R.F. back *sur le cou-de-pied derrière* with sharp *fouetté* movement.

V. Travelling diagonally towards 1, do fifteen small *pas de chat*; on sixteenth beat of section *retiré* L.F. to open position *devant* and *demi-plié* on R.F.

VI. Three *jetés devant*, L.R.L., *jeté derrière* on R.F. on fourth beat, three *jetés derrière* L.R.L., *jeté devant* on R.F. on fourth beat. Repeat whole four times in all.[1]

VII. Travelling slightly diagonally back towards 3: *posé* on L. point, R.F. *sur le cou-de-pied devant*, *tombé* on R.F., L.F. *sur le cou-de-pied derrière*, heads incline to L. on *posé* and to R. on *tombé*. Repeat seven times, on last two beats of section *coupé* on to L.F., raising R. leg *devant* with knee bent.[2]

VIII. Sixteen *jetés devant*, facing 5, starting with R.F. *Posé* forward on R. point in small *arabesque* straight to 5, both arms up, down to L. knee, R. shoulder forward, head inclined to L., arms crossed over breast.

Dance of Two Leaders of the Swan-Maidens.

I. First Leader enters at 3 and travels in a circle passing 4–8–1–5–2–6–3–4. Second Leader enters at 4 and travels in a circle passing 3–6–2–5–1–8–4–3. The step is *temps levé–chassé–temps levé* in 3rd *arabesque* on R.F.–*glissade–jeté en avant* on to L.F. in 2nd *arabesque*. Repeat this six times, making seven in all. Both Leaders are now facing 5 up-stage, placed equidistant on either side of the line 5–7.

II. *Posé* in 2nd *arabesque* on inside foot towards each other, *glissade* out; repeat *posé* on outside foot away from each other, *glissade* towards each other.

III. Travelling down-stage and commencing inside foot, do this step four times to alternate sides: *tombé–développé–tombé–assemblé derrière–entrechat six*. On *tombé développé* pass arms through 5th pos. *en avant* to 4th pos. *en haut*, same arm raised as leg. This movement should be full and with the body. Arms 5th *en haut* for *entrechat six*.

IV. *Temps levé* on L.F., *chassé* R.F., *pas de bourrée dessous*, *glissade*, *posé* in 3rd *arabesque*, both Leaders beginning with R.F. Do this step four times travelling from side to side down-stage.

V. *Posé* in 2nd *arabesque* on outside foot away from each other, *glissade*, and repeat *posé* on inside foot towards each other.

[1] This step (VI) can also be done travelling slightly up-stage.

[2] This step (VII) can also be done across the stage in a straight line.

VI. *Pas de bourrée-jeté en tournant*, four times travelling up-stage and always end facing 5.

VII. *Posé* in 2nd *arabesque* on outside foot away from each other, then *glissade* and repeat *posé* on inside foot towards each other.

VIII. Travelling towards 1, both Leaders commencing R.F.: *posé* in low *arabesque*, arms extended and crossed in low 5th *en avant* with slight waving movement and slowly raising them through 2nd pos. (not too wide), *coupé* L.F. Do this *posé–coupé* seven times, on the eighth time step L.F. across in front, transferring weight on it, R.F. *pointe tendue derrière*, end with arms crossed at wrists in 5th *en haut*, having raised them through 5th pos. *en bas*, *en avant*, to 5th *en haut* crossed at wrists. Leaders exit at 1.

Odette's Variation.

Enter at 3, come to centre, stand on L.F., R.F. *pointe tendue derrière*, arms crossed 5th pos. *en bas*, L. shoulder forward. No music.

On Introduction, *chassé en arrière* with R.F., transfer weight on to it, leaving L.F. *pointe tendue*, *croisé devant*, open arms to side and make one soft wing-like waving movement.

I. *Relevé* on L. point, open R.F. to 2nd pos., arms open to 2nd at same time, R. arm raised higher than shoulder level, *double rond de jambe en l'air en dedans*, close 5th front, *demi-plié*, the R. arm comes down with the leg. Repeat to other side, then once more to first side. Swift *pas de bourrée changé sur place* then *retiré* R.F. (to L. knee) and close it in 5th pos. front *sur les pointes*, at same time take arms to 4th pos. *en haut*, R. arm up, turning head and L. shoulder with very proud movement to 2. Pause.

* Wide *glissade* to L., *posé* on L. point *en attitude*, facing 5, circling first the L. arm over head then the R. so as to end *en attitude croisé*. Repeat from * to R., then "*bourrée*" back on point to centre with one soft waving arm movement and repeat *chassé* back, etc., as in Introduction.

Repeat all from commencement of Section I, but, in place of last *bourrée* back, *temps levé* on L. in *arabesque* to corner 3, run to 3, half-turn to face 1, and "*bourrée*" still further backward to 3 *sur les pointes* with one soft waving movement of arm.

II. *Sissonne en avant* to 1, arms in 3rd *arabesque*, *sissonne ouverte* on R.F. to 1, same arms, *pas de bourrée* under to R., ending with L.F. in low 4th position *devant*, body forward, hands crossed 5th pos. *en bas*, *relevé* on R.F., taking L.F. back with high *développé* to

SOME SETTINGS FOR "SWAN LAKE"

(Above) *Setting for Act One, Scene II, Leningrad Opera and Ballet Theatre,* 1933
(Below) *Setting for Act Two, Leningrad Opera and Ballet Theatre,* 1933

SOME SETTINGS FOR "SWAN LAKE"
(Above) *Setting for Act One, Scene I, Bolshoy Theatre, Moscow*, 1937
(Below) *Setting for Act Two, Bolshoy Theatre, Moscow*, 1937

arabesque, at same time taking arms back slightly below shoulder level and curving body back to raised leg, repeat all, then *glissade* turning to R., *posé* in 2nd *arabesque* on L. point, *temps levé en arabesque* on R.F. towards 4, run to 4, half-turn to face 2, and "*bourrée*" backward *sur place* with one soft waving movement of arms. Repeat the whole of this section on other side, but end with R.F. *pointe tendue croisé devant*, arms in 4th pos. *en avant* in preparation for turns towards 1.

III. Four *posé* turns *en dehors* on L.F., towards 1, two turns, *bourrée sur place* turning to R., with two soft waving movements of arms. Repeat from beginning of this section three times, making four in all; the last time replace *pas de bourrée* with *petits tours sur les pointes* to 1, finish standing on L.F., R.F. *pointe tendue derrière*, L. shoulder forward, arms 4th pos. *en haut*, R. arm up, head to 2. (Frequently this part of the music is cut by one half.) Exit Odette.

Coda.

From the two lines of swan-maidens, the two rear ones from each side run to form a line across the back of the stage. Travelling down to 5, they do:

Step I. *Ballonné* with R.F., *chassé–coupé* twice, *chassé–temps levé* in 3rd *arabesque* on R.F., *pas de bourrée dessous*; repeat all to other side. Separate into pairs, two going to 2, and two going to 1, to rejoin original side lines with

Step II. *Chassé–temps levé* on up-stage foot, same on down-stage foot, repeat to each side.

Step III. *Posé* on inside foot, *retiré* outside foot front of supporting knee, *coupé* on to outside foot, inside foot *cou-de-pied derrière*, *posé* on inside foot, *fouetté* outside foot back. Repeat alternate sides, travelling back until all the swan-maidens are back in their original two lines. As soon as the first four have done the first step twice, the second four begin it, having run from side lines to form line at back; the third four likewise run to form line at back and begin the first step as soon as the previous four have done it twice. When the last four have done the first step twice, they do the third step once to each side, then the second step twice to get back to lines at side.

Step IV. They stand on inside foot, outside foot placed *pointe tendue derrière*. While one Leader and two small swan-maidens enter at 3, with *chassé* on R.F. into 1st *arabesque*, five *temps levés* travelling to 1, *relevé* in 1st *arabesque*. Repeat on diagonal 4–2, then *chassé–temps levé*, *relevé* on R.F. in 1st *arabesque*, same on L.F. *pas de bourrée* to line on O.P. side, Leader up-stage and two small swan-maidens in line with her down-stage. Repeat from Step IV with other Leader and two small swan-maidens commencing at 4.

Step V. (*Corps de ballet.*) During Odette's next step the *corps de ballet* lunge inwards on up-stage foot in *arabesque à terre* with big *port de bras* forward and up, raising down-stage arm as they come up, then repeat on the other foot; the two inner lines comprising two swan-maidens and four small swan-maidens now place themselves diagonally outwards on lines 7–1, 7–2. This takes the whole of her step diagonally 3–1. They stand still during Step VI.

(*Odette.*) Odette enters at 3 travelling from 3–1 with this step: *posé* on R.F., *fouetté* (half turn) to 1st *arabesque* facing 3, *coupé*, half turn, *ballonné piqué*. Repeat six times, run to centre to 1.

Step VI. Commencing 5th pos. R.F., front: *entrechat quatre–relevé–retiré passé derrière* to each side, four *retirés passés derrière*. Repeat the whole of this twice (three times in all) then *en diagonale* to 1, two *posé* turns *en dehors* and series of *petits tours* ending on R.F., L.F. *pointe tendue*.

Step VII. *Corps de ballet* form in three lines of six, doing *chassé–temps levé–chassé–pas de chat* four times, crossing stage; repeat crossing back to places.

Odette runs to centre and with *corps de ballet* does four times a species of *pas de chat* and *coupé* (sometimes a *gargouillade* and sometimes *pas de chat* and *pas de bourrée* are used) only changing feet, taking the front foot back and bringing the other foot on a *demi-plié*, then *bourrée en tournant* on place. Siegfried enters at 1, Benno at 2 and kneels. Odette walks in small circle to R. and steps on to Benno's knee. The *corps de ballet* form in this position:

Siegfried lifts Odette off Benno's knee, turns with her and lowers her on R.F. in *arabesque*, so that she faces him. Odette steps away from Siegfried, who mimes that he loves her and will marry her. Odette turns to R., steps across on R.F., ending in 1st *arabesque* on R. point in front of Siegfried and with large sweeping gestures of her R. arm to 1st *arabesque*, commands her companions to return to the lake. The swan-maidens run off in a line, commencing with the up-stage swan-maiden on the diagonal 1–3; this line is followed by the down-stage swan-maiden of the opposite group of three diagonally to centre, followed by line at prompt side, then line at opposite prompt side, and all exit at 3.

Siegfried tries to restrain Odette from leaving, but, after a poignant farewell, she glides away with a series of *pas de bourrée* travelling backward up-stage and exits at 3. Siegfried and Benno, suddenly conscious of the loneliness of the glade, gaze[1] towards the lake, across the surface of which glide in single file from right to left a number of swans, led by one bearing a crown on its head. All too soon the lake resumes its wonted calm, save where the fitful light of dawn ruffles the surface of the water with rivulets of gold. The curtain slowly falls.

[1] In the Sadler's Wells Ballet production at Covent Garden, Siegfried and Benno gaze upwards at the sky as though following the swans' flight overhead, while the huntsmen enter near 8 and kneel.

CHAPTER XVI

ACT ONE, SCENE TWO: SOME ASPECTS OF PRODUCTION

THE curtain rises on a forest glade, the "wings" formed from trees, the background depicting a lake bathed in moonlight. To the right of the lake is a ruined chapel. The distant back-cloth might suggest a rock-bound shore. Since this is romantic ballet I should like the sky to contain a full moon, lit from behind. It could be slightly dimmed from time to time to indicate the passing of a cloud.

When the curtain rises, one should see a line of white swans gliding slowly over the surface of the lake from left to right, the leader having a miniature gold crown on its head. Not only are the swans traditional, but they serve to explain to the spectator unacquainted with the ballet, the metamorphosis of swan into maiden, and *vice versa*.

As soon as the swans are well across the middle of the lake, the hunting party enter, some singly, some in little groups, carrying crossbows. The usual practice is to rest the bow in the crook of one arm, the butt held in the other hand; to hold a crossbow in one hand, bow downwards, looks slovenly. But it would be more appropriate to rest the bow on the left shoulder, lowering it only when about to aim. Incidentally, it requires an effort of some strength to prepare a crossbow ready to shoot. The head has a stirrup-iron which is slipped over one foot and held firmly to the ground, so that both hands can be used to pull and notch the bow-string.

When Siegfried enters and expresses to his friends a desire to be left in solitude, he gives his hat or plumed cap to one of his nobles, who exits carrying it. It is understandable that Siegfried would not wish to be burdened with a cap during his *pas de deux* with Odette, but would it not be better if he did not wear it in the first place?

As Siegfried makes his way to the lakeside, might he not lightly pass his right hand from left to right, as though he were waving aside a faint curtain of mist. As he lowers his crossbow and aims at a swan, it is presumed suddenly to change into a beautiful woman; but how rarely does Siegfried express surprise! One might suppose that the sudden transformation of swan into maiden was a commonplace.

On her entrance, I think Odette should appear outwardly cold and expressionless, because, although she has changed her form, it is reasonable to suppose that her nature as bird may still linger for a few moments. The rotatory movement of her head is very bird-like, at the same time the movement of her head, drooping as though heavy with grief, and slightly spasmodic, suggests sobbing. On the assumption that the transformation from bird to maiden is not quite complete, her first *port de bras* on her entrance should be markedly wing-like.[1] But, when Siegfried reveals his presence, then the position of her arms and her half-averted face should convey her alarm, indeed her fear. Because she recognizes Siegfried as the huntsman who aimed his bow at her when, in her guise as swan, she was gliding towards the bank.

When Rothbart appears in his form as Owl and Siegfried levels his weapon to shoot him, it is not very clear why Odette should implore the Prince to lower his weapon. It may be she thinks that should the enchanter be killed before she has forced him to release her from his spell, then his spell may become irremovable.

So far, no satisfactory costume has been devised for Rothbart as Owl. Either the mime interpreting the role wears a realistic costume and resembles a giant bird, or suggests a demon king from pantomime, or wears a brown sack-like garment which signifies nothing in particular.

When Odette and Siegfried make their first exit together, I suggest that his attitude should be gently protective, and hers, shyly confiding.

Consider the entry of the swan-maidens. It is essential that their movements should be infused with lyricism, particularly their *port de bras*, for they play an important part in the choreographic score. Unfortunately, these arm movements are frequently so mechanical in execution, so seemingly done "by numbers," so devoid of all poetic feeling, that they suggest a form of drill. Apart from the preening-like gestures which the dancer must sincerely feel to accord them their full beauty, *arabesques* play an important part in the design. In the first *arabesque* position, the arms should be in a straight line, the finger-tips of the front arm in a line with the eyes, and the shoulders square to the direction; if the rear arm is held at an angle the dancer's line is spoilt. In the third *arabesque*, the hands should undulate very gently during the *temps levés* and not writhe, as sometimes happens. The difficulty in *ensembles* is to suggest cohesion without stressing uniformity, which at once reduces the

[1] It is very probable that Odette's *port de bras* have in recent years been influenced by those in Fokine's *La Mort du Cygne*.

maidens to the level of a troupe. Precision of execution and alignment are important, but over-emphasis on precision gives the dancers a mechanical air. The ideal is paradoxical, in that every dancer should preserve her individuality and yet present a complete whole in the mass.

When Benno is the centre of the ring of agitated swan-maidens, it is helpful slightly to dim the lighting, giving the suggestion of a faint mist which might presumably causes Benno to mistake the white-clad maidens for swans.

The episode where Siegfried and Benno seek Odette among the assembled swan-maidens is sometimes carried out in a very casual manner. Siegfried seldom suggests a distracted lover searching for the beloved he fears he may have lost.

The *Pas de Deux* between Odette and Siegfried which follows is important in that Siegfried's growing love for Odette is conveyed by the manner in which he partners her. Odette, who at first courteously accepts his help, begins to trust him more and more as the result of his tender care for her, and is conscious of her growing affection for him. Now and again the swan-maidens intervene and the audience is kept in suspense as to the progress of the romance. A particularly charming pose, which can be very expressive of mutual love, is when Odette, placed in *arabesque,* her arms in fifth position *en haut*, has them gently lowered to the fifth position *en bas* by Siegfried, when he causes her to lean affectionately against him, while he gently sways her from side to side.

The succeeding *Pas de Quatre* is, I think, intended to afford contrast to the preceding love scene between Odette and Siegfried. It is bright, gay, and theatrically effective, although it always seems alien to the general mood. For its complete success the *pas* requires four well trained dancers of under medium height, of approximately equal build, and endowed with a good sense of rhythm. The *pas* must be danced with lightness and brilliance, over-emphasis reduces the *pas* to a music-hall number.

Towards the end of the act, the scene lightens slightly indicating the approach of dawn, and Odette commands her companions to return to the lake. Siegfried, fearful at the thought of being parted from his beloved, tries to prevent her from departing. She herself longs to remain, but cannot prevail against the magnetic force that draws her to the lake. The interpreter of Odette needs to suggest this sense of being drawn two ways, until the enchantment prevails and, extending her arms in a poignant gesture of farewell, she glides backwards towards the lake. She vanishes and at the same moment the first of a line of swans glides across the lake, passing from right to left. Siegfried might clutch Benno with his left hand, while with his right he traces wonderingly the path of the swans as they disappear into the deepening mist.

The wing-like *port de bras* used by the swan-maidens towards the end of this act should become more bird-like, an indication that the maidens are about to resume their life as swans. For the same reason their faces should gradually become less animated and more set. In short, a reversal of the process of swan into maiden which obtained at the beginning of this act.

If the interpreter of Odette is a ballerina of quality, she will not only use the steps and movements of her role to create a fantastic being radiating lyricism and poetry, but also to convey her tranformation from swan into maiden, her first fear of Siegfried, her softening of heart under his tender sympathy for her plight, a sympathy which engenders first her affection and then her love, followed by her pathetic leave-taking as her cruel enchanter forces her to forsake her lover and resume her guise as swan.

CHAPTER XVII

SIMPLIFIED CHOREOGRAPHIC SCRIPT OF "SWAN LAKE" ACT TWO

AT the rise of the curtain a number of guests (presumed to be dressed in the national costumes of Spain, Hungary, and Poland) are seen leisurely walking in couples about the throne-room. There are two pairs of dancers for the Spanish dance, five pairs for the Csardas, and four pairs for the Mazurka.

A page enters at 4 and announces that the Princess-Mother and Prince Siegfried are about to enter. The noble couple are preceded by two pages and attended by four ladies-in-waiting. The ladies and gentlemen present bow as the Princess-Mother and Prince Siegfried enter. They pass to their respective thrones and take their seats. The first page comes forward and announces the arrival of the Would-Be Brides. They enter and curtsey. The Princess-Mother and Siegfried rise from their thrones and descend the dais to greet them. The Princess-Mother asks the Would-Be Brides to dance, then Siegfried conducts the Princess back to their throne and both resume their seats.

The brides form into two lines of three down-stage, each holding a fan in the R. hand. The dance consists in the main of *pas de valse* in diverse patterns, during which the brides either gently flutter their fans or use them in broad sweeping movements upwards and downwards.

Dance of the Would-Be Brides.

I. *Bourrée* on *pointes* to L. to 6, *dégagé* L.F. *pointe tendue* and make an *épaulement* to R. facing 8. Do this step four times in all, alternate sides.

II. Two *pas de valse* making one turn to R. (half turn for each *pas de valse*). Do this four times.

III. Repeat Step I four times as before.

IV. Repeat *pas de valse* turning as in Step II, only twice instead of four times, then do six *pas de valse* alternately to R. and L. without turning, but travelling back to end in formation of two lines on diagonal 3–1.

V. In this formation the down-stage dancers turn to face 4 and the line up-stage face 2. Step on R.F., *ballonné* L.F., *balancé* (all

SOME SETTINGS FOR "SWAN LAKE," FEDOR LOPUKHOV PRODUCTION

(Above) *Setting for Act Two, Kirov Theatre, Leningrad,* 1945
(Below) *Setting for Act Three, Kirov Theatre, Leningrad,* 1945

Coll. Gérard Mulys] [*Photo: Barba, Monte Carlo*

SETTINGS FOR "SWAN LAKE" AS PRESENTED BY THE LITHUANIAN BALLET, THÉÂTRE DE MONTE CARLO, *circa* 1930

(Above) *Act Two* (Below) *Act One, Scene II*

this travelling slightly forward), two *pas de valse* turning to the R. end on same place as at commencement of step. The fan is used in a big sweeping movement upwards in front on the *balancé*. This step travels up or down-stage for each line, making the dancers cross each other. Do this four times. Four *pas de valse* alternately to R. and L., getting into a circle.

VI. Step *temps levé* R.F., *ballonné* L.F., repeat with other foot. Two *pas de valse* turning to R. with sweeping downward movement of the fan. Do this step three times; on the fourth time, instead of two *pas de valse* turning, run to form two straight lines of three as at commencement of dance.

VII. *Dégagé* R.F. *pointe tendue* to R., fan held high in 2nd pos. in R. hand, incline to L. slightly, *pas de bourrée dessous* to L. and pose as before, only L.F. *pointe tendue* to L. with fan now held across front of body with fanning movement. This is done three times to alternate sides, then four *pas de valse* to alternate sides travelling back to form one diagonal line from 3–1.

VIII. Siegfried, having now descended from dais, dances a few steps with each would-be bride in turn down the diagonal line. He does two *pas de valse* turning, finishing with a bow to the bride with whom he has just danced, the bride making a curtsey in return. All the other brides who are not dancing with Siegfried do one *balancé* forward and one *balancé* back, and two *pas de valse* turning to R. After Siegfried has danced with the last bride he walks slowly away towards 1. He is distraught, his thoughts full of the Swan Queen whom he met in the forest. Meanwhile, the brides do eight *pas de valse* alternately R. and L., travelling in a circle led by the bride nearest 3 in the diagonal line; they travel clockwise and end in their original places and in formation of two lines of three down-stage. The bride who leads the circle ends up in back line of three nearest wing. Now they fan themselves more quickly, a reflection of their annoyance at the Prince's lack of interest.

IX. *Dégagé* R.F. *pointe tendue–demi-plié* L.F., fan lowered towards R.F. to 1. *Relevé* in 5th pos., fan brought up to face. This is done twelve times in all.

X. Two *pas de valse* turning to R. Repeat. *Balancé* forward, *balancé* backward. Repeat.

XI. *Ballonné–glissade–entrechat trois* travelling to R., end the *entrechat trois* with L.F. *sur le cou-de-pied devant*, *effacé* to 2, do this step four times in all alternately to R. and L.

XII. Repeat X, only *balancé* forwards and *balancé* backwards once, followed by a *soutenu* to R.

XIII. Repeat XI. Step on R.F., *chassé* on to L.F. Curtsey to Prince who is now standing near 2. The six brides go in a group standing obliquely to the throne near 1.

Now the Princess-Mother rises from her throne attended by Siegfried. She goes towards the brides, thanks them for their dancing, and asks Siegfried to choose from them the one who pleases him the most. The brides now move up-stage and stand near the throne, with the Princess and Siegfried near 2. Siegfried declares that none pleases him and escorts his mother back to her throne, walking back to centre-stage, while the brides walk rather indignantly round the room passing 5 and go towards 2; as they pass 5, Siegfried bows and each bride makes a brief curt curtsey. They eventually sit down on six stools placed from 2 up-stage and watch for the remainder of the act.

A page enters and announces the arrival of two new guests, visitors unknown to the Court. The Princess-Mother commands the strangers to be admitted. All the guests go towards the entrance to the hall to watch the entrance of the strangers. The lights unaccountably dim and an atmosphere of tension is felt. All the guests return to their places. As the two strangers enter, there appears at a window a vision of Odette, who tries to warn the Prince not to be deceived by the visitor's apparent likeness to herself, but Siegfried fails to see Odette's imploring gestures.

The Prince, observing Odile's resemblance to Odette, greets her with unusual warmth and recovers his spirits. Odile curtseys to the Princess-Mother who welcomes her. Then Siegfried turns to Rothbart and enquires: "Who is this lady?" Rothbart replies: "My daughter." Siegfried takes Odile's hand, expresses his admiration of her beauty, and conducts her to an adjoining chamber; as they exit, the vision of Odette vanishes. Odile's father, the Baron Rothbart, sits himself on the Prince's throne and converses with the Princess-Mother, while they watch the dancing, which consists of a series of various national dances contributed by their foreign guests.

Danse Espagnole.

Two Spanish couples run quickly to centre-stage. The two male dancers are in the centre, back to back, facing their respective partners in typical Spanish pose. The men hold their arms above their head, palms outwards; the girls have one arm above the head, the other in front of waist, palms outwards. Throughout the entire dance the couples keep opposite to each other, sometimes changing places.

I. *Dégagé pointe tendue effacé* with up-stage foot making a twist with the hips. Close foot (on ball of foot) to 5th pos. Repeat the *dégagé*, this time closing the foot to 5th pos. with a stamp, and quickly do six *pas de basque* beginning with up-stage foot, making circular movements with the wrists with *épaulement*, arms held in rather forward *demi-seconde* pos. The ladies travel towards each other and the men outwards, so that the couples end with the ladies on the inside and the men on the outside. Make a break of five stamps *dégagé pointe tendue croisé devant* towards respective partners. Repeat the stamps and *pointe tendue croisée*. Repeat the whole step to other side so that the couples end in beginning position.

II. The couples now change sides during a *sissonne retombé* with arms *en haut*, palms outwards. Repeat in same direction. Go round partner *dos à dos* with *coupé* and step outside foot to 4th pos. *front* on ball of foot, outside arm *en haut*, other arm across back. *Pas de bourrée dessous*, ladies approaching each other, men going outwards. Point foot to 4th pos. *front croisé* four times marking the time and opening the position wider leaning back, down-stage arm *en haut*, other across body in front. Repeat *pas de bourrée* and point *croisé* in opposite direction, then a break in 1st pos., facing 5, arms *en haut*. Repeat whole step to other side finishing with the break twice, turning round *sur place*.

III. The ladies, beginning with up-stage foot, do very quick *pas de bourrée* travelling inwards and kneel on one knee *croisé*, and do a circular *port de bras*. They rise and, holding their skirts with both hands, do three walking steps round their partners, going in an outward direction first, then down centre, then they do a *soutenu renversé* outwards. Meanwhile, the two men move towards each other with heel beat followed by stamp, alternate feet repeated several times, they then do three walking steps and *soutenu renversé* with their partners. Repeat whole step, only at end both couples step to 2nd pos. away from each other on outside foot, sliding inside foot up to outside foot and make a *coupé*. Repeat this last movement in same direction.

IV. The couples face each other and work up-stage, the ladies are on the outside. They do a *soutenu renversé*, then place outside foot down-stage, *pointe tendue*, bringing it to the other foot, on ball of foot, place it out again; step on it and repeat this step twice more in same direction. Then, travelling down-stage, all four dancers facing 5, do 6 *jetés* commencing on inside foot for each pair, bringing the working foot *pointe tendue* in 4th pos., front knee slightly bent, making an *épaulement* movement and snapping fingers on each *jeté*.

V. The couples now travel diagonally, the lady on O.P. side going up-stage to 3, her partner down-stage to 1. The couple on P. side, man goes to 3 and the lady to 1. They pass each other back to back with step *temps levé* on up-stage foot for those travelling to 3, *ballonné* with down-stage leg. The opposite for those travelling to 1, raising same arm as working leg on *ballonné*. Step then stamp and repeat this whole step in opposite directions. Repeat in both directions.

VI. Both partners face each other and step with outside foot up-stage in 2nd pos., other foot held *pointe tendue*. Break turning to face diagonally away from each other. Repeat same way.

VII. All four dancers in line now travel down-stage doing quick *pas de bourrée changés*. Point outside foot *effacé* and do three *petits battements sur le cou-de-pied*. Repeat opposite side. Repeat each side again.

VIII. Now the couples cross in pairs, the pair O.P. side passing behind the other couple: *tombé coupé* twice beginning with up-stage foot, one arm in front of body, the other across back, then do a break. Repeat the whole step. The man is travelling backwards and the lady faces him and is travelling forward.

IX. The couples now go round each other in pairs *dos à dos* with a *renversé* movement, stepping on one foot and pointing the other to 4th pos. front, alternate feet six times. The ladies then step to centre with a *développé* front and kneel *croisé*. The men walk and stand back to back in the centre. All the dancers together raise their arms at conclusion.

Csardas.

Introduction of four bars to run from near 1 to

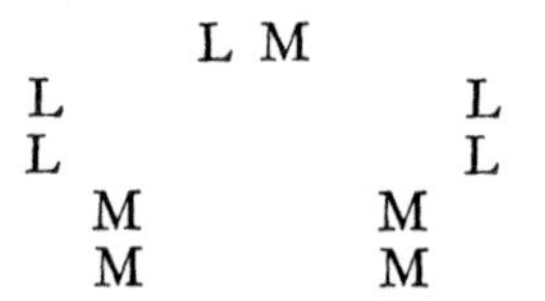

I. Four men travel in towards each other doing *cabriole* with inside foot to side, ending in 2nd pos. *à terre*. Close outside foot to 1st pos. Repeat. Break (4th pos. front with alternate feet; out to 2nd., heels outwards; close in 1st).

II. Four Csardas steps down-stage to 5, commencing outside feet (Csardas step: three *pas marchés*, on the third, lower supporting heel making a beat, and at same time *développé* other leg to 4th pos. front *en l'air*). Four Csardas steps up-stage (turn out towards wings to go up-stage). Two Csardas steps down-stage to meet partners. As the four men begin their 3rd Csardas step towards 5 the ladies do Step I, then Step II, only they do four Csardas steps towards 5 and only two up-stage (turn outwards to wings to go up-stage) to meet partners. As these side couples begin their last four Csardas steps, the centre couple begin and do four Csardas steps down centre of stage, beginning with outside feet. Lady is slightly in front of Man, who holds her round the waist and also holds her right hand with his R. hand. On the last step they both step away from each other on outside feet, closing other foot to 1st pos., and offer R. hands, Lady turning to face up-stage.

III. All the couples placed:

L M M L
L M
L M M L

now do one Csardas step making a half-circle to change places with partner, then one break, both change their direction on the break. Repeat step back to places. Centre couple end both facing 5.

IV. The side couples lunge on to R. leg in deep *plié*, L. knee almost on ground, R. hand at back of head, L. hand at waist, Lady going up-stage, Man down, this is followed by a *développé* front L. leg and two *pas marchés*, L.F., R.F. Repeat in opposite direction. Then three *pas marchés*, R.F., L.F., R.F., finish with *développé* L. leg changing direction of body. Repeat in opposite direction.[1] Centre couple meanwhile do one Csardas step, beginning inside feet, coming towards each other, Man taking Lady round waist, holding her R. hand with his R. hand, end the Csardas step with a little hop on inside foot and make a *dégagé effacé* with outside foot, then six times travelling back to alternate sides holding hands (Man R. hand, Lady L. hand) *petits battements* (back and front) and *dégagé* with small *temps levé* on supporting foot and *épaulement effacé*.

V. Side couples repeat Step IV, only Lady begins down-stage and Man up-stage. Centre couple do two Csardas steps to 5, last one ends with feet together. With a little spring, slide inside feet to 2nd pos., *demi-plié* outside leg. Repeat opposite way. Repeat the first side and break.

VI. The centre couple cross, Lady going L., Man R., with lunge on up-stage leg, *développé* front down-stage leg (facing wings), three walks turning outwards ending with break, having returned to original places. Repeat same way. The side

[1] This description is of the work of the couples on Prompt side.

couples do four Csardas steps in a circle, clockwise round themselves, Lady slightly in front of Man, who holds her R. hand with his R. hand, and has his L. hand round her waist.

VII. Outside couples now go *dos à dos* with double heel clicks four times, then, facing 5, stamp inside feet and place outside foot on ball of foot in 4th pos. back, knee bent, outside arm at back of head, inside arm at waist, bring inside shoulder forward, look at partner. Repeat opposite way and again first way, then mark the rhythm of quick music. Centre couple here step up-stage facing each other in 2nd pos., weight on up-stage leg on *demi-plié* down-stage foot pointed, arms straight, one directed up-stage, the other down, *little *rond de jambe en dehors* with down-stage leg placing it on ball of foot in 4th pos. back, knee bent, position is the same as for outside couples with *épaulement* towards partner. Repeat this step in opposite directions. Repeat three times the last half of this step from *.

VIII. Quick part. Outside couples, Lady with back to audience, Man facing 5, using inside feet place heel on ground and flick toe to where heel was, three stamps R.F., L.F., R.F.[1] making half-turn so that lady faces down-stage and Man up-stage, same opposite direction and repeat both ways (four times in all). Centre couple *dégagé* inside feet and do *pas de bourrée* away from each other, then towards each other, two *cabrioles* crossing each other, three stamps. Repeat back to places.

IX. All couples do flick-flack (*fouettés*) turning on outside foot, three stamps. Repeat all travelling up-stage. Then down-stage twice.

X. All couples do the same here: Man gives R. hand, Lady takes it and spins round under his arm, then ends in front of him, and he, still holding her hand, puts his L. hand round her waist and they both turn, doing either little *cabrioles* or small *ronds de jambe en dehors* with *coupé*. Repeat whole of step.

XI. All couples do two *cabrioles*, three stamps going in opposite directions, Ladies down-stage, Men up-stage. Repeat other way. Repeat both ways.

XII. All couples face each other, stamp and clap, and do the *cabriole* step four times turning, Man holding Lady's waist, Lady has hand on Man's shoulder.

XIII. All couples do Step IX once up-stage, followed by two *cabrioles* and three stamps. The side couples repeat this up-stage. The centre couple repeats it, but travels down-stage.

[1] Described for couples on Prompt side. The ladies are on the inside, men outside.

XIV. Repeat four times first step of quick part, i.e. Step VIII, only this time the arms are crossed akimbo and on the fourth time end with the L.F. *dégagé* to the side.

XV. All couples do four swinging *pas de bourrée* to alternate sides (travelling down-stage).

XVI. Men lunge towards ladies and clap for eleven counts while ladies turn *sur place*. The outside couples end with Lady on one knee looking at partner, and the Man makes a break and stands looking at her. The centre couple finish by the Man taking the Lady's hands and turning her so that they finish with the Lady slightly in front of Man, both stand on L.F., R.F. pointed in *arabesque*, both extend L. arm in *arabesque* to 2 high, Man has his R. arm round Lady's waist and she has her R. hand on his R. hand at her waist.

Mazurka.

Four couples commence near 3 in this formation:

* * * *
* * * *

They travel in a circle anti-clockwise.

I. The Men do two Mazurka steps, the Ladies two *pas de basque*. Then turn *en dehors*, finish with stamp R.F. and clasp open arm facing each other, then *cabriole* step turning with partner, Man has R. arm round Lady's waist, L. arm *en haut*. Lady holds Man's R. shoulder, L. arm *en haut*. This is done four times so that the couples end in the four corners.

II. The two Ladies from 3 and 1 change places with each other with four crisply timed *pas de basque*. Their partners do three single turns *en dehors* (*temps levé–coupé* step) and break. During this, the Ladies at 2 and 4 do four *pas de basque* round their own partners. Now the two Ladies from 2 and 4 do four *pas de basque* to each other's paces, their partners turning *en dehors* with break, while those from 3–1 do four *pas de basque* round the Man they have gone to. Repeat this to finish up with original partner. Man holds Lady's hand, when she does the *pas de basque* round him, he is also doing a *balancé* step *sur place*.

III. The couple at 2 alone. They wheel round to L. and up-stage to centre with eight Mazurka steps for the Man and eight *pas de basque* for the Lady. They face each other and, going in opposite direction (Lady down-stage and Man up-stage) do *cabriole* step sideways ending with feet *à terre*, followed by three stamps. Repeat opposite way. Lady does two *pas de basque* steps round her partner to L., he holds her R. hand *en haut*. They both do two Mazurka steps to 2.

IV. The couple from 1 wheel round L. and come into the centre with Man doing seven Mazurka steps while Lady does seven *pas de basque*. They both do a break facing each other. Then *dos à dos* with arms crossed in front, elbows held high, step to 2nd pos., clicks heels twice, do this six times making two turns in all, then two Mazurka steps down-stage side by side. Then the *cabriole* and stamps, Lady down-stage, Man up-stage, beginning R.F. Repeat other way then two Mazurka steps back to 1.

V. The two couples from 3 and 4 now do: Men four Mazurka steps, Ladies four *pas de basque*, crossing each other so that the couple from 3 ends near 8 and the couple from 4 ends near 6. Then they face each other in pairs, and the Men going up-stage and the Ladies down-stage, they do the *cabriole* step with stamps. Repeat going in opposite direction, Ladies now do four *pas de basque* round their respective partners and all four couples do their Mazurka steps and a break to form a diagonal line 4–2.

VI. They all link up holding hands and wheel round thus clockwise with *cabriole derrière* and two stamps; do this four times. Each dancer faces in the opposite direction from the one next in position. Now the couples separate and with four Mazurka steps open out to the four corners. Now repeat the diagonal line, only this time making it from 3–1. Then do six Mazurka steps and break out to the corners again.

VII. Travelling in a circle anti-clockwise with eight Mazurka steps by Men and eight *pas de basque* by Ladies, holding partner's hand side by side, end in two straight lines, Ladies in front, Men behind. Ladies do four *pas de basque* down-stage commencing R.F., Ladies now do heel clicks (step R.F. to R., click heels twice, step L.F. to L. click heels twice) six times in all, then a break, meanwhile Men do heel clicks six times in all, then four Mazurka steps down-stage to Ladies, then a break.

VIII. The pairs face each other and take both hands and travelling up-stage they all do the *cabriole* step, followed by two steps four times. Now Ladies down-stage, Men up-stage, do the *cabriole* step. Repeat in opposite direction. *Renversé en dehors*, stamp and clap hands, then the *cabriole* step four times, making two turns with partner, Man holding Lady's waist, Lady with hand on Man's shoulder.

IX. All in one line, two Mazurka steps down-stage. Repeat the stamp, clap, and turn. Then all off in a line at 1, doing *cabriole* stamp step four times, finishing up with a series of small *cabrioles* to side.

After return to bow or curtsey to applause, those who have

"SWAN LAKE," ACT ONE, SCENE II. BOLSHOY THEATRE, MOSCOW, 1937

"SWAN LAKE," ACT THREE. BOLSHOY THEATRE, MOSCOW, 1937

danced the national dances take up their position to watch the *Pas de Deux* (*Odile and Siegfried*).

Siegfried enters at 2, Odile at 1, with *temps levé–chassé–temps levé en arabesque*. Meet in centre down-stage. *Relevé* in 5th pos., step back and each makes a little bow, turn up-stage with *chassé–temps levé en arabesque* and run to 4.

I. (*a*) From 4–2, Odile, just in front of Siegfried, *posé* on L.F., R.F. 4th pos. front *en l'air*, *fouetté* back to *arabesque*, *glissade*. Do this step six times in all. Siegfried follows her just behind all the time. Or (*b*) do this step, then Siegfried lifts her with *développé* front R. leg, arms *en haut*, opening out through 2nd pos. In this case the step is only done three times. Run to 1.

II. From 1–2, *glissade–posè* on L.F. in 1st *arabesque* to 6. Supported by Siegfried, with a sharp *fouetté* movement bring R.F. to L. knee, turning so that body faces 5 and head is turned to 1, L. arm 5th *en haut*, R. arm 5th *en avant*. Step on R.F. across in front of Siegfried, *double tour en dehors* on L.F. to 1, end facing 5 with R.F. on L. knee, L. arm 5th *en haut*, R. arm half 5th *en avant*. This step is done three times, run to 2.

III. From 2–4, three *sauts de basque en tournant en dedans*, commence with *chassé* on R.F. to 2nd pos. Siegfried follows Odile back. Odile does *relevé* in 5th pos. and is lifted with *développé* R. leg front, and is carried back to 2. Repeat.

IV. From 2–4, step to 4 on R.F., *cabriole fouetté en arabesque* to face 2, step on L. *pointe* with *développé* R. leg to 4th front to 2, step on R.F. and *posé* in 1st *arabesque* on L. *pointe* to 2. Siegfried does this step just behind Odile without doing the turn and *fouetté cabriole*, instead he steps on R.F. with *rond de jambe en dehors* with L.F., he holds her R. hand with his R. on the *cabriole* and supports her on the *arabesque* at end. Do this three times, then Odile runs to 3, Siegfried steps a little down-stage near 8. Odile does six single *posé* turns *en dehors* and on the seventh a *double tour* ending in back bend, arms *en haut*, caught by Siegfried. He turns her round on *pointe* to 1st *arabesque* to 6. They now walk slowly towards 1, Siegfried takes Odile's R. hand as if to kiss it. Odile suddenly withdraws it, then walks over to Rothbart who has come down from the throne towards 2. Odile does a *glissade* and *posé en lère arabesque* in front of Rothbart supported by him. He whispers to her. Odile goes back to Siegfried who is just off centre-stage, and does *posé en lère arabesque* on R.F. Siegfried holds her R. arm *en haut*. Odile goes forward into a low *arabesque*, Siegfried bringing his arm down so that he places it round her waist, still holding her hand. Odile goes back to Rothbart, this time doing a *posé* in *arabesque* on L. *pointe*, holding

Rothbart's R. shoulder and R. hand with both her hands. Rothbart speaks to Odile with warning movement of index finger of L. hand. Odile indicates, by a slight inclination of her head and by half-looking over her shoulder at Siegfried, that she understands the magician's meaning. During this scene, Siegfried walks a little up-stage, looks round at the guests and at Odile, revealing his admiration of her. Odile does *glissade* towards Siegfried and *double tour en dehors* on L.F. ending with *grand rond de jambe en l'air en dehors* with R. leg, ending in *arabesque* and she leans back on to Siegfried looking fondly at him, arms either in 5th *en haut* back over his head, or R. arm raised to R. side high, Siegfried raising his R. arm, also supporting her with his L. hand. Odile repeats *posé* in *arabesque* on Rothbart's arm. They repeat the mime, and again Odile does *glissade double tour* with *grand rond de jambe* as before. Close feet rather sharply in 5th pos. Siegfried goes towards 1, Odile does a *glissade–posé* in 1st *arabesque* on R.F., being supported by Siegfried at waist. They separate, Prince goes to 1, Odile back to 3, they meet in the centre with Odile doing a *posé double tour en dedans*—on R.F.—ending in 1st *arabesque* to 8, sharply closing feet in 5th pos. again, walk round in a small circle to come towards each other. Odile does a *relevé* in 5th pos. with *développé* L.F. *à la seconde* held by Siegfried with R. hand, his back to audience. Odile does *demi-rond de jambe* with L. leg *en dedans* and bends back supported by Prince. At this moment the vision of Odette appears at back of stage. Odile quickly covers Siegfried's eyes with her hands, so that he shall not see the vision, then she and Rothbart try to send the vision away. Three times Odile goes to drive away the vision and returns with *posé* in 1st *arabesque* into Siegfried's arms, shading his eyes. After the third time, the vision vanishes weeping. Rothbart returns to his seat beside the Princess-Mother. Siegfried has a sense of danger, but fails to observe the vision. Odile and Siegfried now walk to centre. Odile does a *relevé* in 5th pos. and *développé* front R. leg and *grand rond de jambe en dehors en l'air* to *arabesque*. Siegfried now turns her slowly (R.F. *retiré* to L. knee) holding her R. hand *en haut*. She does a *développé* to 1st *arabesque* to 6, *balancés* thus, then goes well forward raising leg in *arabesque*, then Siegfried catches her at the waist with one hand and she promenades thus (1 turn to R.). Then Odile comes up and leans back on to Siegfried with a caressing movement, closes feet in 5th pos. again. They separate: Siegfried goes to 1, Odile to 2, they face each other, walk towards each other. Odile does a *relevé* in 5th, presenting her R. hand to Siegfried with outstretched arm, he takes it with his L. hand. Odile does a *développé à la 2de*, steps towards Siegfried on L.

pointe with a *posé double tour en dehors*, ending in 1st *arabesque* to 6, then on the last beat, *posé* on R.F., turning to L. to face Siegfried, who kneels holding Odile at waist, she is in *arabesque* with both arms in 2nd pos. carried backwards. Their faces are very close together. Odile goes off at 2.

Siegfried's Variation.[1]

Begin at 3. Stand on L.F., R.F. *pointe tendue derrière*, arms in 4th pos., R. arm *en haut*, head turned to R.

I. *Glissade derrière–assemblé–entrechat six–entrechat sept*—three times to 1. Step on R.F. and *chassé* L.F. to 1, and pose in 2nd *arabesque croisée*, rear foot *à terre*.

II. *Pas de bourrée en tournant* to R., end facing 5. *Cabriole* with L. leg in *arabesque*, body leaning over to R., arms in 4th pos., L. arm *en haut*, *coupé* R.F. to 2nd pos. *à terre*, three *pirouettes* ending with *rond de jambe en l'air en dehors* ending to 1, raise R. arm during *rond de jambe* and lower supporting heel quietly at end of it. Do this step three times, ending centre-stage back. Travelling towards 2, *posé* in 1st *arabesque*, take two steps to 2 and *posé* in 1st *arabesque croisée*, then *chassé* L.F. to 1st *arabesque* to 2.

III. *Glissade* back to 4, turning to the R., *cabriole* to 4, back to audience, arms in 4th pos., L. arm *en haut*, lean well back and away from working leg. *Pas de bourrée* turning to R., *cabriole* in 2nd *arabesque* to 2 (slide L.F. back to *arabesque* for the *cabriole*). Do this three times on the diagonal 2–4. *Renversé en dehors–développé effacé* to 1–*pas de bourrée* to 1 (step R.F., L.F., R.F. and closing R.F. 5th pos. front).

IV. *Temps levé–chassé croisé* back R.F. with full movement of body towards working leg. Repeat to L. *Assemblé* front–*double tour en l'air* without changing the feet. Do this three times.

V. Alternate final step:

(*a*) Either repeat Step IV, travelling forward to 5 and ending the *double tour* on the R. knee, *or*

(*b*) Preparation to 2nd pos. *à terre* and *pirouettes sur le cou-de-pied*, *double tour en l'air*, ending in the pose as at the beginning.

Odile (Variation).

Odile walks on to stage at centre, stands on R.F., L.F. *pointe tendue croisée derrière*.

I. *Pas de bourrée en tournant en dedans*, followed by *relevé en attitude en tournant en dehors* followed by *pas de bourrée piqué en tournant en*

[1] The above *variation* is to be danced to original music in the piano score. For alternative versions of Siegfried's *variation*, see *Appendix* A, page 166.

dehors, end facing 5, *dégagé* R.F. *pointe tendue effacé* to 1, *demi-plié* L.F., look towards R.F. (this can be done with a slight spring on L.F. to the *effacé* position in a species of *temps de flèche*). *Rond de jambe en l'air*, R. leg with *relevé* on L.F. *Pas de bourrée dessous* and finish *pointe tendue croisée* as at commencement of dance. The whole step is repeated *sur place*.

II. Travelling towards 4, *posé* in 1st *arabesque* on R.F. *Fouetté dégagé* L.F. to R. knee *écarté* to 2, bringing R. arm *en haut*, L. arm *en avant*. Repeat this, then either repeat it again, or do a *posé* in 1st *arabesque* to 2 on L.F., then walk back to centre-stage to repeat the whole of Step I. End by walking to 3.

III. From 3–1 *pas de bourrée couru* in 5th pos., facing 2. Commence with body leaning slightly forward and *port de bras* from 2nd pos. to 5th pos. *en bas*, pass arms through 5th pos. *en avant*, opening them to 2nd pos., raising and turning head to 5. Six *échappés sur la pointe en tournant* to R., arms in 2nd pos., head turned with slight *épaulement* on each *échappé*. Repeat Step III still on the same diagonal. Then go to 4.

IV. On a diagonal 4–2, *pas de bourrée en tournant en dedans* commencing with L.F. *Grand rond de jambe en l'air en dehors* to 5th *arabesque* with *relevé* on L.F., end facing 2 in *arabesque* on *demi-plié* and immediately do *glissade en tournant*, making a *renversé* head movement and step on R.F. and make an *assemblé*, with L.F., *en tournant en dedans*. Do this step three times in all and go to 2 to prepare for *tours* in a circle.

V. A series of *pas de basque sur les pointes en tournant en dedans* making two circles round the stage and finish down-stage.

Coda.

Siegfried enters at 3 with:

I. A series of six *pas de bourrée grands jetés en 2me arabesque*, beginning on R.F., travelling round the stage anti-clockwise, making a circle and ending near 1. He runs to 3.

II. From 3–1, *temps levé* L.F., *chassé* R.F. Repeat using opposite feet, *assemblé en avant* with R.F., *double tours en l'air*. Do this four times towards 1. Preparation and *tours en dehors sur le cou-de-pied sur place*. Odile enters at 4, walks to centre-stage and does thirty-two *fouettés en tournant en dehors*. Siegfried enters at 4, goes to centre back and, travelling down-stage to 5, does sixteen *entrechats six*. Odile walks back to 4, and, from 4–1, does *posé* on L.F., arms in 4th, L. arm front, R. leg 4th front *en l'air*, *fouetté* back R. leg to *arabesque–chassé croisé* and *pas de chat*. This step is done six times, then she runs to centre down-stage and does a series of *échappés a la seconde*, travelling up-stage facing 5. In the meantime, Siegfried has walked round to centre back stage. Now he follows Odile as she runs down-stage, does preparation and *tours en dehors* supported by Siegfried, who lifts her up with her feet in 5th, legs straight. He puts her down, she steps on R.F. to R., with a *soutenue*. Then she steps towards Siegfried, presenting her L. hand to him with outstretched arm, ending *sur les pointes* in 5th pos. They both make a slight *épaulement*. Odile exits.

Siegfried, in centre of stage, is infatuated with Odile. Rothbart and the Princess-Mother rise and descend from the dais:

R.
S P.-M.

Siegfried expresses his love for Odile, which greatly pleases his mother. Odile enters again at 2 and makes a deep curtsey to the Princess-Mother. Rothbart asks the Prince to swear that he will marry Odile. He replies that he loves her and wishes to marry her, but Rothbart stamps his foot and insists: "Swear that you will marry her!" Siegfried raises his arm preparatory to taking the oath, when he is conscious of a sudden change in the atmosphere. Odile, who is still near 2, points at him and, throwing back her head, laughs derisively at him. The room darkens, thunder rolls, and lightning flashes. Rothbart and Odile run off at 4 during the general confusion of startled courtiers hurrying to and fro and eventually leaving the great hall. The Princess-Mother has swooned away on her throne. Siegfried runs up-stage to where the vision has again appeared weeping in despair and crying "I—must—die", he kneels and entreats Odette's forgiveness. The vision vanishes. Siegfried runs to the throne where his mother sat and finds her dead. Overwhelmed with remorse and despair, he collapses near 8, on the steps leading into the great hall.

CHAPTER XVIII

ACT TWO: SOME ASPECTS OF PRODUCTION

THE curtain rises on the great hall of Siegfried's castle. The walls are of stone and occasionally pierced by arched windows. The lower part of the walls is covered with tapestry depicting battles, tournaments, or scenes of the chase. To the right is a dais on which is set two thrones, one for the Princess-Mother, one for Prince Siegfried, the former being nearest down-stage. Near the thrones are a few chairs for distinguished guests that the Princess may desire to honour, and some velvet covered *banquettes* for her ladies to sit upon; against the walls similar *banquettes* are set at intervals. The stone wall above the tapestry are decorated with shields bearing heraldic devices, and, jutting horizontally from the walls, are short poles supporting knightly banners. From the ceiling are suspended one or more crude chandeliers bearing lighted candles, and the room is warm in the reflected light from a log fire. Such is how I vizualize the setting for this scene.

At the rise of the curtain, guests in the national costumes of Spain, Hungary, Poland (and perhaps Italy, if the *Danse Venetienne* is to be given), would be seen leisurely walking to and fro. The costumes of the several countries should be mingled and not those in the costume of one country grouped together.

Tchaikovsky conceived the guests wearing masks, a device which would enable a guest dressed as Odette to trick Siegfried into believing that the wearer was his beloved, since her features would be concealed by the mask. The guests in the International Ballet's version of this ballet do wear masks, but they are purely for effect and soon discarded.

This act is two-fold in purpose. First, to provide dramatic interest by the duping of Siegfried by Odile, so that he is induced to break his word to Odette that he would ever be true to her. Second, to afford excuse for the introduction of the traditional series of character dances.

When the page announces that the Princess-Mother and Prince Siegfried are about to enter, I should like a herald to appear at the point of entry, which would be immediately opposite the throne, and to mime the blowing of a fanfare on a trumpet to coincide with that rendered by the theatre orchestra.

This entrance would take the form of a short procession, pages singly and ladies walking two by two, preceding the entrance of the Princess-Mother and her son. All the guests should draw aside and bow in greeting as the couple enter, bowing to either side in acknowledgement. If the personnel permits, a man-at-arms could stand at either side of the dais. When the couple are seated on their thrones, a page announces the arrival of the Would-Be Brides. The couple greet them and the Princess-Mother asks them to dance.

It is important, I think, that this number and the succeeding character dances should be rendered so that they appear to be directed simultaneously towards the throne and towards the theatre audience. The dance of the Would-Be Brides is presented here as an *ensemble*, but in the version given by the Soviet Ballet, each bride dances in turn a short *variation* in the hope of winning the Prince's love, an interesting plan since it does convey a sense of rivalry among the aspirants to be the Prince's consort.

What is to be Siegfried's demeanour. I like best the example of Nijinsky who used to sit on his throne, his gaze directed high above the Would-Be Brides' heads, his thoughts clearly far away, Then he would suddenly recollect himself, step down from the dais, and politely dance a few steps with each bride in turn, returning to the throne, his gaze again directed as before. In some productions Siegfried's distraction is conveyed by making him stroll towards the window, which forces him to turn his back upon the brides, a discourtesy ill befitting a reigning Prince.

A page announces the arrival of another guest—an unknown one (he mimes)—and again the herald blows a fanfare on his trumpet. Baron Rothbart (the enchanter in human guise) and his daughter, Odile, enter the hall. At this moment it is usual for a vision of Odette to appear at the window, warning Siegfried not to be deceived by the visitor's apparent likeness to herself. The visitors go towards the dais, where Odile curtseys to the Princess-Mother, who bids her welcome. Siegfried, struck by Odile's likeness to Odette, greets her warmly and conducts her to an adjoining chamber, while Rothbart promptly seats himself on the Prince's throne.

These actions of Siegfried and Rothbart afford examples of extraordinary behaviour. What can the Princess-Mother be about to permit her son to withdraw with a strange woman, and unaccompanied by any chaperon! What, too, is to be thought of a host who calmly forsakes his guests to divert himself in the society of a strange young woman? If it is expedient for them to move from the centre of the action during the rendering of the character dances, could not Siegfried invite Odile to sit beside him and from time to time exchange a few words with her? As for Rothbart, what could be more ill-mannered, not to say presumptous, than for him to occupy the Prince's throne! For this reason I have suggested the placing in the vicinity of the thrones of a few chairs where the Princess-Mother might invite the Baron to be seated.

But to return to Odile, the chief problem of this act from the producer's standpoint. How is she to be presented? It is the usual practice for one ballerina to take the two roles, thus ensuring that Odile shall exactly resemble Odette; moreover, such a proceeding enables the ballerina to demonstrate not only her technical range, but her ability as mime, since she presents two totally different women, their only relation being that facially and physically they are alike.

Normally, the ballerina, when representing Odile, wears a skirt of some colour so that it differs from the white costume worn by Odette, again, the coiffure is more glamorous and the features made up to suggest hardness and brilliance. In short, Odile is depicted as a rather obvious adventuress, and generally one that suggests a period somewhat removed from Renaissance Germany.

One is tempted to ask this question. Would a magician of Rothbart's skill and cunning in his attempt to seduce Siegfried from his allegiance to Odette, instruct his own daughter, or better still his familiar spirit, Odile (whom he has caused to assume the likeness of Odette), to employ such commonplace methods? Would not Siegfried, yearning for the sweet and tender love of the wistful Odette, be revolted by such an obvious appeal to his baser nature?

There are three ways then of presenting Odile. First, in the customary manner as just described. Second, by letting Odile wear Odette's white costume, but having her features masked; in this case the interpreter should be a different dancer so that, when Siegfried has promised to marry her, she raises her mask and reveals that she is not Odette and hence he has been tricked. Third, by being dressed as Odette, and exactly resembling her, since the interpreter is the same ballerina, yet, by some subtle mome, she maintains a mask of tenderness to satisfy Siegfried, but in a mimed aside, proclaims to the audience that she is counterfeit. The last conception is naturally the most difficult, but it could afford a supreme test of a ballerina's art, the ability to combine two persons in one, and without a change of costume. In the realm of drama, the actor has been set a similar problem in dual personality: the roles of Lesurques and Dubosc in *The Lyons Mail*,

[*Photo: Frank Sharman*

"SWAN LAKE," ACT TWO, AS PRESENTED BY THE INTERNATIONAL BALLET, 1947

Produced by Nicholas Sergeyev. Settings and costumes by William Chappell. The part of Odile is taken by Mona Ingelsby

DUSAN RISTIC, SETTING FOR "SWAN LAKE," ACT TWO

As presented at National Theatre, Belgrade, 1951

in which dual role Sir Henry Irving achieved a triumph; admittedly, differences in costumes and make-up were used to distinguish between the two characters.

Rothbart sometimes wears, as in the Sadler's Wells Ballet production, a costume more oriental than European, and occasionally even armour, as in the International Ballet's production. But a suit of mail is a strange costume in which to attend a masked ball; I should prefer a rich costume such as might be worn by a German nobleman of the period.

Now the various character dances follow, and I should like the Master of Ceremonies to call together each group in turn to take up their preparatory positions before their dance. So, first, the Spaniards would assemble, dance and take their seats; then the Hungarian group would do likewise; and finally the Poles.

The *Pas de Deux* by Odile and Siegfried is one of the highlights of this act, because the dance vehicle is employed as a means of captivating Siegfried. It seems to me, therefore, that Odile should begin on a low note and at first emulate the known tenderness and shyness of Odette, then gradually seek subtly to bewitch Siegfried by allowing herself to become more and more radiant, until, like a moth attracted by a shining light, he, too, catches fire from her flame, reflects her mood, and is soon trapped fast in her toils.

During this *pas*, Odile from time to time crosses to Rothbart (now descended from the dais and standing a little to the downstage side of it) who whispers secret injunctions to her, when she rejoins Siegfried and resumes her dance of seduction, which ends with her exit. During this dance the vision of Odette again appears at the window seeking to warn Siegfried of his danger, but he fails to see it, because Odile swiftly engages his attention by lovingly placing her hands over his eyes. That Rothbart, in full view of the assembled guests, should develop his evil plan to cause Siegfried to forswear himself, verges on the ludicrous, and can only be excused on the ground of tradition, or theatrical convention of the period.

Now follow a *variation* for Siegfried, a *variation* for Odile, and the final *coda*. In this last, Siegfried begins with a series of *pas de bourrée—grands jetés en 2me arabesque* which, when well done, conveys a vivid effect of delirious joy. Then Odile enters and does thirty-two *fouettés*[1] *en tournant en dehors*. If these are achieved

[1] At the *première* of the Petipa-Ivanov production of the complete ballet, Legnani danced a series of *jetés en tournant en l'air*. But shortly before or after Legnani left St. Petersburg, these *jetés en tournant* were replaced by a series of 32 *fouettés*, which she had first danced in Petipa's *Cinderella*, which had been withdrawn from the repertory. These *fouettés* were sometimes replaced by other steps, according to the preference of particular *ballerine*. For instance, Vaganova replaced the *fouettés* with a series of brilliant *pirouettes*.

without visible effort and without moving from place, with a subtly graduated *accelerando*, what is basically a mere *tour de force* can be transformed into an expression of mounting triumph, for Odile is now certain of victory. Siegfried replies with a succession of sixteen *entrechats six* travelling on an imaginary line drawn from centre back to down-stage. The complete *pas de deux* is not only technically very brilliant and theatrically most effective, but the steps and movements can also be used to convey admirably a man's infatuation for a woman, and her manifest joy at the success of her wiles.

We now approach the dramatic conclusion to this act. No sooner has Siegfried pledged himself to marry Odile, whom he supposes to be Odette, thus breaking his vow to the latter, than the tender mask she presents to him changes into a cruel, mocking face. Darkness descends, thunder rolls, lightning flashes, and when the scene lightens, Rothbart and Odile have vanished. It might add force to the *dénouement* if, just prior to the descent of darkness, Rothbart and his familiar spirit could suddenly be changed into demons with the legendary scaly legs. It should not be difficult to devise a quick-change costume to achieve this effect, which admittedly demands adroit treatment.

CHAPTER XIX

SIMPLIFIED CHOREOGRAPHIC SCRIPT OF "SWAN LAKE"

ACT THREE

ENTER three swan-maidens from 2. They run to 3 and stand in a diagonal line on L.F. in 1st *arabesque*. *Balancé* back on to R.F., step L.F. and stand in *arabesque*. Repeat *balancé* and hold in *arabesque*.

Enter three more swan-maidens from 1. They run to 4 and stand in diagonal line on R.F. in 1st *arabesque*. All six swans do *balancé* back and stand in *arabesque*. Repeat.

Enter three more swan-maidens from each front corner and stand in diagonal line outside the first two lines in 1st *arabesque*. All twelve swan-maidens do *balancé* and stand in *arabesque*. Repeat.

The formation is thus:

[If full *corps de ballet* of eighteen swan-maidens is used, two sets of three enter together, one set from each side at each entry, instead of six entering only during the third time. The formation would be thus:]

Enter two Leaders. First enters from 2, runs to centre, and turns *sur les pointes*, stands. Second enters from 1, runs to centre and turns *sur les pointes*, stands. While she is doing this, the *corps de ballet* run to form two straight lines near wings from front to back of stage.

Now, as the four lines walk into two straight lines disposed at either side of the stage, the Leaders are standing a little inside their respective lines.

The previous formation becomes this:

6	3
5	2
4	1
12	9
11	8
10	7
L	L

L = Leader

[If the full *corps de ballet* of eighteen swan-maidens is used, the formation will have nine swans on each side.]

The swan-maidens stand on outside foot, the other foot placed *pointe tendue* back, knee bent. Arms crossed 5th *en bas.*

The Leaders interrogate their respective lines in mime:

Leaders: "Have you—here—the Queen—seen?" This is conveyed first by pointing to the line, next to the ground, then indicating the top of the head as though it were a crown, and finally the arms are opened in a gesture of enquiry.

Lines: "We—the Queen—have seen—not." This is conveyed by the swan-maidens pointing to themselves, next indicating the top of the head as though it bore a crown, followed by a slow shake of the head, and a crossing and uncrossing of the hands.

I. *Corps de ballet* in two lines and beginning on outside foot do *posé* in 1st *arabesque* towards the wing, *pas de bourrée dessous–pas de bourrée en tournant en dehors–temps levé–développé*, taking inside foot to 2nd pos., *tombé–chassé croisé–pas de bourrée dessous.* Do this four times in all.

Meanwhile the two Leaders do same steps on opposite feet, just inside the lines and to front of stage.

II. Leaders then go up-stage towards centre with *posé* in 1st *arabesque–chassé–pas de chat*, three times and turn and go back to their original places with four *pas marchés sur les pointes.* They repeat the step towards centre, then run off, one at 1, the other at 2. During this, the *corps de ballet* divide into threes and do the same steps towards and away from the centre and again towards centre, the leaders from the lines being No. 1 and No. 4.

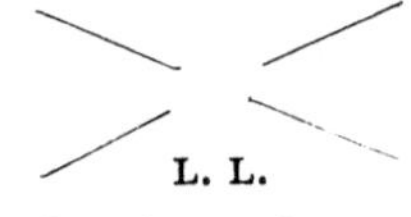

If full *corps de ballet* of eighteen is used, the formation will be thus:

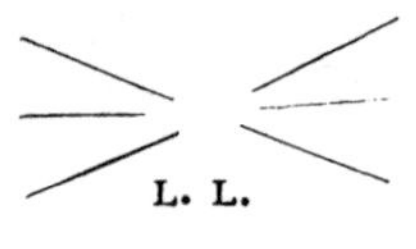

Then four *pas de valse* to centre stage, forming one long line from front to back, stand.

III. Enter six small black swan-maidens from 4. They run in and out between each pair[1] of white swan-maidens, making zig-zag course from back to front of stage. Meanwhile swan-maidens lunge on up-stage leg in 3rd *arabesque* (foot *à terre*) making three arm waves and *relevé* in 5th facing 5, then repeat twice facing alternate ways each time. Then, with four *pas de valse* form into three[2] lines of six, straight across stage, the first line being composed of small black swan-maidens. All do *posé* in 1st *arabesque* on R.F. to 1, *chassé* across, six *jetés en avant* turning, making one turn *sur place*. Repeat three times in all and follow with four *pas de valse*, the twelve swan-maidens going back to their two lines from front to back of stage near the wings, while the six small black swan-maidens waltz off, three going off at 1, three at 2.

IV. (*a*) The twelve swan-maidens, with inside feet, do three *pas de cheval*, then turn and stand in 1st *arabesque*, facing wings, inside foot *pointe tendue derrière*. Repeat three times, then stand still, arms crossed, for the last part of the 1st Leader's *variation*.

(*b*) Meanwhile 1st Leader enters at 3 doing *pas de bourrée–grand jeté en tournant*; on to L.F. *glissade* and *posé* in 3rd *arabesque* on R.F. to 8, repeat twice alternate sides; then travel diagonally back to 3 with *posé*, *petits battements*, and *coupé*; repeat four times in all. Then travel diagonally forward with *rond de jambe sauté* and *posé* in *attitude*, four times in all. Two *posé* turns *en dehors*, *petits tours* and off at 1.

V. (*a*) The twelve swan-maidens do a small *développé* with *pointe tendue* into centre with inside foot, making a low *port de bras* towards foot with inside arm and bend forward of the body, then stand in *arabesque* towards the wing, twice in all and then stand with arms crossed for the last part of the 2nd Leader's *variation*.

(*b*) Meanwhile 2nd Leader enters at 4 and does: *demi-contretemps* with R.F., *jeté* on to L.F., R. leg in *arabesque*, both arms raised to 5th *en haut*, arms straight, *pas de bourrée* commencing with R.F. to 4, finishing R.F. front lowering the arms, *entrechat trois* ending with arms in 4th pos. Repeat three times, then *soutenu*, arms 5th *en haut*, and run to 3. Beginning with R.F. do two *pas de valse sur les pointes* making one turn, take both arms up to R. on 1st *pas de valse*. Do this four times in all travelling diagonally to 1, body facing 2, look to 5, ending in 5th pos. *sur les*

[1] If full *corps de ballet* of eighteen is used there will be four swans between each gap.

[2] Four lines of six if full *corps de ballet* is used.

pointes. *Temps levé* off two feet on to R.F. in 1st *arabesque*, facing 8, *pas de bourrée sur les pointes* to L, lowering arms and turning body towards 2. Repeat *temps levé* in *arabesque* to 8 and *pas de bourrée* to side–*chassé–temps levé* on L.F. in 1st *arabesque* and run off to L. at 2.

The two lines of swan-maidens turn and face up-stage and with four *pas de gavotte* travel to back of stage, and then the two swan-maidens leading the lines meet centre back-stage, so that the swan-maidens form a line of six; they then turn and face front, and in lines of six travel down to front of stage, all facing audience and, with arms round each other's waists, do eight *pas marchés* on the full foot. Meanwhile the remaining six swan-maidens have formed second line facing audience and holding waists, with *pas marchés* travel also to front of stage.[1]

Six small black swan-maidens enter, three from each side at back and form line, when they travel down to front with *pas marchés*. Two Leaders enter, one from each back corner and with *pas marchés* on point meet in centre. All now walk into a group.[2]

The first six make a semi-circle, standing on inside feet, other foot pointed at side, two centre ones have both arms raised overhead at side, the other four have down-stage arm raised. The second six walk into two diagonal lines at each side of the stage, face audience, and stand in sideway bend, on *demi-plié* up-stage foot, *pointe tendue derrière*, arms in 1st *arabesque*. Two Leaders stand in centre of group with arms crossed, down or in 5th pos. *en haut*. The six small black swan-maidens sit on floor in a semi-circle in front, three facing each way.

The group breaks and swan-maidens return to their two lines at side of stage. The two Leaders stand just inside near front. Black swan-maidens form a diagonal line near 2 in front of line of white swan-maidens.

Enter Odette weeping, her head hidden in the crook of her R. arm. She enters at 3 and travels diagonally across to 8, and then from 8 to centre stage. Follows a scene in mime.

Two Leaders stand on either side of Odette and ask her: "What is the matter?"

Odette: "Over there—the one I love—has cast me away—therefore I must die." This is conveyed by pointing off-stage, pressing her hands to her heart then raising her arms above her head and lowering them with the wrists crossed in front of her.

[1] If full *corps de ballet* of eighteen is used, there is another line of six swan-maidens who waltz up-stage to form their line.

[2] If full *corps de ballet* of eighteen is used, the six extra swan-maidens are placed one to each of the diagonals down-stage, two towards centre, kneeling.

Leaders: "No—you—we—will save."

Odette: "No—here—I will die."

Then she goes to 2 and the swan-maidens form a circle round her. They kneel and put their arms round each other and droop their heads to R. Two Leaders go to 4. But Odette breaks through swan-maidens and repeats: "I—here—must die." The six small black swan-maidens again make a diagonal line near 2.

Odette runs towards lake at 4, but is stopped by the Leaders who conduct her back to centre stage, while swan-maidens now form themselves into circular groups of three and four. There is one group in each corner, one centre back, and small black swan-maidens in front corner at 2. At corner 3 there are two swan-maidens only. All stand holding waists. Odette goes and stands in centre of group at 3 and two Leaders complete the group[1] about her.

Enter Siegfried at 6, seeking Odette. He goes first to group at centre back who turn to face him and stand in 1st *arabesque*. He then goes to the small black swan-maidens; they turn. He passes to group at 4; they turn. Finally, he advances to group at 1; they turn and at same time the group about Odette opens into *arabesque*, rear foot *à terre* facing 1. She calls to him. He goes to her and kneels at her feet, when all the swan-maidens sink on to their knees, arms in *arabesque*, front arm to floor. Odette and Siegfried exit centre at 6, followed by two Leaders, or alternatively, they stay on stage, the two leading swan-maidens going off.

Pas de Deux. Odette and Siegfried, with accompanying movements by Leaders and *corps de ballet*.

I. O. & S. They travel from 3–1. Odette does two *pas marchés* R.F., L.F., and is lifted by Siegfried in 3rd *arabesque*, then Odette steps across in front of Siegfried on to L. point, R. leg in low *arabesque* or *attitude*, L. arm on Siegfried's shoulder; she leans back in his arm and he does one turn (promenade) to R. with her *sur la pointe*. Repeat the two *pas marchés* and lift in 3rd *arabesque* to 2, they then walk round up-stage together to 3.

C. de B. They rise from kneeling position and do slowly seven *pas de gavotte*, beginning R.F. The small black swan-maidens pass up-stage on the outside of the white swan-maidens, who are

[1]If full *corps de ballet* of eighteen is used, there is one extra group at 8.

coming down-stage from their groups to form a straight line from 2–3. The groups near O.P. side form a line from 1–4 by those nearest the front going up-stage followed by the others then down-stage to form a line.

II. O. & S. Travelling from 3–1, Odette does *temps levé–chassé–pas de bourrée dessous* to 4th pos. and *pirouetts en dehors* supported by Siegfried. Then she sways four times in his arms in *arabesque* (leg held near ground), Odette remaining on L. point. Repeat still travelling to 1.

C. de B. *Balancé* from side to side turning the body well from side to side, arms crossed 5th pos. *en bas*. Commencing into centre do this eight times, then *port de bras*, i.e. lunge on outside foot in *arabesque à terre*. Come up bringing the inside arm up over head. Repeat to other side (eight counts).

III. (*a*) O. & S. Travelling to 2, *relevé* in 5th and lift on to chest, Odette doing a *développé* to 4th pos. *devant* with R. leg. Siegfried lowers Odette to ground and she steps across him with *posé* on L.F. to *arabesque*, sway four times. Repeat to 1.

(*b*) Walk slowly towards 1, then Odette does a *posé* into low *arabesque* supported by Siegfried, who is kneeling facing 3. Alternatively Odette mimes: "I—here—must die." Siegfred answers: "You—here—die—not. I—you—will save."

(*a*) *C. de B.* Four *pas de valse* each one making half a turn. Commence turning towards wing on outside foot, opposite arm *en haut*, other in 2nd pos. *Port de bras*, i.e. point outside foot *effacé*, take both arms down towards the foot, *pointe tendue*. Come up with arms in 3rd *arabesque* (eight counts). Repeat from beginning on other side.

(*b*) Slow *port de bras*, *effacé* to wings ending in 3rd *arabesque* as above, same on other side, take eight counts for each *port de bras*.

IV. (*a*) O. & S. Travelling back to 3, Odette does *pas de bourrée couru sur les pointes* and *coupé dessous* eight times, then, travelling to 1 to Siegfried, she does five *posé tours en dehors*, Siegfried approaches her

"SWAN LAKE," ACT ONE, SCENE I. CONSTANTINE SERGEYEV PRODUCTION

Setting and costumes by S. Virsaladze, Kirov Theatre, Leningrad, March 10th, 1950

"SWAN LAKE," ACT TWO. CONSTANTINE SERGEYEV PRODUCTION

Setting and costumes by S. Virsaladze, Kirov Theatre, Leningrad, March 10th, 1950

and, on the last turn, she is in his arms. They do the same turn *en dehors* as in Step I.

C. de B. All swan-maidens rest with one foot *pointe tendue derrière* for sixteen counts.

(*b*) O. & S. Then walk again to 1 and *arabesque* as before with Siegfried kneeling. Alternatively Odette mimes: "I—here—must die." Siegfried answers: "You—here—die—not. I—you—will save. I—you—love."

C. de B. All swan-maidens now do three *pas de cheval* (inside arm in front of body, other arm in *arabesque*), turn to face wing in 1st *arabesque*, inside foot *à terre*. Do this step four times in all.

Leaders Two Leaders enter at 4, and, travelling on the line 4–2, do: *temps levé* in 1st *arabesque* on L.F.–*chassé–pas de chat*. Repeat same way. Four *posé tours en dehors* slightly to 1– *relevé* in 5th pos., arms 5th pos. *en haut*; alternatively, instead of last *pas de chat*, do a *coupé dessous*–three *petits tours–relevé* in 5th pos. Repeat the whole step only take the *posé tours* to 2 and end with L.F. *pointe tendue derrière*, arms crossed 5th pos. Or, if doing the alternative version, do *pas de bourrée couru* to 2 and stand as described near 2.

V. (*a*) O. & S. Travelling back to 3, Odette does a series of *temps levés* in 1st *arabesque* on a *demi-plié* on R.F. Then forward to 1 with *posé* turns ending with Siegfried as in Step IV.

C. de B. Hold position in 1st *arabesque à terre* out to wing for nineteen counts (eight and eleven).

Leaders Hold position for nineteen counts (eight and eleven).

(*b*) O. & S. Now they either exit at 1, and enter for the next step at 4, walking across stage to 3; or turn and walk slowly up-stage to 4, then across to 3.

C. de B. All swan-maidens do *posé* on inside foot in 1st *arabesque*, *pas de bourrée dessous* making a quarter-turn, do this four times in all, making a quarter-turn each time, the step comes on alternate feet. Repeat.

Leaders Two Leaders move across stage to 1 with *relevé en attitude* on R.F., one *tour en dehors* on L.F. with arms in 4th pos. *en haut*, R. arm up; do this four times in all. Then *posé* in 1st *arabesque* on L.F. to 6, *chassé croise*–two *posé tours en dehors* to 1. Then *posé* in 1st *arabesque* on L.F., close R.F.–*chassé–temps levé en arabesque* opposite ways, each Leader towards nearest wing, runs off. Alternatively, this last half of the step could be *temps levé* in *arabesque* on L.F.–*chassé–pas de chat–coupé–petits tours* to R., followed by *temps levé* in *arabesque* on L.F., and with a big *chassé–temps levé* in *arabesque*—each Leader exits at opposite wings.

VI. O. & S. Travelling from 3–1, Odette does *relevé* in 5th pos. and *rond de jambe* (R. leg) with *sauté* and lift by Siegfried, then three *petits tours* and lift on to shoulder in *arabesque*, R. leg bent underneath with swaying movement of body and arms. Repeat same way.

C. de B. Repeat lunge into 2nd *arabesque croisée* towards wing, do a *port de bras* bending forward, come up, bring outside arm *en haut*, turn in an up-stage direction to face in, changing arms, so that the position is now *croisé devant* facing in. Then do four *balancés* as in II, commencing on outside foot. Repeat to same side.

VII. O. & S. Odette then does *relevé* in 5th and Siegfried lifts her on to his chest and carries her to 2. *Odette steps across front of Siegfried to his R. and does *posé* on L.F. in *arabesque*, holding his shoulder with L. hand, and his hand with her R. hand. Then *développé* R. leg through to 2, step on it with *pas de chat*. Repeat from *. Odette then *bourrées* round to centre-stage where Siegfried joins her and they form the centre of a group.

C. de B. Four *pas de gavotte* getting into lines of six across the stage. Then eight times *tombé* on to R.F., *posé dessous* on L.F., *retiré* R.F. to L. knee. The small black swan-maidens do *posé–chassé–pas de chat* four times, three of them travelling first to 3 then down-stage close to wings, the other three travelling first to 4 then down-stage close to wing O.P. Then, travelling up-stage and back to their line back-stage, they do *posé* on outside foot, close other to it in 5th pos. arms in 3rd *arabesque*; do this eight times then to Group VIII.

Leaders Two Leaders enter, one at 4, the other at 3, doing eight *pas marchés sur les pointes* towards centre-stage so as to be in front of the lines of six swan-maidens for *posé–retire* step which is done by all white swan-maidens together.

VIII. Walk into group, the six small black swan-maidens sitting in semi-circle on the ground, the white swan-maidens on either side, making a straight line. The position is on a *demi-plié* in 3rd *arabesque à terre* facing in towards centre, body and head inclined. The rest of the swan-maidens make a semi-circle at the back, the two centre ones have both arms up, elbows straight, all the others have down-stage arm in high *arabesque*, other low. The two Leaders stand with both arms up on either side of Odette and Siegfried, who are in the middle of the group. Odette in low *arabesque* leaning on Siegfried's right shoulder.

Rothbart enters at 3. The group divides, half moving towards 2, the other half to 1. Two groups are formed, each group making the same figure only the opposite way. The six small swan-maidens (three a side) are on the ground, sitting back on outside leg, the other extended in front, arms crossed and resting on leg, heads lowered. Behind them stand six white swan-maidens (three a side) kneeling on outside knee, arms in 3rd *arabesque*. In the middle, behind these, stands the two Leaders (one to either group) with arms crossed over chest. Behind them stand six white swan-maidens (three a side) with both arms raised high in 3rd *arabesque* with wrists crossed, inside foot *pointe tendue derrière*.[1] Siegfried and Odette stand near 2. Rothbart separates them. Odette runs to 1 and the group of swan-maidens at 2 run over and join the end of the group at 1, taking up the same positions they had previously assumed on the other side. The line of white swan-maidens at back now have their arms in 1st *arabesque*, R. arm front. The second line, kneeling, hold arms in 3rd *arabesque*. The small black swan-maidens have arms down and crossed. The Leaders have their arms crossed over their chest. Rothbart is now in centre and Siegfried near 2. Rothbart says to Siegfried in mime: "You—swore—to marry—my daughter!" Siegfried answers in mime: "I—love—Odette." Odette runs to Siegfried at 2, and they mutually embrace. Rothbart, with

[1] If full *corps de ballet* are used, there are four white swan-maidens each side kneeling, and five each side standing.

a violent gesture, forces them apart; Odette hurled to 1. Then Siegfried runs towards 1 and joins Odette, and together they defy Rothbart, resolutely raising their left arms in the air and moving towards Rothbart, who, slowly circling, eventually limps off at 3, Siegfried closely following him with repeated thrusts of his L. arm, as though driving him off.

Siegfried runs back to 1 to Odette and they embrace. Then they walk to 2, where she tells Siegfried: "I—must die." She runs to 4, followed by Siegfried, who draws her back. They embrace again. Odette then goes towards 2 and Siegfried kneels and implores her to live. But with a sad expression she repeats: "I—must die" and, making one turn to R., she runs off at 4, and presumably throws herself into the lake.

Siegfried, overwhelmed with despair, buries his face in his hands, then, lowering his hands, he looks sorrowfully at the place where Odette last stood, rises, and turns towards the group at 1, moves down-stage, indicating that he must follow Odette in death, whereupon he runs off at 4, and likewise throws himself into the lake. The light fades as Rothbart appears at 3, and all members of the group now kneel, hiding their faces with L. arm, R. arm placed over heart, then they rise and turn to face 3. All the swan-maidens stand on L.F., lunging forward with both arms extended to 3, head inclined to 3. All stretch up on to R.F., pointing L.F., carrying both arms to R., head facing Rothbart at 3.

The swan-maidens then run in a small circle moving to L. back into the same diagonal lines, lunging forward, while Rothbart withdraws at 3 and staggers off.

The three diagonal lines rise slowly *sur les pointes*, raising both arms over the head (still facing 3), step forward on R.F. again, pointing L.F., and both arms to R. Rothbart has vanished.

The scene is plunged into darkness during which the small black swan-maidens exit, while the two lines take their places for the final group, which consists of two[1] diagonal lines stretching from 4–2, all kneel on R. knee with L. leg extended at back. The arms are in 3rd *arabesque*, facing 4.

As the scene slowly lightens, across the background from 4 glides the shell-like barque bearing Odette and Siegfried, reunited. When the barque reaches the centre background, the two diagonal lines of swan-maidens rise on to L. knee, carrying both arms over the head, and slowly sit on L. knee, both arms extended before them, with the head lowered upon them. As the barque vanishes from sight, the curtain slowly falls.

[1] Three lines if full *corps de ballet* is used.

CHAPTER XX

ACT THREE: SOME ASPECTS OF PRODUCTION

THE setting for this scene is generally the same as that for Act II, except that the lighting is changed, indicative of the approach of dawn. It would, however, be an improvement and afford variety if a new scene depicting another part of the lake-side were used, as in the Petipa-Ivanov production.

The curtain rises on an empty stage and then the swan-maidens enter from different directions in groups of three. The step they use is a *balancé* followed by a stand in *arabesque*, which has something of a bird-like character, and at the same time suggests sadness, because the maidens are concerned and anxious about the non-arrival of Odette.

This sense of dejection is again emphasised when, standing on one foot with the other extended to the fourth position back, *pointe tendue*, allowing the knee to bend, the swan-maidens are questioned by the Leaders as to whether they have seen Odette.

Now follows an unexpected effect. When the swan-maidens form into one line from up-stage to down-stage, some swan-maidens in black-dresses run in and weave in and out of the line like a dark serpentine rivulet.

The sustained mood of sadness marches to its climax with the arrival of Odette, who enters weeping, her head bowed and resting in the crook of her arm. When the two Leaders hurry to her side and sympathetically enquire as to the cause of her grief, she reveals that Siegfried has forsworn her, in consequence of which she must die. The swan-maidens, deeply shocked by the news, form a protective circle about her, expressing their sorrow in their drooping heads.

Suddenly, Odette, in a frenzy of despair, breaks through the circle and runs towards the lake, as if about to cast herself into the water, but the two Leaders bar her path and gently conduct her away from the lake-side, where the swan-maidens again form a circle about her. This desperate act of Odette to end her life as a result of the downfall of her dearest hopes can be very moving, but it must be kept in a lyrical mood and not allowed to become melodramatic.

Now Siegfried enters in search of Odette. His walk should be depressed and hesitant, his expression pale and distracted. He goes from one group to another seeking his beloved, but each of the first three groups he approaches, in succession indicates a direction contrary to where Odette is, as though refusing to help him whose shameful conduct has so injured their Queen. But the fourth group at 1 indicate that Odette is at 3.

Odette's love for Siegfried is too deep for her to remain long indifferent to his presence and she calls to him (in mime). He goes to her and kneels at her feet, in the hope that she will pardon his unwitting betrayal of her. The swan-maidens add their own entreaties by kneeling with their arms in *arabesque*, the front arm inclined towards the ground.

The *Pas de Deux* by Odette and Siegfried has all the poignant character and urgency of a last farewell meeting between two lovers, one of whom is about to die as a result of the other's error, a fact known to both of them. This *pas* is made even more moving by the choral use of the *corps de ballet* who glide about the lovers, powerless to stay Odette's cruel fate yet giving expression to their sad thoughts by the use of the *arabesque*, which, in its constant association with the swan-maidens has the force of a *Leitmotiv*.

Later, Rothbart tries to overcome Odette's love for Siegfried by reminding him that he had sworn to marry his daughter, Odile. When Siegfried declares that he loves Odette alone, this impassioned declaration breaks down all reserve between Odette and Siegfried and they fall into each other's arms.

Now follows the scene in which Rothbart, enraged, hurls the lovers apart. This needs to be done with authority and well-simulated fury. But the lovers unite and with upraised left arm threaten Rothbart to such good purpose that he limps away, circling slowly in the manner of a bird on the defensive.

Again the lovers embrace; this has a more moving effect if done slowly and gently. Then Odette, overcome with sadness in the knowledge that the moment of her death is fast approaching, walks a few paces with Siegfried, striving to put a brave face on her dark thoughts. Now she stops and with a fatalistic air mimes: "I—must die." For a brief space Siegfried tries to deter her from her thoughts of suicide. But, repeating the declaration (in mime): "I—must die," she makes a sudden turn as though to snap the agony of waiting, runs towards the lakeside, and is seen to leap into the lake.

Siefried, horror-stricken at the fatal act which Odette, impelled by some all powerful agency, has just committed, is filled with despair. Life which, a short while since, appeared so beautiful, has now lost its savour. Deprived of Odette, he has no longer any desire to live, and, steeling himself for a moment, he, too, runs to the lake and seeks Odette beneath its waters.

It would, I think, add to the dramatic value of this scene if the audience could see how the action of the lovers affected Rothbart. Normally, Rothbart is merely a sinister watcher of the double tragedy. Yet, with his magical powers, he must be well aware that if Siegfried sacrifices his own life for love of Odette, then, he, Rothbart, must himself die in consequence; so runs the mystic law. Consequently, the enchanter's increasing apprehension and fear should be clearly visible in his features and in his trembling limbs. Lastly when Siegfried takes the fatal leap, one should see Rothbart's strength fast ebbing as he staggers away, presumably to die in some secret retreat.

The diagonal lines of semi-recumbent swan-maidens, who resemble large white flowers, make a beautiful picture, which is completed by a vision of the reunited lovers, seated in a fairy barque, drawn over the lake, one imagines, by unseen swans. It is imperative that the barque should be mounted on wheels so arranged that the tiny craft glides past without any jolts or pauses, to vanish into the night. The barque should be lit so that it appears to glow as if with an inner radiance, which also reveals clearly the faces and forms of the lovers. But it frequently happens that the frail barque hesitates and stops, and that only the faces of the two lovers are lit, as if they had encountered a beam of light. The lovers' gaze should be directed very slightly upwards as though fixed upon some beautiful distant land slowly appearing on the horizon.

CHAPTER XXI

SEVENTY-FIVE YEARS OF "SWAN LAKE"

SWAN LAKE, first produced in 1877, with choreography by Reisinger, at the Bolshoy Theatre, Moscow, is still performed with unfailing success in both Moscow and Leningrad today, although its structure, both musical and choreographic, has undergone many changes.

The succeeding Moscow productions of 1880 and 1882, in which the choreography of Reisinger was replaced by that of Olaf Hansen, have already been described. Since none of these found favour with the public, *Swan Lake* was removed from the repertory and consigned to the oblivion of the archives of the Bolshoy Theatre, where it remained for some ten years, as though awaiting the composer's death, when, like another Sleeping Beauty, it would again wake to life at the loving touch of Petipa and Ivanov, a ballet reborn and endowed with a new, hitherto unsuspected beauty which was the fruit of their care and devotion.

As the reader is aware, the first production of *Swan Lake* at St. Petersburg, in 1894, consisted of Scene II only. The complete ballet, like the single second scene, was presented at the Maryinsky Theatre, in 1895, with choreography by Petipa and Ivanov. This edition remained in force for thirty-eight years, until February 13th, 1933, when the desire for change and reform, engendered by the Soviet régime, spread to the Ballet, and inspired a new conception of *Swan Lake*, known as the Vaganova version.

This production was the joint work of the ballerina and People's Artist of the Republic, Agrippina Vaganova, and the painter, V. V. Dimitrev; the later being responsible for designing the settings and for the idea of transferring the period of the action, which Tchaikovsky had placed in the days of chivalry, to the eighteen-thirties, the epoch of the Romantic Period.

In this production Prince Siegfried becomes a German Count residing in an ancient castle. A storm rises and some of the Count's friends enter with a dead swan, the sight of which inspires him with thoughts of hunting. But some young people arrive and beg the Count to stay with them. He consents, but, not given to merrymaking, soon grows bored. The guests dance a Polonaise and leave. The Count, left alone, takes a musket and goes hunting. His friends see him in the distance and decide to follow him.

[*Photo: G. L. Manuel Frères, Paris*

OLGA SPESSIVTZEVA AND SERGE LIFAR AS ODETTE AND SIEGFRIED

[*Photo: Maurice Seymour, Chicago*

ALICIA MARKOVA AS ODETTE

In "Swan Lake," Ballet Theatre production, New York, 1942

The second scene of the first act takes place by the lake-side, with much of the action associated with Act II, except that the Count is armed with a musket instead of a crossbow.

The second act shifts the action to the castle hall, the Count having planned a fancy-dress ball at which all the guests are to come in mediaeval costume. Here again the theme follows the usual course. Rothbart becomes the Duke Rothbart, a penniless nobleman, who hopes to improve his position by marrying his daughter, Odile, to the Count. Among the guests is a girl dressed to represent a swan. The Count goes towards her, but she disappears. Then Odile asks him to dance, which he does. But the swan-girl re-appears and the Count, pushing Odile aside, goes in search of her. In his eagerness he hurries out of the castle to the amazement of his guests.

The final act returns to the lake-side. A swan enters in great distress for Rothbart has been hunting and wounded her. Now comes the Count still searching for the swan-girl. He runs towards the wounded swan and, taking her into his arms, tries to tend her, but she dies. The Count, greatly distressed, stabs himself and leaps over the cliff. Later, the guests find his body.

Not only was Tchaikovsky's period of action altered and the ballet divided into three acts instead of the original four, but also the sequence of the music, the order of the numbers being arbitarily changed. As regards the choreography, Vaganova retained the best features of the Petipa-Ivanov production and introduced certain elements of her own, including four new *variations*. Again, the dual role of Odette-Odile was divided between two ballerine: Odette, strangely designated "a swan," being taken by Galina Ulanova, while the role of Odile was interpreted by O. T. Jordan. Prince Siegfried was interpreted by Sergeyev. A particularly odd feature of this production was the introduction of realistic touches in a romantic theme, for instance, in the first act the neck of the dead swan was daubed with blood, while Odette's last act costume was similarly treated.

During the Second World War the Ballet Company attached to the Kirov Theatre was evacuated to Molotov, and *Swan Lake* was again presented in the Petipa-Ivanov tradition. But when the Germans were driven from Russia and the Kirov Theatre Company returned to Leningrad, a new version of *Swan Lake* was devised by Fedor Lopukhov; this was presented on June 22nd, 1945. Here, again, the basis of the production was the Petipa-Ivanov choreography, to which was added several new features.

For instance, in Scene II, during the *pas de deux* between Odile and Siegfried, Rothbart appeared and disappeared at different parts of the stage by means of traps, an artless device intended to suggest Rothbart's hovering about the lovers in the guise of an evil phantom. Scene III began with a scene of the knighting of Siegfried, while the Dance of Masquers was replaced by an *entrée* of huntresses. Moreover, Rothbart played a much more active part in this act; he was even accorded a solo dance following the Mazurka. In Scene IV the *ensemble* of the swans was changed; Rothbart was seen casting a spell upon them and there was a stern contest between the magician and Siegfried during which the former's wings were torn off and cast into the lake, wherein the magician perished. At this moment of victory the sky was flushed with the roseate light of dawn and the swans became young women, by the rather commonplace device of discarding the feathers of their tutus. Today the Lopukhov version survives only at the Kiev Theatre of Opera and Ballet.

On March 20th, 1950, Konstantin Sergeyev restaged *Swan Lake* at the Kirov Theatre, basing his production on the Petipa–Ivanov tradition, but adding some *ensembles* of his own to the last act, with a view to heightening its alternating poignant and foreboding atmosphere.

Let us return to the original home of *Swan Lake*—Moscow. After the success of the ballet at St. Petersburg, the Petipa-Ivanov production was reproduced at Moscow for the Coronation festivities, with the participation of the Moscow ballet company; the part of Odette-Odile being taken by Pierina Legnani. According to Svetlov, she danced beautifully, although certain partisans of the Moscow Ballet, such as Mukhin, resented her visit and attempted to decry her performance, saying: "The production of this work will afford opportunity for Moscow to be astonished that the St. Petersburg public, which has seen Taglioni, should have evinced such rapture over Mlle Legnani, who is endowed with neither a good figure nor a pleasing appearance, and whose dancing is quite ordinary." But, notwithstanding the success of the production, the Moscow directorate made no attempt to reinstate the ballet in its repertory.

It was not until January 24th, 1901, at the invitation of V. A. Teliakovsky, that the ballet was once more revived. This time, the production was entrusted to A. A. Gorski, a cultured and talented *maître de ballet* and a former pupil of Petipa. The role of Odette-Odile was danced by Giuri, a charming and gifted dancer in the Legnani manner. The *Novoye Vremya* said of the dancer: "Giuri, despite her slender legs and fragile and delicate appearance, invested her graceful body with an extraordinary softness of movement. The production was marked by an innovation introduced by Teliakovsky, an invitation to distinguished painters, as opposed to professional designers for the theatre, to collaborate in theatrical productions. The designers of the settings for the 1901 Moscow production of *Swan Lake* were R. Y. Golovin, K. A. Korovin, and Baron Klodt. The general view of the critics was that Teliakovsky's courageous innovation marked a retrograde step in the history of Russian design for the theatre. Happily, the public thought otherwise. Golovin and Korovin will be remembered as the designers for Diaghilev's first production of Stravinsky's *L'Oiseau de Feu.*

Among other interpreters at Moscow of the famous role of Odette-Odile was Ekaterina Geltser, now People's Artist of the Republic, the daughter of the Vasily Geltser who collaborated with Tchaikovsky and Begichev in the writing of the scenario. According to Bakrushin,[1] she always paid particular attention to the musical aspect of a role, and she now insisted upon many former cuts in the music being restored. As a result of this the variation, *The Swan's Last Song*, previousiy omitted, and one of the best numbers in the ballet, was replaced. Almost simultaneously, the same *variation* was restored in the St. Petersburg production, at the instigation of Olga Preobrazhenskaya.

Then came the debut of Thamar Karsavina as Odette-Odile on October 24th, 1908. Bakrushin declares that this dancer with her simplicity, charm, and deep emotional feeling realized Tchaikovsky's conception to perfection. As the spectator watched Karsavina dancing, he entered into the mood of Tchaikovsky's music. The same writer observes that although Karsavina "did not exhibit an extraordinary ability as technician or mime, the spectator admired her dancing, believed in the expressiveness of her interpretation, and surrendered himself to the warmth of her emotions." No less unforgettable was the contrast between Odette and Odile which Karsavina so brilliantly stressed. While the former evoked sincere sympathy and love, the second aroused an intense feeling of antipathy. Her Odile suggested something artificial, not a human being, but a seductive chimera fashioned by evil spells.

In 1920 the Bolshoy Theatre, partly under the increasing pressure of new movements in the theatre, and partly conscious of the need for a stimulus in the form of fresh ideas, invited Stanislavsky and Nemirovich-Danchenko, the directors of the Moscow Art Theatre, to join forces with them, an invitation which was accepted.

Among the proposals submitted by Nemirovich-Danchenko was a new production of *Swan Lake*, which, having been decided upon, was carried out by him personally, working in collabora-

[1] *Tchaikovsky's Ballets and their Stage History.*

tion with A. A. Gorski. Several changes were introduced, one of particular interest being an endeavour to reduce the traditional walking about and running into the wings. The Dance of the Dwarfs in Scene II was restored, also the original tragic ending as conceived by Tchaikovsky. The setting for Scene I, by Lavdovsky, was retained, but there were new settings by A. A. Arapov for the remaining three acts.

The role of Odette-Odile was divided between two ballerine, by which means both could appear on the stage at the same time in certain episodes. The *première* took place on February 24th, 1920, Odette being danced by the newly graduated E. M. Ilushenko, and Odile by M. P. Reisen. As Ilushenko had not yet acquired the high degree of technique essential to the role, certain steps were made easier for her, but, according to Nemirovich-Danchenko, she gave a very finished lyrical portrait of Odette. Reisen's Odile was very successful in creating an impression of cruel beauty. Originally, it was intended that both Odette and Odile should wear large swan's wings which the dancers were to agitate while dancing, but these were found impracticable and discarded after the dress rehearsal.

An unusual feature of this production was Gorski's restoration of the long omitted *Masquers' Dance* (*Tanez Masok*), which is how Tchaikovsky visualized the opening of the scene set in the great hall of Prince Siegfried's castle. Further, Gorski introduced into this act a quite new character, a jester,[1] a role created for, and danced with great success by, Vasily Yefimov. This character is retained in contemporary performances of the ballet at Moscow.

However, notwithstanding the high hopes placed on the new production, it failed to please and was withdrawn a year later. Bakrushin[2] attributes its non-success to a lack of unity of conception between *maître de ballet* and decorative artist.

On February 19th, 1922, *Swan Lake* was revived by Gorski in accordance with the 1901 production, the roles of Odette-Odile being fused and danced by M. R. Kandaourova, while the part of Prince Siegfried was taken by Asaf Messerer. The settings by Arapov were discarded and replaced by the former scenes. The only memory of the Nemirovich-Danchenko production was the *Dance of the Dwarfs* and the tragic end to Scene IV, both of which were retained.

In this production, Asaf Messerer, the first Soviet-trained male dancer, sought to replace the conventional mime by expressive gesture. For instance, in the well-known episode where his companions are about to shoot at the swans, he replaced the

[1] Also introduced into the current Leningrad presentation, Sergeyev production.

[2] *Tchaikovsky's Ballets, and their Stage History.*

traditional sequence of seventeen gestures, by running towards his companions, stopping them, and taking a crossbow from one of the huntsmen. When they mimed: "What is the matter?" he merely pointed in the direction whence the Queen of the Swans was expected, and she made her entrance. Again, in the third act, when Siegfried presents Odile to his mother, and mimes a conventional series of gestures: "I–her–love–and—her–will marry," Messerer simply conducted Odile to his mother and mimed: "Here she is." Then he kissed his mother's hand and knelt on one knee before her, to receive her consent and blessing upon the proposed union.

Swan Lake had its first performance outside Russia in 1888, perhaps inspired by the tour of Western Europe which Tchaikovsky began on November 27th of the previous year. After visiting Berlin, Leipzig, and Hamburg, he passed to Bohemia, having been invited to conduct at Prague. The first concert took place at the Rudolfinium on February 19th. The second was given at the Narodny Divadlo (National Theatre), two days later, and was unusual in that it was part concert, part theatrical performance. The musical section consisted of the *Serenade for Strings*; the last movement of the *Third Suite*; a piano solo by Ziloti consisting of three excerpts from *Eugène Onegin*; and the *Overture 1812*. Then followed what the composer himself described in his *Diary* as a "splendidly staged" second act of *Swan Lake*.

The choreography was by Augustin Berger, while the three principal roles were partially naturalized. Odette was interpreted by the prima ballerina, an Italian, Giulietta Paltrinieri-Berger; Prince Siegfried became Prince Jaroslav and was rendered by A. Berger; while Benno, renamed Zdenek, was taken *en travestie* by Marie Zieglerova. The *corps de ballet* were variously described as Fairies, Swans, and Spectres. The ballet was not conducted by the composer, but by a Czech musician, Adolf Cech, presumably because Tchaikovsky found it difficult to adapt himself at short notice to the rearrangement of his score, the dances being as follows:

Entrée dansante	G. Paltrinieri-Berger and *corps de ballet.*
Valse	
Adage	
Variation dansante	G. Paltrinieri-Berger.
Pas d'Action	G. Paltrinieri-Berger, A. Berger, *corps de ballet,* and six pupils of the ballet school.
Valse des Fleurs	*Corps de ballet.*
Grand Ensemble.	G. Paltrinieri-Berger, *corps de ballet,* and pupils of the ballet school.

The scenery was the usual stock setting supplied by a Vienna firm and was selected from the range of Forest, Garden, Palace, Village Green and so forth.

The complete ballet, arranged in 4 acts and 6 scenes, was given at Prague for the first time on June 27th, 1907, the choreography being by Achille Viscusi.

In England, *Swan Lake* was not seen until 1910, when it was presented as the chief attraction of a twice daily programme at the Hippodrome, London, the first performance being given on May 16th. The company consisted of "twenty of Russia's acknowledged greatest dancers including Mdlle Preobrajensky (*sic*), Mdlle Ludmila Schollar and M. George Kiakscht."

It is of interest to quote *The Times*' notice. "The ballet is in two scenes lasting an hour. First, there is the Festival at the Prince's Castle, beginning with a defiant Mazurka. The Prince while entertaining his friends is summoned to the Palace to meet his bride; of course he refuses to go, and the guests make the Preceptor, who brings the message, tipsy for his pains. An orthodox *Pas de Trois*, a lively *Czardas*, and a *Pas de Deux* were all danced with the kind of finish and ease which effectively conceals the art. Special mention must be made of Mlle Schollar. The scene ends with a *Torch Dance*, and a flight of swans, which entices the Prince to take his arquebus and go after them to the lake with his friends. Once there the swans appear as damsels—guarded, when transformed, by an owl 7 feet high with vast wings, which he flapped when there was room. Mlle Preobrajensky evidently has the whole technique of ballet-dancing at her fingers' ends, or rather at the tips of her toes, and added to this she is an artist in mime. She is able to traverse all the most difficult passages of her art with a freedom and accuracy which make her effects quite complete. We have seen the ballet steps made more fascinating, but no execution more perfect than Mlle Preobrajensky's. The neatness and ease of her toe-dancing are astonishing. M. Georges Kiakscht made no mistake in any of his dances, and the whole performance—the *Swan Dance, the Pas d'Action,* the *Pas de Trois,* the *Variation* and *Coda* in the second scene—was admirably carried out by those concerned." From this it would appear that the production consisted of a series of *divertissements* from the first three scenes, presented partly in the castle grounds, and partly in the lakeside setting, and given a semblance of continuity by an adaptation of the theme.

The complete ballet was first presented in England by the Vic-Wells Ballet at the Sadler's Wells Theatre, London, on November 20th, 1934, with scenery and costumes by Hugh Stevenson. The choreography was reproduced by Nicholas Sergeyev, former *régisseur* at the Maryinsky Theatre, St. Petersburg, while the principal roles of Odette-Odile and Prince Siegfried were taken by Alicia Markova and Robert Helpmann respectively. A new and more elaborate production with scenery and costumes by Leslie Hurry was presented by the same company at the New Theatre on September 7th, 1943; the ballerina was Margot Fonteyn. The International Ballet also presented a full-length production, by Nicholas Sergeyev, of *Swan Lake*, with settings and costumes by William Chappell, the first performance[1] being given on March 18th, 1947, at the Adelphi Theatre, London.

In America, *Swan Lake* was first performed on December 19th, 1911, at the Metropolitan Opera House, New York. The writer has not been able to discover a copy of the programme of the first performance, but a later programme gives the cast as follows: Katerina Geltzer, prima ballerina from the Imperial Opera, Moscow (*Odette-Odellia*); Mikhail Mordkin (*Siegfried*); Alexander Volinine (*Benno*); Kiprion Barbos I (*Wolfgang*); Mlle Pantaliwea (*Queen*); M. Trojanowski (*Von Rothbart*). The production was described as "a fairy-tale ballet by Marius Petipa, rearranged by Mikhail Mordkin," who, an enigmatic footnote explains, "has taken certain liberties in condensing the acts to comply with American conceptions of stagecraft." The settings were by James Fox, resident designer to the Opera House.

Chicago had its first sight of *Swan Lake* in 1930, in the form of Act I, Scene II, only, presented at the Chicago Civic Opera by Laurent Novikov with Ruth Pryor and Edward Caton.

In France, *Swan Lake* was given for the first time by Diaghilev's Ballets Russes at the Théâtre du Casino, Monte Carlo, on April 13th, 1912. This production was in two acts and three scenes. The cast was: Matilda Kshesinskaya (*Queen of the Swans*); Vaslav Nijinsky (*Prince*); Serge Grigoriev (*Evil Genie*); Mlle Kulczucka (*Princess-Mother*); Mme Astafieva (*Prince's Fiancée*); M. Semenov (*Prince's Friend*); and Enrico Cecchetti (*Master of Ceremonies*). On the 27th there were some changes in the cast; Odette was taken by T. Karsavina, the Evil Genie was Kovalsky, and the Princess-Mother was interpreted by Lydia Nelidova. On May 3rd, Nijinsky was replaced by Adolph Bolm.

The ballet was not given again at Monte Carlo until December 18th, 1923, the cast being: Vera Trefilova (*Queen of the Swans*); Anatol Wilzak (*Prince*); Serge Grigoriev (*Evil Genie*); and Jean Jazvinsky (*Prince's Friend*). The production was again in two acts and three scenes. The *Pas de Trois* (Act I, Scene II), was danced by Ludmila Schollar, Ldyia Sokolova, and Stanislas Idzikowski. The *Danse Espagnole* was rendered by Maria Dalbaicin and Leon

[1] The first English production to include the *Danse Venetienne*.

Woizikowsky. The *Csardas* was led by B. Nijinska and N. Kremnev. The *Mazurka* was danced by Mlles, L. Tchernicheva, Dubrovska, Maikerska, Allanova, and MM. Slavinsky, Zverev, Jazvinsky, and Fedorov.

On May 11th, 1925, there was a production styled *Le Bal du Lac des Cygnes* which consisted of the following six *divertissements*: 1. *Danse des Cygnes*; Mlles. Nikitina, Devalois, Savina, Gevergeva, Soumarokova, Coxon, Chamie, Klemetska, Zalevska, Nikitina II, Soumarokova II, Nemtchinova II. 2. *Adage*; Alicia Markova, Nicholas Efimov, and Constantin Tcherkas. 3. *Danse Espagnole*; Lubov Tchernicheva, Leon Woizikowsky. 4. *Mazurka*; Mlles. Dubrovska, Danilova, Maikerska, Komarova, MM. Slavinsky, Zverev, Jasvinsky, Fedorov. 5. *Pas de Deux*; Vera Nemtchinova, Antoine Doline (*sic*). 6. *Czardas*; Lydia Sokolova, Nicholas Kremnev, Mlles. Gevergeva, Soumarokova, Chamie, Klemetska, MM. Lapitsky, Savitsky, Kochanovsky, Domansky.

Le Lac des Cygnes was given on April 11th, 1925, with Nemtchinova and Dolin in the principal roles, and again on the 16th. The following year, the ballet was given once, on January 24th, as a Gala Performance in honour of S. A. S. Prince Louis II, with Nemtchinova and Serge Lifar as Odette and Siegfried. In 1927 there were six performances during January and April; three performances in April, 1928; but nothing in 1929, when the Diaghilev Company ended with the death of its director.

On April 24th, 1930, the Ballets de Vera Nemtchinova presented a one-act version of *Swan Lake*, with settings and costumes by Khoudiakov, the roles of Odette and Siegfried being taken by Nemtchinova and Anatole Obukhov.

In 1932, René Blum, who had long been Directeur de la Comédie at the Casino, Monte Carlo, established with Colonel de Basil a company called Ballets Russes de Monte Carlo, which, on April 21st, presented a one-act version of *Swan Lake* with settings by Visconti and Geerto; the principal dancers were Felia Dubrovska and Valentin Froman. In 1933, on April 20th, this version was revived, the principal dancers were Danilova and Lichine. The ballet was revived during the 1934 season, with a new setting by K. Korovin, the principal dancers being Danilova and Boris Kniasev. The ballet was not given during the 1935 season, but revived the following year, on April 9th, with settings by Visconti and costumes by Mme Karinska; the principal dancers were Nemtchinova and Anatol Obukhov. For the 1937 season, the ballet was revived on April 3rd, the production being staged by N. Zverev, and provided with a new setting by Emile Bertin; the principal dancers were Nana Gollner and Michel Panaiev. For the 1938 season the ballet was revived on April 7th, with Markova and Panaiev; on the 16th, Danilova replaced Markova. In 1939 the principal dancers during April and May were Markova and Panaiev, Danilova replacing the former on May 13th.

There was no ballet season again until 1942, when Les Nouveaux Ballets de Monte Carlo, directed by Marcel Sablon, staged a one-act version of *Swan Lake* with choreography by Suzanne Sarabelle after Ivan Clustine (a version unknown to me), the principal dancers being Suzanne Sarabelle and Edmond Linval. The following year, on February 6th, saw a new one-act version with choreography by Marie-Louise Didion after M. Petipa, and staged with a setting by Charles Rouz and costumes by Mme Vialet; the principal dancers were Didion and Christian Arnaud, the latter being replaced on May 2nd by Boris Trailine. On July 22nd, 1942, there was presented a new one-act version by Nicholas Zverev, the principal dancers being Marcelle Cassini and Gérard Mulys.

During 1945, E. Grunberg took over the direction of the company, now called Le Nouveau Ballet de Monte Carlo, which presented on December 25th a new one-act version of *Swan Lake* with Ludmila Tcherina and Edmond Audran as principals. On April 14th, 1946, the same version was revived with Yvette Chauviré and Youly Algaroff in the chief roles. In 1948 the company was renamed Le Grand Ballet de Monte Carlo, the director being the Marquis de Cuevas. This company presented a one-act version of the ballet on April 2nd, with Rosella Hightower and Andre Eglevsky; the setting was by Eugene Dunkel.

Swan Lake was revived at the Paris Opéra on January 2nd, 1936, by Serge Lifar, in connection with the visit of Marina Semeyonova. Only short excerpts were given and by three dancers: Semeyonova, Lifar, and Efimov. Later, the part of Odette was taken by Suzette Lorcia. Scene II was presented at the Opéra on January 23rd, 1946, the production being by Victor Gsovsky. The principal dancers were Chauviré, Dynalix, Vaussard, Peretti, and Efimov.

In Denmark, *Swan Lake* (*Svanseoen*) was first performed at the Royal Theatre, Copenhagen, on February 8th, 1938, the production consisting of Scene II, to which was added the *Pas de Trois* from Scene I. The setting and costumes were by Poul Kanneworff. Margot Lander was Odette, Leif Ornberg was the Prince. The production was by Harald Lander after Petipa-Ivanov.

In Italy, as in France and Denmark, the complete *Swan Lake* has never been given. At the Teatro alla Scala, Milan, a one-act version of the ballet (*Lago dei Cigni*) was first performed by the

Diaghilev Company during the season 1926–1927; the principal roles were danced by Olga Spessivtzeva and Serge Lifar; the setting was by K. Korovin. The ballet remained unperformed until December 31st, 1949, when the one-act version was revived with certain modifications by Margarete Wallmann. The principal dancers were Chauviré and Skouratov; the setting was designed by Alexandre Benois.

The ballet was presented at the Teatro Reale, Rome, during the 1937/8 season in a version consisting of three scenes, the whole lasting one hour. This production was staged by Boris Romanov, after Petipa-Ivanov; the settings and costumes were by Prince Mario Cito-Filomarino. The principal dancers were Attilia Radice and Anatole Obukhov.

The ballet was also presented in a one-act version during the May Festival at Florence, 1939, on the occasion of a visit by René Blum's Ballets Russes de Monte Carlo; the principal dancers were Mia Slavenska and Michel Panaiev.

*In Riga, *Swan Lake* was first presented by the Latvian Ballet, at the National Theatre in 1926. The production, after Petipa-Ivanov, was by Alexandra Fedorova, formerly of the Maryinsky Theatre. The settings and costumes were by E. Vitols. This production was so successful that it was given thirty times—an unprecedented number for Riga—in one year. Fedorova herself was Odette.

In November, 1934, the Latvian choreographer and *premier danseur,* Osvalds Lemanis, devised a special arrangement of *Swan Lake,* the principal changes occurring in Scenes I and IV. It is of interest to record that the death of Odette was succeeded by an apotheosis formed of "swans" soaring skywards. The principal roles were taken by Edite Pfeifere (*Odette*), Helénè Tangijeva-Birzniece (*Odile*), and Osvalds Lemanis (*Siegfried*).

In Sweden, *Swan Lake* (*Svansjön*) was first performed at the Royal Opera, Stockholm, in 1942, the production consisting of Scene II only. The choreography was by George Gé after Ivanov. The setting and costumes were by Gunnar Tandberg. The principal roles were taken by Britta Appelgren (*Odette*), Teddy Rhodin (*Siegfried*), and Julius Mengarelli (*Benno*). This version was also given at Göteburg in 1943, with Nina Gabay as Odette.

The complete ballet was given for one performance only at the Royal Opera, Stockholm, in 1948. The production was by Albert Kozlovsky after Petipa-Ivanov. The principal roles were taken by Elsa-Marianne von Rosen (*Odette-Odile*), John-Ivar Deckner (*Siegfried*), and Per Arne Oarsebo (*Benno*).

At Malmö, Scene II was given for the first time in 1952. The

DANILOVA AND YOUSKEVICH AS ODETTE AND SIEGFRIED

[*Action photo: Roger Wood*

MARGOT FONTEYN AS ODETTE

production was by Carl Gustav Kruuse after Petipa-Ivanov, with Inga Bergren as Odette.

In Yugoslavia, *Swan Lake*, in full, was first performed at the National Theatre, Belgrade, on July 1, 1925, the choreography being by Alexander Fortunato after Petipa-Ivanov. The settings and costumes were by Vladimir Zedrinski. Odette was first interpreted by Jelena Polyanova and later by Nina Kirsanova, Margareta Frohman, Janja Vasiljeva, Natasa Boskovic, and Nada Arandjelovic respectively. The first Siegfried was Alexander Fortunato, the role being later taken by Anatolij Ukovski and Milan Ristic. Up to February 21, 1941, this production was given 103 times.

After the Second World War, the ballet was revived on December 18, 1951, the production being by Nina Kirsanova after Petipa-Ivanov. The settings were by Dusan Ristic, and the costumes by Milica Babich-Jovanovich. Odette was taken by Jovanka Bjegojevic, and later by Katarina Obradovic and by Milica Jovanovic; Odile by Vera Kostic; while Siegfried was taken first by Branko Markovic, later by Gradimir Hadzislavkovic. Up to July 15, 1952, the production has been given 20 times.*

* *
*

An examination of the foregoing list of the *premières* of *Swan Lake* in different countries reveals the surprising fact that, outside Russia, the first complete presentation of the ballet in Europe was at London in 1934. The second, or lakeside, scene, has long formed part of the repertory of most companies, both State and privately owned.

Passing from the ballet proper to the two chief characters, there is a long line of Odettes-Odiles and of Siegfrieds. Among the many renderings of the dual role of Odette-Odile, I can mention a few representative names only: P. M. Karpakova (1877), Pierina Legnani (1895), A. A. Giuri (1901), Ekaterina Geltser, Olga Preobrazhenskaya, Matilda Kshesinskaya, Vera Trefilova, Thamar Karsavina (1908), Anna Pavlova, M. R. Kandaourova (1922), Olga Spessivtzeva, Alicia Markova (1934), Margot Fonteyn (1939), Beryl Grey (1942), Moira Shearer (1946), Violetta Elvin (1942), Mona Inglesby (1947), Nana Gollner, Galina Ulanova (1929), Olga Lepeshinskaya, Irina Tikhomirnova, Marina Semeyonova, Natalia Dudinskaya, Maya Plisetskaya.

*The matter contained within this asterisk and that on page 154 was added at the time of going to press, and the names therein are therefore not included in the Index.

Among well-known interpretations of the principal male role may be mentioned those of Pavel Gerdt (1895) Mikhail Mordkin, Vaslav Nijinsky, Asaf Messerer (1922), Anatol Wilzak, Anton Dolin, Vakhtang Chabukiani, Dudko, Alexei Yermolayev, Konstantin Sergeyev,[1] Robert Helpmann (1934), Paul Petrov, Alexis Rassine, Michael Somes, John Hart, John Field. Nijinsky's rendering made a deep impression upon me for its evocation of the romantic mood.

The names of those dancers who have taken the role of Odette or of Siegfried in Scene II only of *Swan Lake*, or in a one-act version of the ballet are legion. Among Odettes there have been Vera Nemtchinova, Alexandra Danilova, Yvette Chauviré, Felia Dubrovska, Irina Baronova, Tamara Toumanova, Mia Slavenska, Attilia Radice (1937), Margot Lander (1938), Patricia Bowman, Colette Marchand, Natalie Krassovska, Rosella Hightower, Elaine Fifield. The Siegfrieds include Stanislas Idzikowski, Serge Lifar, Anatole Obukhov, Michael Panaiev, Igor Youskevich, André Eglevsky, Walter Gore, Gérard Mulys.

Markova's rendering has a special place in the history of English Ballet, not only for its distinguished qualities, but because she was the first English ballerina to dance the dual role of Odette-Odile, a particularly difficult task in 1934 when there was no contemporary rendering of the complete role outside Russia which was available for examination and study.

Russia apart, the finest rendering of Odette to be seen in Europe or America today is that of Margot Fonteyn, which is not only beautifully danced, but in which each step and every movement are so invested with meaning and mood that they contribute to the evocation of a haunting and most lyrical portrait of the unfortunate Odette, doomed to alternate between the states of swan and maiden. This superb quality of interpretation has not been attained overnight, it is the outcome of years of constant thought, study, and application all directed to the evolution of what was at first no more than a sketch into a complete and finished portrait. One feels that Fonteyn has not only lived the role but even penetrated the soul of it.

I venture to suggest that early measures should be taken to ensure that Fonteyn's interpretation, now in its prime, be preserved by film and sound track to serve as a model and inspiration to English Odettes in course of development and of those to come.

If *Swan Lake* offered a ballerina the role of Odette alone with its infinite possibilities of expression in terms of dance and mime, it must be accounted a masterpiece, but when to this are joined the additional opportunity afforded the ballerina of interpreting

[1] Considered to be the most distinguished Siegfried on the Soviet stage.

another great role, that of Odile, a completely different character, to say nothing of the contrasting styles in choreographic approach of Ivanov, the creator of Odette, and Petipa, who conceived the role of Odile, then *Swan Lake* must rank as an outstanding example of a ballet in the romantic tradition, a ballet which certainly upholds, perhaps at times even excels, its classic prototypes—*La Sylphide* and *Giselle*.

APPENDICES

A. ALTERNATIVE CHOREOGRAPHIC VERSIONS OF CERTAIN STEPS AND VARIATIONS

B. ORIGINAL SEQUENCE OF NUMBERS IN TCHAIKOVSKY'S SCORE OF "SWAN LAKE" AS COMPOSED FOR THE FIRST PRODUCTION AT MOSCOW, 1877

C. BIBLIOGRAPHY

APPENDIX A

ACT I. SCENE I. ENTREE FOR SIXTEEN PEASANT GIRLS.

Another version of this is that in which sixteen dancer peasant girls come in in four separate entrances, each with some flowers; in this case the dancers of the *Pas de Trois* do not appear until their dance begins. In such case the whole of the music is used. Also, the Tutor distributes coloured ribbons to each peasant girl, perhaps a relic from the first Petipa-Ivanov production in which a maypole was brought on and danced round.

ACT I. SCENE I. PAS DE TROIS. ALTERNATIVE VERSION 4TH STEP. 2ND GIRL'S SOLO.

*Another version of 4th step of 2nd Girl's solo is: commence in 5th pos., R.F. back. *Relevé* on L.F., *retiré* R.F. to back of knee, close R.F. to 5th pos. back. Repeat *relevé* this time R.F. to front of L. knee, body inclined towards R. side, arms 4th *en avant*, R. arm across body. *Relevé* R.F., *retiré* L.F. to back of knee, *rond de jambe en dehors* with R. leg, body inclined to L. for last two steps, arms in 4th *en avant*, L. arm across body, position of body for the *rond de jambe* slightly *éffacé* to 1. Do this step four times in all to alternate sides, or three times and *temps levé en arabesque* on L.F. and run to 3.

ACT I. SCENE II. ODETTE: FIRST ENTRANCE. ATLERNATIVE VERSION.

In the Sadler's Wells production at Covent Garden, Odette runs to 7 and turns slowly *sur les pointes* in 5th pos. Siegfried follows her and she runs to 2. He goes to 2. Siegfried asks Odette why she flees from him. She runs *sur les pointes* from him towards centre and does one *soutenu* and two wing-like movements of arms in 2nd pos., while Siegfried runs round her to R. This is repeated three times across front of stage 1–2, then continues on as at *.

ACT I. SCENE II. WALTZ BY SWAN-MAIDENS. ALTERNATIVE VERSION.

Based on that produced by Nicholas Sergeyev for the Sadler's Wells Ballet, and designed for twenty-six or eighteen dancers; the following description is for twenty-six dancers, the formation at commencement is three lines from 7–5; there are two outside lines of nine dancers each, and a centre one of eight dancers : i.e. four small swan-maidens (popularly styled "cygnets") and four tall swan-maidens.

The four small swan-maidens are foremost in the centre line and four tall swan-maidens behind with the two swan-maiden Leaders standing Nos. 7 and 8 in the line.

Description of the Work of the Centre Line of Eight Dancers.

I. Consists of *balancés* as in the version described on page 97, each dancer in the line going the same way, i.e. towards 1. This is done the same number of times.

II. The same as on page 97, the dancers running out in opposite directions: the 1st to the L., the 2nd to the R., and so on, then back and again out and back to the line.

III. *Pas de bourrée–posé en arabesque*, arms carried back to low 2nd pos., eight times in all on same feet, the 1st, 3rd, 5th and 7th dancers travelling in a circle (outside the moving lines at the sides) passing 1–8–4–7, and the 2nd, 4th, 6th and 8th dancers travelling in a circle passing 2–6–3–7. They meet up-stage and come down-stage in two lines, the 1st and 3rd dancers being joined by the 2nd and 4th to form the first line and the 6th and 8th dancers being joined by the 5th and 7th to form the back line. The two lines are now in the order from O.P. side

7—5—6—8
3—1—2—4

and fairly down-stage.

V. The front line of four small swan-maidens does *rond de jambe* to each side with *temps levé* on supporting foot, *assemblé* and *relevé en arabesque*, both arms raised. Repeat. During this the back line of tall swan-maidens does the preening *port de bras* opposite ways in pairs, each pair steps on to foot nearest wing first, then the other way. Then the front line does *glissade* up-stage step and *fouetté sauté en tournant* to face 5. Repeat up-stage other side, then *posé* in *arabesque–chassé–pas de chat* twice down-stage, during this the back line passes down-stage between the dancers of the front line who are passing up-stage, with *posé en arabesque–chassé–pas de chat* thrice, then they do *pas de bourrée courru* in 5th pos., going back facing 5, arms crossed over chest.

VI. Now the front line do *relevé* in 5th pos., arms raised high to sides, lunge *croisé* on R.F., arms crossed over chest, half-turn to L., *relevé*, lunge *croisé* on L.F. Repeat other way. Repeat each side again. The back line does the same series of movements but commences with lunge instead of *relevé*.

VII. Now two small swan-maidens in the front line and two tall swan-maidens from the back on each side do *chassé–temps levé* in 1st *arabesque–chassé–pas de chat* three times, forming into two lines from 7–5 crossing. Then they cross with same step again, done three times. Then two small swan-maidens in the front line and one tall swan-maiden from each side cross again, while two swan-maiden Leaders go up-stage for their *variation*.

Description of Work of the Two Outside Lines of Nine Swan-Maidens which occurs at same time as the above work of the Centre Line of Eight.

I. *Chassé–temps levé* on up-stage foot in 1st *arabesque–pas de chat*, closing arms to 5th *en bas* on *pas de chat*. Do this four times. This is done travelling out towards wings.

II. Then six *petits jetés devant* round each other in small circles in pairs, the 1st swan-maiden turning in the direction of the up-stage foot, the 2nd swan-maiden follows her round, beginning with down-stage foot; then 1st swan-maiden does *posé* in 1st *arabesque* on L. *pointe* towards the wings, *chassé croisé* R.F.; 2nd swan-maiden does the *posé* on R. *pointe* inwards towards centre and *chassé croisé* L.F.[1] Repeat II.

III. *Chassé–temps levé* in 1st *arabesque* on R.F.,[1] *pas de chat*, do this four times in all, travelling in towards the centre of stage getting into lines of three, so that the formation becomes:

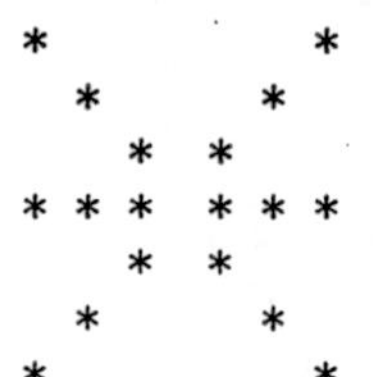

the leaders of the two lines lead the first three towards the centre, the 4th in the line becomes the leader of the next three, and so on; for the 4th time all swan-maidens do a *soutenu* outwards.

IV. Travelling away from centre and back into the original two lines with *pas de bourrée–posé* in *arabesque* on up-stage foot, taking arms to a low 2nd pos., a little back behind shoulder line. Do this four times on the same foot.

V. *Posé* on inside foot on *pointe* with *rond de jambe en l'air en dedans* with outside leg, passing arms through 2nd pos., end in 5th pos. off *pointes*, body and head *croisé*, inclined inwards, arms in 5th pos. *en bas*, hands crossed at wrists. *Posé* in 1st *arabesque* towards wings on outside foot, *pas de bourrée dessous sur les pointes*. Do this four times in all, always on same side.

[1] This is the foot used by the dancers on the Prompt side. O.P. side uses opposite foot.

VI. Lunge *croise*, the two swan-maidens at head of two lines make the lunge on inside foot *croisé*, arms in crossed 5th pos. *en bas*, the 2nd swan-maidens in the lines on outside foot and so on down the lines. *Relevé* in 5th pos., arms 5th pos. *en haut* with elbows straight and palms turned outwards, everyone is now in one straight line, repeat the lunge the opposite side, arms and body the same, do this lunge four times.

VII. *Temps levé* on outside foot, *fouetté derrière* inside foot, do this three times on alternate feet, *pas de bourrée dessous sur les pointes*. Repeat to same side.

VIII. *Chassé–temps levé* in 1st *arabesque–pas de chat* three times, dividing into threes as before, only the 3rd down the line leads the threes this time and going towards centre, the formation is:

Same step going to straight lines, then the preening *port de bras* four times, commencing stepping on to inside foot, end with weight on inside foot, other *pointe tendue derrière*, arms in crossed 5th pos. *en bas*. During this *port de bras* the two small swan-maidens and one tall swan-maiden on each side are crossing for the third time while the two swan-maiden Leaders run outwards and up-stage to take positions for *variation*. Thus the lines on each side nearest wing contain nine swan-maidens and the inside lines one tall swan-maiden and two small swan-maidens.

This *variation* is the same, with the exception that Step I is done four times on alternate feet, then, instead of *pas de bourrée–grand jeté en tournant* up-stage, they use outside feet and do *chassé–temps levé* in 1st *arabesque–pas de chat*, four times travelling up-stage and finish ready to repeat Step I. For Step VII, the two swan-maiden Leaders join the inner lines made by the two tall swan-maidens and four small swan-maidens, so that at the end of the waltz there are four lines of swan-maidens well out towards the wings, the two lines nearest the wings on each side containing nine swan-maidens and the two inner lines four swan-maidens, the Leaders being down-stage. All stand on outside feet, the inside foot *pointe tendue derrière*. Benno enters at 1. Siegfried at 2. They look down the lines of swan-maidens, Benno down P. side, Siegfried O.P. side, then they change over, Benno finishing near centre as in other description.

As Odette runs down-stage to sink on to the ground, the swan-maidens move so that there are three pairs of swan-maidens in line on each side with three huntsmen between them and a group right down-stage on either side, which consists of two small swan-maidens seated on the ground, each inclining body to the other, legs outwards, one swan-maiden kneeling in centre slightly at rear with both arms extended diagonally upwards, two swan-maidens kneeling a little outside but behind the seated swan-maidens, with arms in 3rd *arabesque* away from centre of group. Two tall swan-maidens stand between the three kneeling swan-maidens with both arms diagonally upwards to either side, the whole group faces slightly inwards.

In the description of the *Pas de Deux* of Odette and Siegfried, note the different movements made by the *corps de ballet* in Section II. They do the same step, i.e. a series of *temps levés* in 1st *arabesque*, only the *corps de ballet* take up the formation of threes at the end of the step, instead of the two diagonal lines from 1–3 as in the other version:

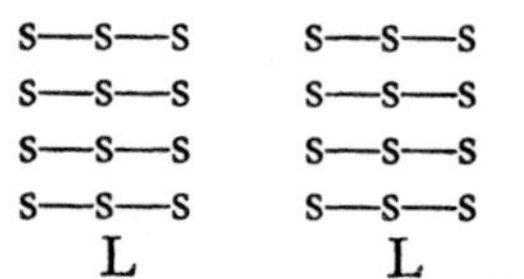

with the extra tall swan-maidens and small swan-maidens forming the two front lines of threes and the two swan-maiden Leaders centre front of foremost line. The group of four tall and four small swan-maidens do their *temps levés en arabesque* crossing down-stage in two straight lines of 4 to take up their formation described above. The order of the two front lines of four is: two small swan-maidens leading each side, then the leading swan-maidens, and last in the line is the extra tall swan. The leading swan-maidens step forward at the end of the step to the positions in figures shown above.

They stand thus during Step III and at the end they walk to one diagonal line from 3–1, and one straight line near wing on P. side, the diagonal contains eighteen *corps de ballet* and the straight line four small swan-maidens and four tall swan-maidens. They perform the lunge and *ports de bras* as described in Step IV, the straight line of eight swan-maidens doing it facing inwards towards the centre-stage. At Step VI the eight swan-maidens go off and the eighteen swan-maidens repeat the lunge and *port de bras* only facing 1, then they move so as to make one straight line near the wings 1–4. They do a *port de bras*, opening their arms through 5th pos. *en haut* and 2nd pos. to crossed 5th pos. *en bas*.

Step VIII, the eighteen swan-maidens form two diagonals, 3–1 and 4–2, all standing as described, but all on straight supporting leg, not graduated in height.

During the *Pas de Quatre*, etc., until the *Coda*, the eighteen swan-maidens stand in two lines at right angles to stage as before.

The *Coda* is the same as that described on page 105, only in Step I each line of swan-maidens contains three from each side and the entry, at Step IV, of small swan-maidens and swan-maiden Leaders now have two tall and two small swan-maidens from each side. Step VII: the eighteen swan-maidens standing nine on each side do *chassé–temps levé* in 3rd *arabesque–glissade* to alternate sides four times, travelling from their lines near wings to form three lines of six swan-maidens across stage from 6–8, getting to this last formation by going in a circle in threes, the 1st swan-maiden taking the place of the 3rd and so on; when they have got to the three lines from 6–8, they do the same step three times more (making seven times in all), one down-stage to five, one up-stage to 7, and the third down-stage to 5, stop with foot pointed 4th back before beginning next step. The four small and four tall swan-maidens cross with this step and cross back to places. The last *port de bras* in Step V is done with nine swan-maidens forming the two lines near wings from 2–3–1–4, and the inner lines 1–3–4–2 contain the four small swan-maidens and four tall swan-maidens, the leading swan-maidens coming third in each diagonal line.

ACT II. DANSE ESPAGNOLE: ALTERNATIVE VERSION BASED ON SERGEYEV RECONSTRUCTION).

Two Spanish couples run on and pose *écarté* in pairs

Y G Y G
1 2 4 3

Take up *écarté* position with a *port de bras*.

I. Twelve quick *pas de basque* to change places, arms held above head rather in the manner employed in Scottish dances 1 2 4 3

Partners again face each other and take position with a *port de bras*. Repeat back to places by same route.

II. Quick *pas de basque* to change places again, 3 and 1 using opposite feet, step up stage on *demi-plié*, draw up other foot and stamp, taking arms from 2nd pos. to *attitude*, with a flick of the wrists; 2 and 4 do same only facing partners, 2 and 4 do quick *pas de basque*, changing places with each other. Nos. 2 and 4 kneel and do several big *ports de bras* circle-wise, while 1 and 3 do quick *pas de basque* round them, making a figure ∞ ending beside their own partner. Now all travel upstage facing in pairs, step up stage, draw up other foot and make a *développé devant relevé*; repeat same side. Repeat the taking of position.

III. *Sissonne retombée* twice crossing, 4 and 3 ending O.P. side, 1 and 2 ending P. side. Now, making *coupés dégagés*, go round together, youth with hand at back of girl's head, partners facing each other. Repeat the taking of position. Repeat whole step back to places.

IV. Partners face in pairs and travelling up stage do *soutenu renversé en dedans*, changing arms while turning; end with front foot placed on ball of foot in 4th pos. front, close it in to other foot, take it out to 4th pos. again, and again close it in. Repeat step three times in all. Now all using same feet travel down stage to 5, doing 4 times on alternate feet a small sprung *pointe tendue* to 4th pos. front, slightly *croisé*, taking both arms, palms down, down body to working leg.

V. In pairs *dos à dos, rond de jambe en dedans* with *temps levé*
↖ ↗
followed by *balancé* forward and backward 1 2 4 3, repeat passing on the other side of partner.
↘ ↙

VI. Quick *pas de basque*, 1 and 3 travelling round themselves, 2 and 4 making a circle, 2 passing outside 3, and 4 passing outside 1, each with partners together again, girls to the left of their youths; now, continuing the *pas de basque* in a circle, 1 and 2 travelling anti-clockwise, 3 and 4 clockwise. End facing 5, youths just behind girls, cross doing 6 times *tombé croisé coupé* back. Now go round in pairs with a small spring *pointe tendue* front 4 times run to centre, youths face each other and take up a *position effacée*; girls kneel in front of them but a little outside.

ACT II. DANSE VENETIENNE (DANSE NAPOLITAINE)

Arranged for four couples. Youths carry mandolines; girls tambourines. Run on and stand across back.

Y G Y G Y G Y G
1 2 3 4 5 6 7 8

Girls stand with both hands on R. hip, tambourine in R. hand. All stand in 4th pos., L.F. front.

I. *Dégagé coupé* twice, three stamps. Repeat this step 7 times with three *dégagés coupés* before the stamps. The two centre couples lead round followed by the two outside couples, 3, 4 and 1, 2 coming down stage and going off to R.; 5, 6 and 7, 8 going off to L., all end in a square:

1, 2 7, 8
3, 4 5, 6

II. The partners cross to each other's places, girl passing up stage of youth, with a kind of waltz step, that is, they rise in 5th pos., then cross with three steps turning; one long step on *demi-plié* taking 2 beats, followed by 2 steps. Repeat. Then the partners cross back to places, girl passing in front of youth with *tombé croisé*, *coupé derrière* 8 times, travelling sideways facing 5.

III. Turning round each other, making two turns in all, with *dégagé* R.F. front, *plié* L.F. 4 times and 4 *jetés derrière*. Do this three times in all, then 5 *jetés derrière*, travelling out to the corner, ending with an *assemblé*. Now all four couples are near the four corners; youths nearest the centre, girls nearest to the wings.

IV. All do 8 *ballonnés* towards centre, hopping on L.F., girl has R.H. on youth's shoulder and tambourine in L.H. The pairs now go *dos à dos* making half a circle round each other, the girl having put tambourine now into R.H. and swinging arms from side to side, youth plucks strings of mandoline. Repeat this step out to corner.

V. Girl hops round *en dehors* on L.F., arms in 2nd pos., R. leg raised and bent. Boy lunges on to front foot and plays, marking the time with heel beats on front foot. Both come *dos à dos* with 4 hops in *arabesque* forward and 4 hops in *attitude devant*, backwards. Repeat the hops turning. The two front couples turn and do *jetés derrière* up stage, while the two back couples come down stage passing between the others doing *dégagé pointe tendue* front with two hops on supporting leg to alternate sides

↑ 2, 1 ↑ ↑ 8, 7 ↑
↓ ↓
3 4 6 5

Repeat this figure to end in the beginning places in the square.

VI. All do *glissade derrière*, *jeté derrière* alternate sides commencing R.F. Travel in a circle anti-clockwise back to places. Youths now mark the time as in Step V. Girls face youths, point foot *croisé* front, *effacé* back with hops. Repeat step V, then *balancé* turning. All do 8 *jetés derrière*, running up stage to starting place, only girls now on right of youths: 2, 1 4, 3 6, 5 8, 7

VII. *Echappé sauté* to 2nd pos., *temps levé* raising leg *croisé devant*, *balancé* turning 4 times. Then *dos à dos* making one turn. Girls do *balancé* turning, youths lunge and beat time with heel. Youths now lunge, girls kneel facing youths.

ACT II. PAS DE DEUX (ODILE AND SIEGFRIED) ALTERNATIVE VERSION 2ND STEP.

From 1–2, *glissade–posé* on L.F.–*grand battements à la seconde* R. leg, *fouetté dégagé* to 1st *arabesque* to 6, step on R.F. across in front of Siegfried, *double tour en dehors* on L.F. to 1, end facing 5 with R.F. on L. knee, L. arm 5th *en haut*, R. arm half 5th *en avant*. This step is done three times, run to 2.

ACT II. SIEGFRIED: VARIATION. ALTERNATIVE VERSION.[1]

Stand near 3.

I. *Glissade–entrechat six en tournant–glissade–posé en arabesque* R.F. to 8, L. hand at waist, R. hand *en haut*, in high *arabesque*. Do this four times alternate sides, travelling diagonally sideways down-stage, end near 2.

II. From 2–4, do *temps levé–chassé* backward *effacé* on to R.F., *temps levé* R.F., *coupé–fouetté* back L.F., step on to L.F., *soutenu* to L. *entrechat huit* facing 2. Do this step three times, then go to centre-stage back.

III. Travelling from 2–5, do *temps levé–chassé* to 4th pos. front L.F., same R.F.–*coupé–assemblé* front R.F.–*double tour en l'air* ending on R. knee. Preparation for *pirouette sur le cou-de-pied*, ending on *demi-plié* on L.F., R.F. *arabesque à terre*. Repeat the whole step on same side, ending last *tour en l'air* on R. knee, L. arm at waist, R. arm *en haut*.

ACT III. SIEGFRIED: VARIATION. ANOTHER ALTERNATIVE VERSION[2].

Glissade derrière to R., *double cabriole* facing 1, *fouetté, dégagé* to 1st *arabesque,* ending to 6. *Glissade derrière* to R., *pose* on R.F., L. leg to *arabesque*, body facing 2, R. arm in 5th *en haut*, L. arm in *demi-seconde* pos. Do this three times, then *pas de bourrée, grand jeté* towards 2 in 2nd *arabesque croisée*, arms *en attitude*, L. arm up. *Pas de bourrée* to 2, small *assemblé*. Preparation and *tours en dehors sur le cou-de-pied* to L., ending with *grand rond de jambe en dehors* ending *croisé* to 2. *Glissade* turning to L. and travelling well across stage to 1. Repeat the small *assemblé* at 1 and *pirouettes sur le cou-de-pied* to R. with the *rond de jambe renversé* ending to 1. Run up-stage to 7. **Temps levé–chassé–coupé–assemblé to* 5–*double tour en l'air*. Repeat the *double tour en l'air*. Repeat from* then preparation and *double tour sur le cou-de-pied, double tour en l'air* falling on R. knee.

[1] Included in Sadler's Wells Ballet production at Covent Garden. This variation is danced to an interpolated piece of music by an unknown composer (?Riccardo Drigo).

[2] This *variation* is danced to an interpolated piece of music by an unknown composer (?Riccardo Drigo).

APPENDIX B

LE LAC DES CYGNES

A Grand Ballet

In Four Acts

Music by P. Tchaikovsky

Arranged for the piano by N. Kashkin

Jürgenson, 1st Edition, *circa* 1878, publication No. 2950

The following is the original sequence of the numbers in each act according to Tchaikovsky's score for the first production of the ballet at the Bolshoy Theatre, Moscow, 1877.[1]

Act I

No. 1. Scene (*Allegro*).

A party of villagers come to congratulate the Prince upon his birthday. His tutor, Wolfgang, bids them entertain the Prince with dances. The peasants consent. The Prince orders them to be given wine. The servants obey. The village girls are presented with flowers and ribbons.

No. 2. Valse. Corps de ballet

No. 3. Scene (*Allegro moderato*).

A runner[2] announces the approach of the Princess-Mother. The retainers put everything in order. The tutor endeavours to assume the demeanour of a very busy man.

No. 4. Pas de Trois (*Allegro moderato*).

No. 5. Pas de Deux (*Tempo di Valse ma non troppo vivo, quasi moderato*).

No. 6. Pas d'Action. (*Andantino quasi moderato*).

The tutor, inebriated, dances and provokes laughter by his clumsiness. The tutor whirls and falls.

No. 7. Scene.

Darkness begins to fall. One of the guests suggests a final dance to the clashing of their drinking-cups.

[1] The sequence of numbers as re-arranged for the Petipa-Ivanov production at the Maryinsky Theatre, St. Petersburg, 1895, is given in the piano score of *Swan Lake* edited by Peter March, and published by the Tchaikovsky Foundation, New York, 1949.

[2] That is, a messenger.

No. 8. Dance with drinking-cups. (*Tempo di Polacca*). (Bells).
No. 9. Final Scene.
A line of swans passes across the sky.

Act II

No. 1. Scene.
No. 2. Scene (*Allegro moderato*).
The Prince and Benno enter.
The Owl appears (p. 71).
No. 3 *Allegro*.
A group of swans glide over the surface of the lake.
No. 4. Dances of the Swan-maidens (p. 78). (*Tempo di Valse*).
Moderato assai graziozo (Odette's Variation).
Vivace. Dance of the Cygnets (p. 82).
Adagio (*Andante*) (p. 84).
Allegro (p. 98). No longer used.
General Dance (*Tempo di Valse*). Valse of Three Swan-maidens (p. 90).
Coda. *Allegro vivo* (p. 92).

Act III

No. 1. *Allegro giusto*.
No. 2. Dances of the Corps de Ballet and of the Dwarfs. (*Moderato assai*).
Ballabile. (*Allegro vivo*.)
Trio (Dwarfs) (p. 100).
No. 3. *Allegro*.
A Flourish of trumpets announces the arrival of new guests. The Master of Ceremonies goes to meet them; the Herald announces their names to the Princess-Mother.
The old Count enters with his Wife and Daughter. They bow to the Princess-Mother. The Daughter dances.
No. 4. Scene.
The Princess-Mother calls the Prince aside to inquire which of the prospective brides pleases him.
Baron Von Rothbart comes forward with Odile (p. 110). The Prince is astonished by her resemblance to Odette.
No. 5. Pas de Six.
Variation I. *Andante con moto* (p. 115).
Variation II. *Moderato* (p. 117).
Variation III. *Allegro* (p. 118).
Variation IV. *Moderato* (p. 119).
Coda. *Allegro molto*.

No. 6. Danse hongroise. (*Allegro moderato.*)
No. 7. Danse espagnole. (*Allegro non troppo.*)
No. 8. Danse napolitaine.
No. 9. Mazurka.
No. 10. The Princess-Mother is delighted that the Prince is attracted by Odile, and consults Wolfgang about it (p. 139).
Valse (p. 140).
The Prince kisses Odile's hand.
Allegro vivo. Rothbart's Variation (p. 141).

ACT IV.

No. 1. Entr'acte.
No. 2. Scene (*Allegro non troppo*).
Odette's swan-maidens are concerned as to where she is (p. 145).
No. 3. Dance of the Cygnets.
No. 4. Odette runs in and acquaints her friends of her misfortune. The stage darkens. A storm begins. *Allegro vivace* (p. 154).
No. 5. *Andante.*
Final scene.
The Prince runs in.
"Oh, forgive me," says the Prince (p. 158).
Odette falls into his arms. (*Alla breve moderato e maestoso* (p. 160).
Moderato. Swans appear on the surface of the lake (p. 164).

APPENDIX C

BIBLIOGRAPHY

Abraham, Gerald (Editor). *Tchaikovsky: A Symposium*, Lindsay Drummond, 1945.

Bakrushin, Y. A. *Alexander Alexeyevich Gorski*, Moscow-Leningrad, 1946.

Bakrushin, Y. A. *Tchaikovsky's Ballets and their Stage History* (*Baleti Tchaikovskogo i ik scenitcheskaya Istoriya*) in Shaverdyan, *Tchaikovsky and the Theatre* (*q.v.*).

Benois, Alexander. *Reminiscences of the Russian Ballet*, 1941.

Blasis, Carlo. *Dances in General, Ballet Celebrities, and National Dances* (Russian text), Moscow, 1864.

Bogdanov-Berezovsky. *Galina Ulanova*, 1949.

Borisoglebsky, M. *Materials for a History of Russian Ballet* (*Materiali po Istorii Russkogo Baleta*), 2 Vols., Leningrad, 1938.

Brodsky, A. M. *Tchaikovsky on the Stage of the Kirov (formerly Maryinsky) Theatre of Opera and Ballet,* 1840–1940 *(P. I. Tchaikovsky na stsenye Teatra, Operi, Baleta Imeni S. K. Kirova,* 1840–1940), Leningrad, 1941.
Evans, Edwin. *Tchaikovsky*, Dent, 1906. Revised 1935.
Glebov, Igor. *Lebedinoye Ozero.*
Grimm, Jacob. *Teutonic Mythology.* Trs. S. Stallybrass, Vol. IV., 1888.
Hapgood, I. F. *The Epic Songs of Russia*, New York, 1886.
Karsavina, Tamara. *Theatre Street*, Heinemann, 1930. Revised, Constable, 1948.
Khudekov, S. B. *Istoriya Tanzev*, Vol. IV., St. Petersburg, 1917.
Laroche, H. A. *From My Recollections of P. I. Tchaikovsky (Iz moikh vospominany o P. I. Tchaikovskom)* in *Syeverny vestnik*, Vol. II., St. Petersburg, 1894.
Newmarch, Rosa (Editor). *The Life and Letters of Peter Ilich Tchaikovsky* [by Modeste Tchaikovsky]. Edit. from Russian, Lane, 1906.
Newmarch, Rosa (Editor). *Tchaikovsky: His Life and Works, with Extracts from his Writings and the Diary of his Tour Abroad in* 1888, Grant Richards, 1900; Revised, William Reeves, 1908.
Petipa, M. *Memoirs*, St. Petersburg, 1906.
Pleschayev, A. A., *Nash Balet*, St. Petersburg, 1899.
Rimsky-Korsakoff, N. A. *My Musical Life*, Knopf, New York, 1923.
Shaverdyan, A. I. (Editor). *Tchaikovsky and the Theatre– Essays and Materials (Tchaikovsky i Teatr: Stati i Materiali)*, Moscow-Leningrad, 1940.
Skalkovsky, K. A. *V Teatralnom Mirie*, St. Petersburg, 1899.
Slonimsky, Y. *Maîtres de Ballet (Mastera Baleta)*, 1937.
Valts, K. *Sixty-Five Years of the Theatre*, Leningrad, 1928.
Weinstock, Herbert. *Tchaikovsky*, Cassell, 1946.

PERIODICALS

Annual of the Imperial Theatres, Seasons 1893–94; 1894–95.
Biriuich (Herald) *of Petrograd State Theatres*, No. 7, Dec., 1918.
Modern Chronicle (Sovreminnaia Letopis), No. 35, 1869, Contains Laroche, G. A., *Teatr Kasenny i Teatr Narodny*).
Modern News, Feb. 26th, 1877.
Moskovskie Vedomosti, 1875.
Russkie Vedomosti, No. 49, Feb. 21st. 1877.
Theatre Gazette, Feb. 22nd, 1877.
Vsemirnaya Illustratsia, April 23rd, 1877.

INDEX

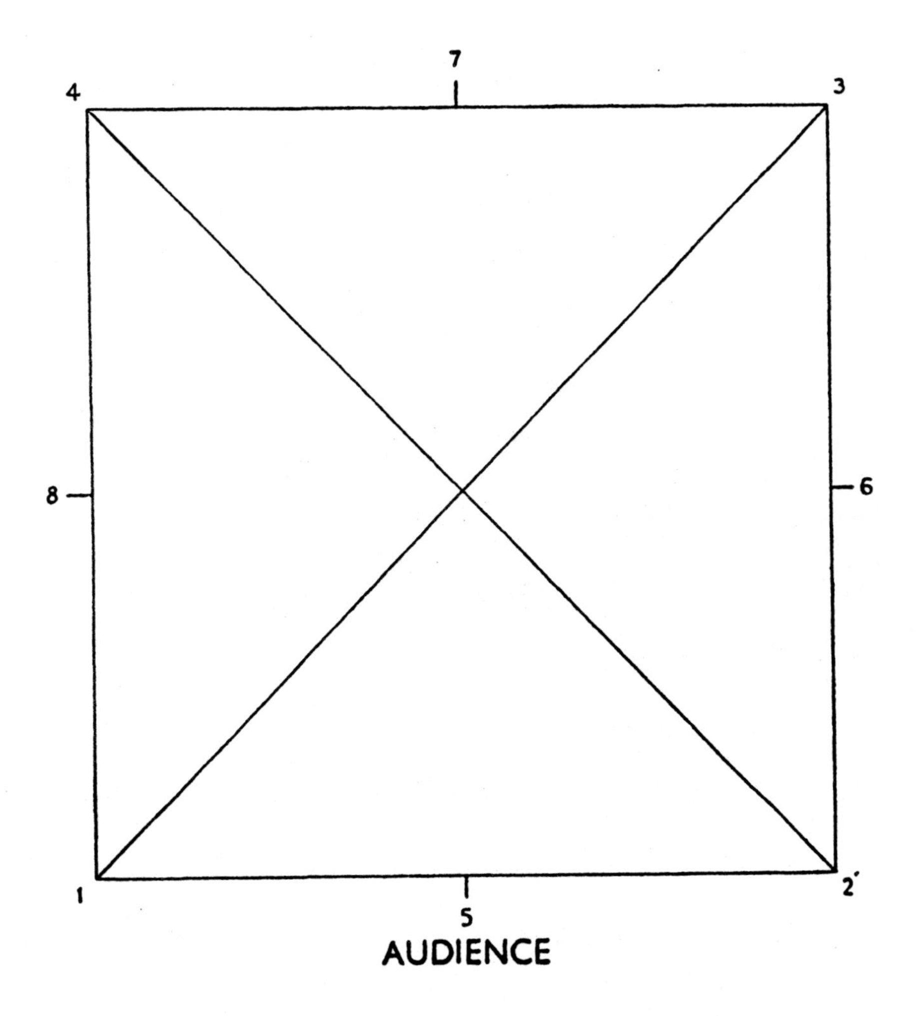
7
4
3
8
6
1
2
5
AUDIENCE